The Cambridge Introduction to
Contemporary American Fiction

The Cambridge Introduction to Contemporary American Fiction explores fiction written over the last thirty years in the context of the profound political, historical, and cultural changes that have distinguished the contemporary period. Focusing on both established and emerging writers – and with chapters devoted to the American historical novel, regional realism, the American political novel, the end of the Cold War and globalization, 9/11, borderlands and border identities, race, and the legacy of postmodern aesthetics – this Introduction locates contemporary American fiction at the intersection of a specific time and long-standing traditions. In the process, it investigates the entire concept of what constitutes an "American" author while exploring the vexed, yet resilient, nature of what the concept of home has come to signify in so much writing today. This wide-ranging study will be invaluable to students, instructors, and general readers alike.

Stacey Olster is Professor of English at Stony Brook University, a former Fulbright Fellow Scholar, and an award-winning teacher. She is the author of *Reminiscence and Re-Creation in Contemporary American Fiction* and *The Trash Phenomenon: Contemporary Literature, Popular Culture, and the Making of the American Century*, and the editor of *The Cambridge Companion to John Updike* and *Don DeLillo: Mao II, Underworld, Falling Man*. Her articles on contemporary American literature and culture have appeared in essay collections and journals such as *Modern Fiction Studies, Critical Inquiry, The Review of Contemporary Fiction, Michigan Quarterly Review*, and *Critique*.

The Cambridge Introduction to
Contemporary American Fiction

STACEY OLSTER

Stony Brook University

CAMBRIDGE
UNIVERSITY PRESS

CAMBRIDGE
UNIVERSITY PRESS

University Printing House, Cambridge CB2 8BS, United Kingdom

One Liberty Plaza, 20th Floor, New York, NY 10006, USA

477 Williamstown Road, Port Melbourne, VIC 3207, Australia

4843/24, 2nd Floor, Ansari Road, Daryaganj, Delhi – 110002, India

79 Anson Road, #06–04/06, Singapore 079906

Cambridge University Press is part of the University of Cambridge.

It furthers the University's mission by disseminating knowledge in the pursuit of
education, learning, and research at the highest international levels of excellence.

www.cambridge.org
Information on this title: www.cambridge.org/9781107049215
DOI: 10.1017/9781107278813

First published 2017

Printed in the United Kingdom by Clays, St Ives plc

A catalogue record for this publication is available from the British Library.

ISBN 978-1-107-04921-5 Hardback
ISBN 978-1-107-62717-8 Paperback

To the Olster-Mizrahi-Olanoff clan,
proof that quality does indeed trump quantity

Contents

Acknowledgments

I kvetch, therefore I am. It thus is fitting that I thank those who suffered the three-year kvetchathon that accompanied work on this project, however much word count limits restrict me to those who most, to paraphrase Faulkner, endured: as always, my sister, Deborah Olster (m.s. to my d.s.); the Thoroughly Unpleasant Professor Pizarro (Will to my Grace, Joaque to my Stace); Ronald Gordon (1 to my 1A, or was it 1A to my 1?). Thanks as well to all the various keepers: Ray Ryan, at Cambridge University Press, for keeping the faith; Marlon Ross and Tracey Walters, for keeping me honest; Ralph Clare, for keeping me going through *Infinite Jest* (no joke); Marjorie Parsons, in the United States, and Nathalie Cochoy, in France, for keeping the International Society of Scholarly Cheerleading afloat; the Versluys-Eeckhout Belgian Connection, for keeping me supplied with my drug of choice (chocolate); and the Upper East Side Dream Team, for keeping body and soul together. Special thanks to Benjamin Edwards for generously allowing his amazing artwork to be used as a cover image. Finally, to the memory of Richard Levine and Felice Levine: Let a thousand flowers bloom in Fenway Park.

Brooklyn, New York
2016

Introduction: From Sweet Home to Homeland

> "Home is a failed idea."
>
> – Don DeLillo, *Mao II* (1991)

Bill Gray, the reclusive writer who utters these words in Don DeLillo's novel, knows whereof he speaks. His ex-wives want nothing to do with him. His adult children mock him as mythical. Yet his remark about the failure of home does not refer to the upstate New York abode that houses his decades-in-the-making third novel and makeshift family of amanuensis who cooks and Moonie who cleans that live there with him as the book opens. On the contrary, the presence of a guest at dinner inspires Bill to toast the place as "feel[ing] like home" (67). What prompts Bill's more anguished words about home is the fact that he is forced to leave them on an answering machine, a device that severs all personal connection between speaker and listener. More to the point, as he goes on to say, the same device that generates a whole new kind of loneliness can also be accessed in Brussels to blow up a building in Madrid, thus replacing the idea of home as a zone of comfortable boundaries by the reality of a homeland that needs to be secured. This in a book published ten years before 9/11.

I open my description of what constitutes contemporary American fiction with reference to DeLillo's 1991 work because of how well it recapitulates the concerns of fiction written in the previous decades and how much it anticipates those that fiction in the two decades to come will explore. A "new communist element" and specifically not a "new fundamentalist element" (123), the Beirut terrorists in *Mao II* are political and historical throwbacks to Cold War binarism, the most recent form of that Us/Them dynamic that, as scholars have argued, has long been at the heart of American exceptionalism. Culturally, however, they testify to what a spokesperson terms the "many things Beirut has learned from the West" (129). Glued to VCRs, on which they watch footage of themselves in scuffed khakis shooting at local militia and, later, shooting at blown-up photographs of the local militia's leaders, the terrorists occupy a war-torn city that functions as a "millennial image mill" (229), a postmodern paradise in which all national differences have collapsed. Movie posters advertise films everywhere even though nowhere can there be

1

found anything that remotely resembles a movie theater. Signs for a Western soft drink – Coke II – resemble signs for China's Cultural Revolution. Boys stationed at checkpoints wear uniforms pieced together from Syrian, American, Lebanese, French, and Israeli garments. Indeed, more than just having learned from the West, DeLillo implies, Beirut is indistinguishable from the West – and from the US in particular. Introduced as having "sunk to the status of less developed country" (5), the US in this book *is* "just like Beirut," as the novel's refrain asserts (146, 173, 176), what with tent cities in Tompkins Square Park recalling refugee camps and cabdrivers sporting licenses that confound the "normal sequence" of given name and surname (148). And not just Beirut, as the portrayal of Times Square and Trafalgar Square and Tiananmen Square as interchangeable locales confirms.

In refusing to state explicitly that the year in which his novel is set is 1989, DeLillo recognizes the idiosyncratic element behind all attempts to date contemporary American literature with respect to the history of globalization. As Paul Giles argues, many different years can be, and have been, used to define the beginning of the contemporary period: the 1971 announcement of Richard Nixon that the United States would no longer redeem currency for gold, which ushered in an era of fluctuating exchange rates; the 1981 inauguration of Ronald Reagan, whose free-market philosophies increasingly drew the country into the global marketplace; the 1989 fall of the Berlin Wall; and the end of the Cold War (13–14). Nevertheless, from a postmillennial perspective, the connection between globalization and what he terms the current "deterritorialization of American literature" is beyond dispute (1). Such certainty in the impact of the political/historical on the cultural differs markedly from the hesitance shown by Amy Hungerford when commenting in 2008 upon "the period formerly known as contemporary": "Political watersheds are one thing, but cultural or aesthetic ones quite another, and it was not immediately clear – nor is it clear now – that, to borrow a turn of phrase from Virginia Woolf, literature changed, even if the world did, on or about 9 November 1989" (410). By the second decade of the twenty-first century, that impact is much more clear. The loss of American confidence that Dave Eggers addresses by way of an IT supplier sent to Saudi Arabia in *A Hologram for the King* (2012) is the same loss queried by John Updike in *Rabbit at Rest* (1990) after the bipolar politics of the Cold War have given way to an economics of "Japan, and technology, and the profit motive" (272): "what's the point of being an American?" (442–43).

Part of the urgency behind that question stems from the fact that the collapse of the very physical boundary between East and West in 1989 was followed by later events and phenomena that lent themselves – rightly or wrongly – to interpretations of other forms of collapse: the 2001 destruction of the World Trade Center (another collapsed boundary); the 2000 dot-com bust and 2008 economic meltdown (collapsed economy); the 2008 election and 2012 reelection of Barack Obama as president (collapsed racial binaries); global warming and climate change (collapsed ecosystem). Part is a function of earlier demographic shifts that collapsed the boundary between center and periphery and complicated all assumptions about the Eurocentric character of the nation: according to recent statistics cited by Richard Gray, 7.5 million foreign-born individuals entered the US legally between 1990 and 1997, many from outside Europe, accounting for 29.2 percent of the population growth; by the middle of the twenty-first century, nonwhite and Third World ethnic groups will outnumber whites (22). Writing in 1987, Gloria Anzaldúa described the US-Mexico border as *"una herida abierta"* (an open wound) where "the lifeblood of two worlds merg[es] to form a third country – a border culture" (3); addressing the American Studies Association in 2004, Shelley Fisher Fishkin quoted Paul Lauter depicting the entirety of America as part of a "world system, in which the exchange of commodities, the flow of capital, and the iterations of cultures know no borders" (21).

If literature is conceived as one such iteration of culture, the question to which such interrogating of America as a distinct entity leads is what constitutes an American author. Asking "What's in a Name?" in her own ASA presidential address, Janice Radway proposed doing away with the adjective entirely, based on the belief that the "perpetuation of the particular name, 'American,'" supports the notion of an "imaginary unity" that should be prevented "from asserting itself in the end, again and again, as a form of containment" (2–3). Focusing more specifically on the question of "[w]hat exactly is 'American literature'?" Wai Chee Dimock followed with two more: "Is it a sovereign domain, self-sustained and self-governing, integral as a body of evidence? Or is it . . . more like a municipality: a second-tier phenomenon, resting on a platform preceding it and encompassing it, and dependent on the latter for its infrastructure, its support network, its very existence as a subsidiary unit?" (1).

Still in the making, contemporary American fiction does not constitute the kind of "sovereign domain" alluded to above, as the wide range of established and less established authors included in this study makes clear. It resists categorization by way of authorial birthplace or citizenship or residence: too many writers have been born in one place and raised in or emigrated to another. Indeed, the older model of immigrant writers leaving one nation and settling in another – whether by intent (the Havana-born Cristina García and St. Petersburg–born Gary Shteyngart brought by their parents to the US as children) or accident (Ha Jin already in the US on a student visa when the

Tiananmen Square protests occurred in 1989, Aleksandar Hemon stranded in Chicago when the siege of Sarajevo began in 1992) – has been complicated by other kinds of geographical movement. Some writers born in the US have been raised elsewhere only to return to the US. One thinks, for instance, of Julia Alvarez moving between New York and the Dominican Republic, Teju Cole between the US and Lagos, and Claire Messud between Connecticut, Australia, and Toronto. Others roam more peripatetically. Jonathan Littell, born in New York City, raised in France, currently resides in Barcelona while holding dual American and French citizenship. Mohsin Hamid, born in Lahore, bouncing between the US and Pakistan from the age of three through his twenties, becoming a naturalized British citizen in his thirties, now lives in Lahore. Jhumpa Lahiri, born in London, raised in Rhode Island, moving from Brooklyn to Rome, recently returned to the US to teach at Princeton. As a result, the earlier narrative that traced the struggling immigrant's journey from old to new land, what Bruce Robbins calls the "immigration as redemption" pattern (1100), has been joined by the triangulated narrative that, as Caren Irr argues, exposes the slender lines that separate expatriate, émigré, and migrant (179–81).

At the same time, the contemporary American fiction included in this study avoids the limitless horizons that hemispheric denotes. While it expands the definition of "US" beyond the contiguous states, it still adheres to the historical particularities and politics of the nation that is comprised by those states. Such specificities explain the inclusion of Junot Díaz and Jessica Hagedorn, to take two examples. When Díaz opens *The Brief Wondrous Life of Oscar Wao* (2007) by tracing the "*[f]ukú americanus*" back to its port of entry, Santo Domingo (1), he refers to the intertwined histories of the US and the Dominican Republic, from the settlements established by Columbus in 1492 to the fiscal control exercised by the US between 1905 and 1941, from the Spanish soldiers left there in 1493 to the US Marines dispatched there from 1916 to 1924 and, again, in 1965. Likewise, when Jessica Hagedorn quotes William McKinley's justification-by-God's-grace speech of 1898 in a novel that opens in 1956, she recalls in *Dogeaters* (1990) the history of the Philippines as a US protectorate, an imperialist past that lives on as cultural imperialism long after the islands' 1946 independence, as emblematized in *Dream Jungle* (2003) by the making of *Napalm Sunset*, a fictionalized Vietnam War movie based on the actual Vietnam War movie, *Apocalypse Now* (1979), that was filmed in the Philippines. By contrast, such specificities do not characterize a writer such as Caryl Phillips, born in St. Kitts and raised in Leeds, whose fiction focuses much more on the connections between the West Indies and England, despite the fact that a novel such as *Dancing in the Dark*

(2005), which portrays the life of Bert Williams, a Broadway entertainer born in the Bahamas, would seem to qualify him as relevant.

In examining the fiction of writers who expand the notion of what constitutes contemporary American fiction beyond those with indisputable Americanist pedigrees (Joan Didion descended from a member of the Donner-Reed party, Thomas Pynchon from a patentee and treasurer of the Massachusetts Bay Colony) or those born in the US to immigrant parents (such as Gish Jen and Oscar Hijuelos), this study takes heed of an important point that David Cowart makes when querying the applicability of those postcolonial paradigms that scholars so often employ: "Though not necessarily inclined to sacrifice separateness and difference on the altar of cultural osmosis, these [immigrant] writers seldom dwell on a perceived marginalization" (*Trailing* 3). Many, as he goes on to say, deliberately resurrect the oldest American tropes or rewrite the most canonical American texts, as evidenced by Chang-rae Lee's appropriation of *All the King's Men* (1946) in *Native Speaker* (1995), to which one might add *The Scarlet Letter* (1850) in Bharati Mukherjee's *The Holder of the World* (1993) and *The Great Gatsby* (1925) in Joseph O'Neill's *Netherland* (2008). A similar recognition, I would argue, must be maintained when dealing with American fiction written during the period of contemporary globalization. For all the adjectives proposed by scholars to denote the cultural artifacts produced over the last quarter of a century ("cosmopolitan," "planetary," and, appropriating a term coined by Randolph Bourne in 1916, "transnational"), and for all the different models used to replace a US nation conceived as a container (intertwined networks for Radway, set and subset modules for Dimock), the novelists who actually compose American literature do not always follow suit.

For regionalist writers, this can mean subordinating the global to the local, as occurs in a novel such as Richard Russo's *Empire Falls* (2001), its suggestive title and origins in the closing of a Maine textile mill and shirt factory by a multinational corporation notwithstanding. It also can mean extrapolating from the local to the national, as occurs in Frederick Busch's *Girls* (1997) and *North* (2005), in which the upstate New York act of rescue, typically the return of a lost body, functions as an act of citizenship, a function of the body politic. For immigrant writers, it even can mean affirming the act of becoming a legal citizen, as happens in Shteyngart's *The Russian Debutante's Handbook* (2002), in which no amount of theme-park simulation can dispel the hero's sensation of being the "Live Jew of Birkenau" during a trip to an Auschwitz turned into a tourist attraction (429), and Hemon's *Nowhere Man* (2002), in which the authorial alter ego from a Yugoslavia that no longer exists remains a "Nobody" forever aspiring to be "Someone Else" (180), in effect a country of one, "the Bosnian," as Jozef Pronek's habitual difficulty with articles attests (146, 156). Fully aware of what the actuality of the United States as nation is, many writers still are reluctant to dismiss the ideal of what America represents. Nothing suggests more succinctly the US as fallen nation than the two cones of a nuclear plant and the floating detritus of "Eden's waste" that greet the eponymous narrator of Mukherjee's *Jasmine* (1989) upon her illegal entry into Florida (96). Yet nothing more celebrates "the promise of America" than the pregnant character's departure for California on the book's last page to give birth – in an appropriation of one of the oldest American literary tropes – to what will be the latest incarnation of herself (214). Likewise, nothing conveys more clearly the current status of the United States as sovereign state than the scene near the end of O'Neill's *Netherland*, in which Hans van den Broek, a Dutchman living in London after a sojourn in New York City, goes to Google Maps to look for a cricket field he has helped to carve out in Brooklyn a few years earlier, only to find no trace of his labors and, once he veers upward into the atmosphere on his laptop, "no trace of nations, no sense of the work of man. The USA as such is nowhere to be seen" (252). That being said, nothing establishes more joyously Hans's status as a "naturalized" American than the scene in which this analyst so resistant to all things "fantastical" (103), so fearful of batting "the American way" (50), finally slams a cricket ball into the air much like a baseball, and does so "without injury to my sense of myself" (176).

The tremendous productivity of the novelists discussed in the chapters to follow proves their resistance to the affliction that plagues Bill Gray – to return to *Mao II* for a moment – an author as demoralized by terrorism's usurpation of writers' ability to "alter the inner life of the culture" and commercialism's wholesale "incorporat[ion]" of writers as he is paralyzed by the modernist weight of Joyce and Beckett (41). The variety of position statements composed by today's novelists, in fact, signals an equally varied range of concerns when addressing what many specifically identify as American in nature: from the "billion-footed beast" stalked by Tom Wolfe in his "Literary Manifesto for the New Social Novel" (45) to the hypertext advanced by Robert Coover as an "inevitab[le]" medium for future narrative (9), from the single entendres David Foster Wallace dared US fictionists to adopt to extricate themselves from the "deep doo" of a postmodernism mired in televisual self-reference ("E Unibus" 184) to a maximalism that transcends identity politics Bharati Mukherjee sought from immigrant writers barred from a nativist minimalism ("Immigrant" 28–29), from the "empathizing" prescribed by William T. Vollmann when diagnosing the "disease" of "American Writing Today" (330) to the "plagiarizi[ng]" redefined by Jonathan Lethem as forming "the actual and valuable material of all human utterances" (including his own, as the appended key to every source he "stole, warped, and cobbled together" to make his essay proves) ("Ecstasy" 68). No longer dwelling on the question of what is left to write in the manner of John Barth's "Literature of Exhaustion" (1967) – which never was really about actual creative exhaustion but the perceived threat of it, a feeling that the "Literature of Replenishment" (1980) portrayed as hardly unique to the twentieth century – these novelists write, whatever doubts they may harbor about the current state of the novel. No longer bemoaning an anxiety of influence, they affirm what Lethem termed the "*ecstasy of influence*" (67). Some do more than that. Tim O'Brien asserts "story-truth" as "truer sometimes than happening-truth" (203). Carole Maso offers writing that provides not just a model "for how to live" but a model that can "teach us how to better live."

It is with the aim of exposing readers – specialists and nonspecialists alike – to that wide range of American fiction that this study, in turn, is offered. In so doing, I am aware that comprehensive can never be exhaustive, that determining what for practical purposes must be left out and what kept in has been part of the balancing of depth and coverage that has informed this project from the start. To that end, my focus has been on the novel rather than the short story collection, my emphasis typically on an author's exemplary work (or works) rather than list of works. That some of those authors appear in more than one chapter testifies not just to my admiration of their talents but to the diversity of their talents and the fact that the sensibilities of writers can change over time. For every author such as Gore Vidal, whose seven-part chronicling of a nation evolving from republic to empire is as consistent in *The Golden Age* (2000) as it is in *Washington, D.C.* (1967) – the path of Burr not taken as unlikely to have been much different from the path that was taken – there is an author such as Susan Sontag, whose early eliding of history through dreamscape frames in *The Benefactor* (1963) and *Death Kit* (1967) is completely upset when *The Volcano Lover* (1992) presents the 1799 Neapolitan Revolution as proof of the nightmare that is history. The same applies to those authors approached in ways deliberately meant to unsettle expectations, as illustrated, for example, by my consideration of Jonathan Lethem and Paul Auster as political novelists and Ann Beattie and Stephen King (yes, that Stephen King) as writers of historical metafiction.

And, to state the obvious, I also recognize the inherently self-defeating element of any study that includes the word "contemporary" in its title: today's contemporary is, after all, tomorrow's antediluvian. That being said, it is not with any view toward supplanting the work that precedes this study that I add my voice to a conversation initiated by Tony Tanner's *City of*

Words: American Fiction, 1950–1970 (1971), Frederick R. Karl's *American Fictions, 1940–1980* (1983), and Marc Chénetier's *Beyond Suspicion: New American Fiction since 1960* (1989), and continued in single-authored texts by Kathryn Hume, Kenneth Millard, and Patrick O'Donnell and essay collections edited by scholars such as Malcolm Bradbury and Sigmund Ro, Jay Prosser, and John N. Duvall. Chénetier, who replaced the idea of a mainstream perpetually reconstituting itself by absorbing eruptions into its wake with a mainstream consistently pulling away from expected currents, abjured the idea of looking at literary history in terms of forward progress. "'Revolutions' in the novel," he wrote, "are often just as much a 'return to' as a 'breaking away from'" (13). In situating this study as part of what, at this point in time, can be deemed a history of contemporary American literary histories, I see myself engaged in a similar endeavor, of pushing what follows the "since" in the subtitles of earlier scholarship – 1960 for Chénetier and Hume, 1970 for Millard, 1980 for O'Donnell – further along chronologically so as to explore the changes and continuities, additions and alterations, displayed by American fiction. I thus begin with chapters that focus on the contemporary novel's updating of genres that occupy a prominent place in the American literary canon, notably the historical novel, regional realism, and the political novel. The next chapters focus on the contemporary novel in the context of recent history, in particular on its interrogating of what is (and is not) specific to those events or phenomena – such as 9/11 and globalization – said to distinguish that history. The last chapters focus on the contemporary novel's depiction of American identity, from the role played by border and race to the role played by documents and mere happenstance in the determination of subjectivity. A conclusion turns to aesthetics to explore the future of the contemporary American novel – as postscript hypertext or digitally designed novel, as genre novel, as post-postmodern novel.

All of which brings me to the title of an introduction – which takes a text rather than a year as its rough starting point and ends with a term attributed new meaning in the US after 9/11 – that might serve as a subtitle to my entire book. "It wasn't sweet and it sure wasn't home," says the last of the Sweet Home men in Toni Morrison's *Beloved* (1987), to which Sethe, who has suffered every form of brutalization and humiliation on the plantation of that name, responds, "But it's where we were . . . Comes back whether we want it to or not" (14). Much as the idea of home has for centuries. Bridget Bennett, in fact, traces the ability of the imagination to create or re-create a home out of the most unlikely conditions back to the earliest settlers for whom the transformation of a previously unfamiliar landscape into a home was a crucial element of colonization and ultimately nation building, as her discussion of one of the foundational texts of American literature, Mary Rowlandson's 1682 captivity narrative, makes clear (328–33). It is that legacy that the young soldier of Kevin Power's *The Yellow Birds* (2012), returned from Iraq to "the emptiness [he] still called home" in Virginia (111), invokes when recalling the "early English settlers [who] took it as the farthest point they'd go upstream, the geology of the place preventing them from having any choice other than the one wherein they said, 'We are lost; therefore we will call this home'" (133). The word "homeland," however, has no such lineage. A term never used by presidents prior to George W. Bush when referring to the US in times of world crisis and hence recent to the American lexicon, as Amy Kaplan argues, its Old World assumptions about fixed origins, common bloodlines, and shared mythic past are as antithetical to the exceptionalist notion of America as New World as are its diasporic connotations of a deeply rooted past from which one is severed (84–90). Bracketing an introduction to an introduction to contemporary American fiction with reference to home and homeland, then, expresses the contextualizing of that fiction as both of a specific time and of a specific set of traditions that informs the whole study.

It also expresses the vexed nature of what home, broadly defined, has come to signify in so much of that fiction – a Kentucky plantation on which boys hang from the most beautiful sycamore trees in Morrison's book, a Fifth Avenue mansion within which brothers try to barricade themselves in E. L. Doctorow's *Homer & Langley* (2009), a temporary shelter with attached mortgage to the realtor in Richard Ford's *Independence Day* (1995), a crumbling wreck from which the narrator in Mat Johnson's *Loving Day* (2015) seeks to liberate himself – and the resilience the idea of home displays. When the mixed-race protagonist of Johnson's novel opts to burn down the Philadelphia ruin he has inherited at the book's opening – an eighteenth-century estate haunted by ghosts that literally sits upon a hill in the text's Americanist characterization – he discovers that the building consistently referred to as his "father's house" is impervious to flames. When he makes inquiries about moving it elsewhere, he is told that, for all its rotting foundation and cracked walls, the house could be taken "halfway around the world and it would hold" (256). But when it finally is removed to Malaga in the book's conclusion to serve as home for a mixed-race community whose members wish to "keep it safe" (285), he learns that the "house [that] is still there" that also is a "house [that] will always be here" might be an edifice worth preserving (275). And left with the land on which that property sat, he remains with a place on which to build.

Chapter 1

History and the Novel

> We are sui generis, Homer, he said. Unless someone comes along as
> remarkably prophetic as we are, I'm obliged to ignore our existence.
> – E. L. Doctorow, *Homer & Langley* (2009).

Homer Collyer, introduced as "the blind brother" in the opening line of
E. L. Doctorow's novel, refuses to follow suit. In contrast to his sibling,
Langley, who omits the Collyers from his "forever up-to-date newspaper"
because their uniqueness precludes their reduction to those Universal Forms
at which his compilation aims (176), Homer opts to record the brothers'
history and reclaim it from the tale of two recluses into which local reporters
have already turned it. "For," as he explains, "what could be more terrible than
being turned into a mythic joke?" (200). In so doing, this contemporary
namesake of an ancient Greek chronicler exposes the difference between the
seeing brother blinded by myopia and the sightless brother who possesses true
vision. Defending their Fifth Avenue home as "our inviolate realm" (90), and
fortified by a belief in Emersonian self-reliance, Langley pays for his unilater-
alism with his life – buried under tons of American junk after accidentally
setting off a trip wire for one of the booby traps meant to preserve the border
between inside and out. Aware that every act of self-reliance "was in service of
our ruination" (200), Homer, however, recognizes the brothers' implication
in the world beyond their doorstep. When a French journalist expresses
surprise at the heavy shutters attached to their once-great mansion, given
that the United States, as compared to Europe, does not seem to have "enough
history" to warrant such protection, Homer corrects her assumption: "Maybe
there is enough history to go around" (185). And armed with such understanding, Homer can foresee two alternatives for the Collyer history and, by
extension, US history: an "end-of-the-line" or a "supreming of the line,
a flowering of the family tree" (177). Steadfast in his antiquated convictions,
Langley can only orchestrate "the means of our last stand" (201).

I quote deliberately here because of how well Doctorow's re-creation of
these two actual figures evokes one of the most oft-cited characterizations of
the contemporary period, Francis Fukuyama's *The End of History and the Last*

Man (1992). To be sure, this was hardly the first time that a *fin-de-millénaire* period produced cries of historical demise, as evidenced by Henry Adams's equally well-known dictum with respect to an earlier turn of the century: "Only in 1900, the continuity snapped" (457). Indeed, American millennialism, the prevailing idea of history since the colonial era, was predicated on an end to history, and the ambivalence generated by an apocalyptic finale to be followed by a paradisiacal restoration. What distinguished the 1989 article in which Fukuyama's claim first appeared was the way its celebration of the "universalization of Western liberal democracy as the final form of human government" that the end of the Cold War heralded ("End" 4) – so different in tone from the fears of nuclear annihilation inspired by that war's onset – concluded with a lamentation for the "end of history" as "a very sad time" (18). At issue, as Walter Benn Michaels correctly observes, was nothing less than American identity and the ideals by which that identity was defined: "insofar as the end of the Cold War (at least as Fukuyama understands it) means that the Russians *have* come to believe in them (and the end of history means that *everyone* has come to believe in them), the distinctiveness (the Americanness) of the American Creed has disappeared" (*Shape* 25).

In theory, such challenges to national identity should have been devastating to the writing of American historical novels, coming on the heels of those challenges posed by postmodern theorists who queried both the narrative of history (reduced to emplotment by Hayden White, a *grand récit* replaced by *petits récits* according to Jean-François Lyotard) and the historical novel's ability to represent the past at all, given, as Fredric Jameson famously wrote, the "new and original historical situation in which we are condemned to seek History by way of our own pop images and simulacra of that history, which itself remains forever out of reach" (25). The novel as genre, after all, has been the literary form most associated with the rise of modern nation-states since their late eighteenth- and early nineteenth-century inception. The historical novel in particular, as defined by Georg Lukács, was devoted to bringing a nation's "past to life as the prehistory of the present" (53), specifically, by presenting nationhood as the product of, on the one hand, turbulent transformations and, on the other, a developmental national history within which those transformations were given meaning (23–26). And yet the contemporary American historical novel has flourished over the last two-and-a-half decades. Multivolume works composed by both older and younger writers (the last three volumes of Gore Vidal's seven-part American Chronicle and five volumes of William T. Vollmann's Seven Dreams series; James Ellroy's Underworld USA, Madison Smartt Bell's Haitian Revolution, and Kevin Baker's City of Fire trilogies) were joined by single volumes composed by the most unlikely of writers (Susan Sontag, Stephen King). Fictional biographies of iconic figures (Martin Luther King in Charles Johnson's *Dreamer* [1998], Sojourner Truth in Jacqueline Sheehan's *Truth* [2003]) were complemented by fictional biographies of unknown figures (Mamah Borthwick Cheney, Frank Lloyd Wright's mistress, in Nancy Horan's *Loving Frank* [2007]) and legendary figures (John Henry in Colson Whitehead's *John Henry Days* [2001]). Chronicles of New York City produced an ongoing saga, from New York City in the Gilded Age (E. L. Doctorow's *The Waterworks* [1994], Marge Piercy's *Sex Wars* [2005]) and the turn of the century (Caleb Carr's *The Alienist* [1994] and *The Angel of Darkness* [1997]) to New York City throughout the twentieth century (Colum McCann's *This Side of Brightness* [1998]) and over multiple centuries (Pete Hamill's *Forever* [2002], Edward Rutherfurd's *New York: The Novel* [2009]).

In emphasizing the process by which history is constructed and the role played by the chronicler, the contemporary novels in the discussions that follow recall many classic American novels – Hawthorne's *The Scarlet Letter* (1850), Melville's *Israel Potter* (1855) – that subvert their own authority by discrediting the texts, often "found" texts, cited in their introductory frames. At the same time, the eschewing of complete relativism that often infuses their metafictional representations of history gestures toward the "new commitment to the materiality of history" that Peter Boxall sees emerging in the most recent twenty-first-century treatments of the past (12). The first set addresses the contemporary challenges to national identity as Thomas Pynchon, Bharati Mukherjee, and Toni Morrison return to the colonial period during which that identity became established and complicate a developmental national history by situating it as part of globally intertwined histories. The second set re-creates the lives of historical American figures, beginning with those presented by T. Coraghessan Boyle, Joyce Carol Oates, and Ann Beattie as what Joan Didion termed "Michelin[s] to [their] time and place" (*White* 57), and ending with the central figures of the Kennedy assassination chosen by Don DeLillo, Norman Mailer, and Stephen King for their role in the 5.6 seconds that, in DeLillo's view, "broke the back of the American century" ("American Blood" 21; *Libra* 181). Finally, the third set explores American literary history by way of rewritten canonical texts and homages to canonical American authors, acts of legitimizing and ironizing that, as performed by Frederick Busch, Charles Johnson, and Michael Cunningham, enact what Linda Hutcheon has termed the "politics of parody" (93–117) while contesting the entire ideal of aesthetic autonomy.

The Way We Were(n't)

Set in 1786, Thomas Pynchon's *Mason & Dixon* (1997) opens with a nation "bickering itself into Fragments," even with "the War settl'd" (6); it ends with the decision of Charles Mason's two eldest children to stay in Philadelphia after his death and "be Americans" (772). Yet "What is an American?" – the question posed by Crèvecoeur four years earlier – is hardly apparent. As the recollections of the Reverend Wicks Cherrycoke that form the bulk of the novel make clear, even while proclaiming themselves "Americans All" prior to that war of independence, the colonists have very little sense of national identity. Some are defined by way of regional origins: "New-Yorkers in Georgia, Pennsylvanians in the Carolinas, Virginians ev'rywhere" (570). Others are cultural hybrids whose identities vary according to partic-ular context: the Virginian George Washington displays an old pitman's lilt to the British Dixon, but sounds like an African to Pennsylvanians; his African American servant Gershom is also a *yarmulke*-wearing Jew. Far from being a nation distinct unto itself, a paean to all things "new" as Crèvecoeur claimed (38–39), Pynchon's America is but "a Patch of England, at a three-thousand-Mile Off-set" (248), whose dissidents' original impulse, as scholars of the American Enlightenment have long argued, was restorative in nature, namely, the return of those liberties traditionally granted all British subjects by England's constitution.

In Pynchon's depiction, in fact, the establishment of a Visto, or line, that sends Charles Mason and Jeremiah Dixon to America in the first place only exposes the vexing contradictions at the heart of exceptionalist American ideology. This America, as Dixon reports prior to the men's departure, is a place where colonists are "inclin'd to kill the People already living where they wish to settle" (248), a New World only insofar as such settlement would later be justified by the rhetoric of Manifest Destiny. Filled with hirelings, indentured servants, and contractual agents, not to mention those Africans who form the economic basis of the trade the colonists are attempting to protect from British interference, America is, as the melancholic Mason notes, just "[a]nother Slave-Colony" (248). As such, it is no different from the Cape of Good Hope to which the men journey to observe the Transit of Venus in the novel's first section, and different from the US of Pynchon's earlier works only in extending enslavement beyond binary opposition (Elect/Preterite in *Gravity's Rainbow* [1973], gender in *Vineland* [1990]). "Who is unique?" asks Pynchon in this novel. "Who is not own'd by someone?" (551).

More to the point, the Visto by which Mason and Dixon are to resolve formally an eighty-two-year-old contested boundary (1681–1763) exposes the artificiality of *all* national boundaries. For if, at the end of the duo's labors, "there exists no 'Maryland' beyond an Abstraction, a Frame of right lines drawn to enclose and square off the great Bay" no more "than there exists any 'Pennsylvania' but a chronicle of Frauds committed serially against the Indians dwelling there" (354), there exists no "America" beyond the mapping of America, a pictorial rendering much like the colored "Pen-and-Paper Representation" drawn by Dixon (687), making the birth of the nation less a question of politics – "no taxation without representation" – than of aesthetic delineation. Far more solid and not melting into air, to rephrase Marx and Engels, is the Visto that eventuates in an eighty-mile-long shopping mall (701), Pynchon's emblem for the period of late capitalism, in which globalization has shifted power from nation-states to huge conglomerates.

Nowhere is that shift better illustrated than in the depiction of the East India Company, located "ev'rywhere, and [in] Ev'rything" (69), "richer than many a Nation, yet with no Boundaries," with individual outposts that all perform "the Doings of Global Trade in miniature" (140, 159), and typifying the new decentered and deterritorialized apparatus that Michael Hardt and Antonio Negri have called "Empire." It is to the East India Company that Pynchon attributes every abuse of power that, in earlier works, he ascribes to the State – illegal searches, impounded property, violations of civil liberties – but with one important difference. The "stately Finger" in *Gravity's Rainbow* that points to a "city of the future" in which "there is noplace to hide" and IG Farben is *"the very model of nations"* may reflect the paranoia of characters who think that Providence is always giving them the finger (566). The "Invisible Hand," in *Mason & Dixon*'s appropriation of Adam Smith, with whose workings one dare not interfere is indubitably "a superior Power,— not, in this case, God, but rather, Business" (411). No wonder Dixon feels discomfort with interstitial spaces in such an "all-business world" (164), in which Lord Pennycomequick reigns as "global-Communications Nabob" (721). Conceptually unable, in Jameson's terms, "to map the great global multinational and decentered communicational network" in which he feels himself ensnared (44), he cannot locate himself, either perceptually or cognitively, in a mappable external world. The only question that remains is whether the "overhead view" of that world that he must produce as part of his employment will represent an alternative "World he could escape to, if he had to" (242), or remain a miniaturized version of the one in which he finds himself already embedded.

The nationally constructive role that cartography plays in Pynchon's version of American origins is assumed by embroidery in Bharati Mukherjee's *The Holder of the World* (1993), which returns to a still earlier period

(1632–1750) to expose "the tangled lines of India and New England" by way of two characters (11): the "pre-America American" Hannah Easton, who journeys from Brookfield to England to India and then back to Salem; and the "post-deEuropeanized American" assets hunter Beigh Masters ("Holders" 19), who offers her reconstruction of Hannah's life as "the real story of the brave Salem mother and her illegitimate daughter" from which Nathaniel Hawthorne "sh[ied] away" (284). That story is not, however, a cautionary tale about "those who step over the border" (148), as the many instances of miscegenation (Hannah's mother and a Nipmuc brave, Hannah and a Hindu raja, Beigh and an Indian computer programmer) and parallels between Mary Rowlandson and the *Ramayana*'s Sita might suggest. Rather, it is a tale that harks back to Columbus's mistaking New World natives for South Asians, and proceeds by way of spatial and temporal juxtaposition to reveal "the story of North America turned inside out" (160). On the one hand, the Taj Mahal arises on the banks of the Yamuna while the first Masters to arrive in America erects a log cabin next to a hog pen. On the other hand, India in the 1690s experiences "late-stage capitalism" just as the US does in the 1980s (101), with multinational chains stretching up and down the Coromandel Coast "like condos on the Florida coast" and outsourced manufacturing nearly shutting down the British clothing mills (102). In this novel's unsettling of center and periphery, England is "dead, finished, washed up"; the New World is "for losers" (102); and India is ruled by a man who sits on a throne over which is suspended a golden replica of the globe, a "mobile fit for an emperor who ha[s] seized all other empires contained in the universe" (263).

The aesthetics that govern such collapses and collisions derive from two main sources. One is Mughal miniature painting, whose multiple narratives and separate foci still insist upon simultaneity and "the interpenetration of all things" ("Four-Hundred-Year-Old" 27–28), a perspective reinforced by the many examples of embroidery that punctuate the text – the sampler of tropical setting and dark-skinned people that the young Hannah stitches, the skin grafts with brightly colored threads that she later practices on squirrels, even the "word pictures" that form the "rampant embroidery" by which her adventurer husband woos her (63, 68) – emblems of the narrative that Beigh herself is in the process of fashioning. If such interlacing makes for a history "as tightly woven as a Kashmiri shawl" (189), the virtual reality program that Beigh's lover, Venn, is perfecting facilitates a much more interactive model of history, a history of "a billion separate information bytes" and an infinity of possible permutations (7) – yet not, significantly, histories of equal integrity. As Beigh realizes, after the donning of headgear and electronic gloves leaves her spending ten seconds with a Century 21 agent in Kansas City, "data are not neutral" (279). Judgment matters. In the "sinner's alphabet" of seventeenth-century New England (41), "A" may be for "Adulterer," "B" for "Blasphemer," and "I" for "Indian lover," but in the "subversive alphabet" that Hannah is taught by her mother, "*A*" is for "Act," "*B*" is for "Boldness," and "*I*" is for "Independence" (54).

For all its celebration of multiple perspectives, then, the book avoids a relativistic perspective. It is this avoidance that enables Mukherjee, the Brahmin who emigrates from Calcutta to Canada to Iowa, to characterize what is an American in a way that Pynchon, the descendant of Puritans who arrive on the *Arbella*, does not. In contrast to those who, alternately, trade on or sack the Coromandel Coast and "ha[ve] no home, no loyalties except to themselves" (182), Hannah has a very clear sense of America as home, which she asserts on two crucial occasions: when confronting a Muslim general in the middle of battle who mistakenly refers to her as "English" (247), and when imploring her Hindu lover to "[c]ome home with me" instead of continuing a battle he cannot win (255). Mukherjee is aware, of course, that what enables Hannah to make these declarations is the fact that she is a *white* American, secure in the belief that "[n]othing could happen to her, not from alien enemies" (244), and confident that she can negotiate an end to war with an emperor older than the Massachusetts Bay Colony. Yet what makes an *American* to Mukherjee ultimately has less to do with the fixities of race or birthplace and more to do with those fluidities that know no borders. The New World "Firsters" of 1630 who believe "that the first time anything had been made, built, eaten, sold or raised was inevitably the best" engage in a form of "idolatry" (72, 73) no different from that of Old World Indians who are shackled by "blood-memory" and subscribe to divine fate (253). Hannah – orphaned as Easton, adopted as Fitch, married as Legge, made consort as Salem Bibi and imperial fetish as Precious-as-Pearl – who is forced to recognize that "[e]verything was in flux" while living on the Coromandel Coast, learns in India that "[t]he survivor is the one who improvises, not follows, the rules" (234). It is this willingness to transform and, if need be, transgress that characterizes those Mukherjee terms "'Americans' in the making," regardless of "whether or not they ever make it" to America's shores ("Four-Hundred-Year-Old" 27). When Hannah finally returns to Salem with her mixed-race daughter, Pearl – to whom she gives birth, fittingly, while in transit, "somewhere in the South Atlantic" (284) – she can set up a household in which "seditious sentiments were openly aired," however much their utterances of "We are Americans to freedom born!" miss the point that Americans are not so much born as constantly reborn (285).

None of the characters in Toni Morrison's *A Mercy* (2008) is afforded such liberty because all are portrayed as implicated in a seventeenth-century global economy that stretches from Angola to Portugal to Barbados to America, in which "[r]um rules, no matter who does the trading" (31), and "tobacco and slaves [are] married, each currency clutching its partner's elbow" (14). They are not yet implicated in a wholly racialized economy, however, as an early reference to the union of "blacks, natives, whites, [and] mulattoes – freedmen, slaves and indentured" who mount Bacon's Rebellion (1676) attests (10). Territory is "ad hoc," land claims are "fluid" (13), and Virginia is "still a mess" (11). Unlike the Calvinist Massachusetts, defined by religious piety, and the Catholic Maryland, distinguished by trade with foreign markets, Virginia – the setting for Morrison's City upon a Hill – is introduced as a wilderness, sixty acres of which the "ratty orphan" Jacob Vaark and his wife try to cultivate (12), "mindful of a distinction between earth and property" (54), aided by a racially mixed group of other orphans and strays who view themselves as forming a "small, tight family" (58). The mouths of the serpents on the gate of this Edenic garden end in flowers, not fangs.

The fact that it is Jacob's inheritance – which is to say ownership – of those acres that allows him to erect that gate in the first place testifies to the doomed nature of his exceptionalist exception: Florens, the black girl whose braided narratives comprise the book, records her history with a nail on the walls and floor of the deserted house that Vaark erects as a monument to himself but never lives to see. Likewise, for all his disdain of "wealth dependent on a captured workforce" and belief that those who work his own land have arrived there through acts of "rescue" (28, 34), each of the individuals that make up his workforce arrives in payment of a debt. Florens is accepted as part payment from a Portuguese plantation owner, the mentally touched Sorrow in exchange for a lumber purchase, the indentured Willard and Scully in a "land-for-toil trade" with a neighbor (148). Even Rebekka, the mail-order bride for whom Jacob advertises, requires a "reimbursement" to be made to her parents (74). Only Lina – "rescued" after her Native American village is decimated by measles (44, 46) – he admits to having "purchased outright and deliberately" (34), and for Lina passing through the "sinister gate" adorned with "[t]wo copper snakes" is tantamount to "entering the world of the damned" (51).

The pride that cometh before the fall Morrison traces to the Vaarks' presumption of self-sufficiency; the Fall itself she portrays as given, inevitable in a market economy: Jacob can no more resist the "fever of building" after his visit to the D'Ortega plantation than he can the smallpox fever that eventually kills him (89). Yet the fever that leaves him, much like the first Slothrops of

Gravity's Rainbow, felling trees in large numbers to build a bigger double-storied house for which the childless couple has no use attests to what Morrison, in interviews, has cited as an especially American characteristic ("Toni Morrison"). This fever does not originate in Jacob's viewing of those luxury items, dismissed by him as "useless baubles," that make the Portuguese slave owner's domicile look like "a place where one held court" (19, 14). It springs instead from the competitive instincts awakened by having bested D'Ortega in a business deal, reminding Jacob, "not for the first time, that only things, not bloodlines or character, separated them" (27), specifically, things that can be denoted as "mine" (62) and that, as evidenced by the more satisfying plan to enter the Barbados rum trade that Jacob "fondle[s]," appeal to masculine desire (35).

No woman in the novel can escape masculine desire, or the violence that so often accompanies it. Florens's mother experiences a forced "breaking in" upon her arrival as a slave in Barbados (165–66); Lina is brutalized with fist and whip while living among the "kindly Presbyterians" (47). Even Scully, a man, is molested at age twelve by an Anglican curate, who then flogs him to conceal the circumstances of their union. At the same time, no woman during the period in which the book is set (1682–1690) can exist independent of male protection, subject as all women are to the doctrine of coverture. The one belief that the "exiled, thrown-away women" who journey to America with Rebekka in steerage (82) and the Anabaptist churchwomen already living there share concerns "the promise and threat of men": "Here, they agreed, was where security and risk lay" (98). Rebekka thus understands the relative safety that marriage affords her as a *feme covert*, a legal being by virtue of her existence having been incorporated into that of her husband: "Wife beating was common, she knew, but the restrictions – not after nine at night, with cause and not anger – were for wives and only wives" (94–95). She also understands the precarious situation she faces after the death of that husband leaves her "a widow [who] was in practice illegal" (98), a state of affairs even more threatening to the "three unmastered women" and infant daughter who remain on Vaark's property and who, "belonging to no one," will "bec[o]me wild game for anyone" in the event of Rebekka's death, subject to "purchase, hire, assault, abduction, exile" simply for being "[f]emale and illegal" (58). As Florens's mother states in the book's final chapter, "There is no protection. To be female in this place is to be an open wound that cannot heal" (163).

Mukherjee comes to a similar conclusion near the end of her novel, when Hannah challenges the Mughal emperor to identify who has "poisoned the hearts of men" and locates the blame in "anyone who confuses protection with power" (*Holder* 268). But in having Florens's mother qualify her assertion with the phrase "there is difference," Morrison offers a more nuanced view of the acts of mercy that are still possible in a country not yet codified (*Mercy* 166), acts that, however compromised or self-serving, nonetheless bypass all those binaries that would come to serve as foundation for the patriarchal nation. A white girl accused of witchcraft "[r]isks all" to facilitate the escape of the black girl, Florens, whose presence has deflected interest from her (160). A man, Scully, afraid of losing the earnings that will free him from servitude to a woman, tries "when possible and in secret" to "soften or erase the hurt" inflicted when, in the absence of alternative models, that widowed woman starts beating and mistreating the other women who work for her (155). And one white man takes one black child in payment for another white man's debt because the child's mother sees him as someone who, in contrast to her Portuguese owner, has the look of a man who "did not want" and can therefore view her daughter "as a human child, not pieces of eight" (163, 166). Florens's mother errs, of course, in assuming that a lack of sexual desire signals an absence of desire – Jacob, as the rest of the book shows, has tremendous wants; he just prefers not to see in person the shackled human beings who satisfy them. Yet she is correct in recognizing Jacob as a man who understands that "there was no good place in the world for waifs and whelps other than the generosity of strangers" and that those bound to adults, in any way, are, at the very least, "less doomed" (32). To be sure, such acts of human responsibility, without the cement of clan or kin, can go only so far in creating the kind of imagined community by which Benedict Anderson has delineated nationhood, but, in Morrison's return to the colonial past, the affiliations to which they lead are, as Scully and his aptly named partner Mr. Bond realize, "enough to imagine a future" (156).

American Icons

The future envisioned by the Americans in T. Coraghessan Boyle's work typically joins the utopian socialism of the nineteenth century with the religious fervor of the seventeenth. The homes these dreamers create, however, expose the discrepancies between aim and actuality. Nothing better illustrates the irony – and resultant tragedy – of those discrepancies than the life of architect Frank Lloyd Wright (1867–1959), who acclaimed a "true home" the "finest ideal of man" in his *Autobiography* (1943) just prior to asserting the need to gain his own freedom through divorce and who designed Prairie houses around a central hearth and integrated family space despite having little use for the six children in his own family (163). His "fictional re-creation" (n. pag.) in *The Women* (2009) extends Boyle's fictionalized biographies of health guru (and cornflakes inventor) John Harvey Kellogg in *The Road to Wellville* (1993) and sex researcher Alfred C. Kinsey in *The Inner Circle* (2004) in order to address "the same old conundrum: how to build what he saw in his mind's eye" (368). In this instance, though, the lens through which the life is filtered belongs to the invented figure of Tadashi Sato, the sole non-Western apprentice to work with Wright in America. Much like the self-styled "pioneer" Kinsey, as parsimonious in his personal habits as he is profligate in his sexual desires (*Inner* 394), Sato's Wright is an embodiment of American contra-dictions: a "rugged individualist" resembling the "lone cowboy[s] of the Wild West films" (*Women* 225); a celebrity self-promoter and con man only exceeded in his efforts by P. T. Barnum; a preacher's son who literally founds his City upon a Hill, Taliesin, as a house on the brow of a hill in Wisconsin and approaches all stimulants with an attitude that is "almost Puritanical" (222). Unlike Kinsey, revered *like* a "master" by those "disciple[s]" that form his inner circle and loved as both a surrogate father and "in the way a patriot loves his country or a zealot his God" (*Inner* 97, 260), Wright actually functions *as* a "Master" to those young "acolytes" who – desperate to "believe in a vision, belong to something greater than themselves" (*Women* 172, 171) – arrive at Taliesin to begin their Fellowships with "*Daddy Frank*" (19), after having paid a steep tuition for the privilege of doing so, only to find themselves peeling onions like galley slaves. In this servitude they are preceded by the women of the novel's title, each of whom Wright installs in Taliesin, first as mistress and later as domestic drudge, and replaces in conformance to his expressed need for public "adornment[s]," not "anchor[s]" (269).

More than a function of personal pathology – Wright as mama's boy whose perfect woman is the employee who "scrubbed and washed and ironed" like an "artificial mother" but with whom, unlike his overbearing real mother, he never has to interact because she is near-deaf (204) – what enables Wright to abscond with these women regardless of existing marital status is the pre-rogative of modernist genius: "He saw what he wanted and he took it. That was his nature. That was his right" (89). What enables him to discard them with impunity is his credo to "never look back" (64), the quality of American "moral frontiersmanship," to borrow a phrase of Joan Didion's (*White* 57), that leads Wright to view the conflagration of Taliesin I as an opportunity to build a grander Taliesin II, and the burning of Taliesin II due to faulty wiring as the chance to erect a still grander Taliesin III, with no thought at all to his own contributing role in the homes' destruction.

These felt prerogatives, significantly, are not portrayed as a function of gender. All three women who come to call Taliesin home entertain their own delusions of artistic greatness – Olgivanna the avant-garde *danseuse*, Miriam the expatriate aesthete, Mamah the feminist translator – most of all the delusion, as the Swedish feminist to whom Mamah is devoted writes, of love as a "formative art, instead of a blind instinct of procreation" (334). And all three women, like Wright, presume that an aesthetic sensibility makes them superior to those "ordinary people" who "had neither insight nor originality or any sense of the world" (369). What they fail to understand, as the massacre at Taliesin that forms the novel's climax illustrates, is how dangerously a hierarchy based on aesthetics perpetuates already existing hierarchies of race and class. Mamah is fully aware that lecturing her Barbadian servant Carleton on women's rights while he is on his knees scrubbing the fireplace, "as if he were bowing to her in subjugation, as if he were a slave in the old South – a darkie – and she the overseer's wife" (418), is fraught with racial overtones. Yet she does so anyway as part of her mission to educate the black man whose treatment of his wife she finds "*primitive*" (417) – wholly unaware that Carleton, a proud graduate of Combermere School in Bridgetown, is engaged in his own mission to educate his "bush nigger" wife in the proper use of the King's English (418). Forced by Mamah's continued behavior to recognize that, far from having entered the "inner sanctum, the place where the white elite lived" (407), he is still a boy looking into the big house of the British landowner to see how the whites take their tea, Carleton responds accordingly while serving tea at Taleisin. He takes, in a deliberate return of all the Americas' repressed, the "closest thing to a tomahawk he could find" to Mamah and her children (435), and then sets fire to the house originally built to dissolve the boundaries between inside and out but whose organic architectural design has been consistently belied by the actions of the people who occupy it.

The longing for home that animates the two very different women at the center of Joyce Carol Oates's *Blonde* (2000) and Ann Beattie's *Mrs. Nixon* (2011) originates in homes that are horribly fractured and matures in a midcentury America that sanctifies domesticity. The illegitimate Norma Jeane Baker (1926–1962) shuttles between orphanages and foster homes after her mentally unstable mother tries to kill her in a bathtub of scalding water; she marries at sixteen, believing that "a woman's work inside the home is not work but sacred privilege and duty" (*Blonde* 153). Orphaned at eighteen, the farmer's daughter Thelma Catherine Ryan (1912–1993) marries Richard Nixon ten years later and becomes a woman who "internalize[s] the expectations of her time and enact[s] them meticulously" (*Mrs.* 78). Yet each woman also displays a yearning that, as Beattie writes, is "a necessary component to Americans' conception of themselves," for "[s]omething always has to be the faraway green light at the end of the dock" (216). One ends up a star, literally unable, after leaving the studio that has just changed her name to Marilyn Monroe, to determine "*[w]hich way is home*" (*Blonde* 218); the other a cipher, one of the few first ladies without a memoir to her name, her White House code name of "Starlight" notwithstanding.

To the end of making Monroe's story the story of postwar America, Oates, while hitting all the familiar notes (daddy complex, substance abuse, studio commodification), focuses on what distinguishes this particular film sensation from those who have preceded her. The "Marilyn Monroe" that, as Oates has it, is "born in the New Year of 1950" with the release of *The Asphalt Jungle* is both a Hollywood invention linked to the "new city" of Los Angeles "INVENTING ITSELF" after the Second World War with "no backward look" and the bombshell whose explosion onto the scene coincides with a season of clandestine nuclear testing (*Blonde* 244, 207). The public hysteria generated by her appearances is likewise "some new lurid development in the history of mankind," a new "Church of Fame" no longer confined to those grotesques of Nathanael West who come to California to die but extending to fans worldwide (513), from the Japanese crowds that form "a great multi-headed beast, rapt and expectant," outside her Tokyo hotel, demanding "*Mon-chan!*" (467), to the mobs of American GIs in Korea that seek to tear her limb from limb as she hangs out a helicopter blowing kisses at them.

In this postwar period, however, the Blonde Actress, as Monroe is denoted for most of the novel, is not the only figure whose existence depends upon a public ravenous to affirm its own self-image. The Ex-Athlete (Joe DiMaggio) is an "American icon" by virtue of baseball (376), "his ticket up and out" having made him "one of the winners of the great American lottery" (399). The Playwright (Arthur Miller) "exude[s] an air of the West" (despite being born in New Jersey) and the look of a "man with no family" (despite a mother, father, wife, and children very much alive) by virtue of his parents having "their idiosyncratic Jewish surname Americanized and their gnarly Jewish roots extirpated" (513, 495). The President (John F. Kennedy) bears a "great American name," belongs to a "tribe of the blessed" (688), and is "a great man, a war hero, a figure of History, a Prince" (689), specifically the Dark Prince whose kiss will transform Monroe's Beggar Maid into a Fair Princess.

But in depicting a woman whose entire existence is predicated upon the degree to which she is the object of male desire, as the first shot of the sleeping Angela in *The Asphalt Jungle* makes clear, *Blonde* goes beyond Oates's portrayal of American politics and eros as "the negotiating of power" in *Black*

Water (1992), her fictionalized account of the 1969 Chappaquiddick accident that led to the drowning of Mary Jo Kopechne (53), to expose those dynamics of power as steeped in American misogyny. Trapped in an overturned car that is slowly filling up with water, and waiting for the help she assumes the Senator (Edward Kennedy) who has left her behind will bring, Kelly Kelleher keeps reminding herself, "You're an American girl" (*Black* 18, 149, 152), as a way of convincing herself that no harm can befall "a young princess in a fairy tale" (60). The Blonde Actress, by contrast, sees herself as "*only an American,*" which is to say only "*[s]kin deep*" with "*nothing inside me, really*" (*Blonde* 227), because she grows up thinking of her vagina as "an empty cut, a nothingness" (287), surrounded as she is by men who view the female body as, alternately, a "joke" (as the photographer who positions her nude body in the most vulnerable state possible claims [230]) or a slimy and stinky "fish" (as the sons of Charlie Chaplin and Edward G. Robinson assert [336]). The hint of private parts provided by a subway grating updraft in *The Seven Year Itch* (1955) does not offend because they belong to The Girl with No Name, as the character the actress plays is called, and daily peroxide applications have burned away all odors. The brazen adultery of Rose Loomis in *Niagra* (1953), though, requires punishment at the hands of her cuckolded husband: "*No man is equal to her. She has to die*" (600). And so does the Blonde Actress, whose "rich rank female odor" has become (736), by the end of the book, the embodiment of "Evil [that] has come home to America" to the government agent who has pledged to serve his country during "these inter-ludes of false peace" and whose surveillance of the actress highlights the element of voyeurism in all the gazing at her through camera lenses (644). Having inherited his father's "patriot pride" along with his "pioneer wisdom," the Sharpshooter injects a fatal dose of liquid Nembutal into her heart, secure in the belief, also passed down patrilineally, that "*[t]here is always something deserving of being shot by the right man*" (641).

The most revealing shot of Mrs. Nixon, in Beattie's retelling, is the one taken with the "pop of a flashbulb that might as well be an assassin's bullet" (*Mrs.* 231), in which the Nixons line up as if they are a "chorus line, or paper dolls," for the final photograph of the family in the White House (229). More than hyperbole, as evidenced by Beattie's mention of the historical figures reduced to two dimensions in Tom Tierney's books of paper dolls, the image conveys the scaling down to the point of invisibility, the strategy of "protective coloration" (or, perhaps better, beige-ification), adopted by Mrs. Nixon in order to transform herself into a "generic president's wife" (207). For, as the imagined life that Beattie constructs makes clear, giving up a (brief) career as movie actress (a bit part in a 1935 film of *Vanity Fair* cut) with marriage to an ambitious politician does not mean that Mrs. Nixon gives up performing. It just means limiting that career to a single role, regardless of whether the character is agreeable or disagreeable, and making consistency a measure of success.

Beattie, whose earlier novels (beginning with her first, *Chilly Scenes of Winter* [1976]) chronicle the generation that came of age in the 1960s, freely acknowledges how uncongenial to her sensibilities she finds Mrs. Nixon, referring to her as "my nonmother," trapped in a life that both Beattie and her own mother were able to escape as young women (263). But she returns to the image of paper dolls – figures one picks, dresses, and, most important, "*animate[s]*" (261) – when explaining that it is precisely Mrs. Nixon's remaining a minor figure hovering in the background of historic events – forgotten quite literally at times (left behind in Iowa during a 1960 stump stop, omitted in her husband's 1974 farewell speech to the White House staff) – that makes her one of the kind of characters that writers love. Their silence frees writers "to project onto them" (122), or, as Beattie says of herself, "to play out scenarios from outside my experience, limning someone dissimilar from me with whom I nevertheless empathize" (77). Indeed, in a contemporary "Age of Memoir," in which novelists increasingly turn to historic figures in order to compete with authors writing "me-moirs" of "people no one would have heard of until they read the book" (75), someone like Mrs. Nixon is especially prized. The relative absence of information about her life forces Beattie to re-create that life by joining factual research with her own "experience of literature" (79). Mrs. Nixon thus emerges – in a technique that Beattie, in a nod to old Polaroid cameras, terms "justifying the image" (81) – by way of the plays in which she performs while in college and community theater (A. A. Milne and Martin Flavin), dramas staged during her lifetime (Henrik Ibsen and Tennessee Williams), other novels about historical figures (Oates on Monroe, DeLillo on Lee Harvey Oswald), and, most of all, Beattie's analyses of short stories (Maupassant, Chekhov, Joyce, Hemingway, Salinger, Yates, Calvino, Carver, Barthelme). In contrast to Mrs. Nixon, who "might have been a storyteller" had she spoken more for the record and less in the most banal of clichés (28), and Richard Nixon, who "liked to fabricate stories, and if he hadn't been president, many of his fictions would be highly hilarious" (6), Beattie, through her metafictional meditations, reminds readers that there was a time when the short story "had a job to do" (59), namely, "showing people how their base desires might lead to disaster" (60). Updated a century, and expanded to the length of a novel, the story that Beattie tells shows how women "can say two seemingly contradictory things at the same time, and be true to no one, including themselves" (85–86), and, in the case of Mrs. Nixon, how a woman who never permitted herself to smoke in public can still die, largely unnoticed by the public, of lung cancer in Park Ridge, New Jersey.

As the shooter accused of perpetrating one of the most galvanizing events of postwar American history, Lee Harvey Oswald (1939–1963), the central figure of Don DeLillo's *Libra* (1988) and Norman Mailer's *Oswald's Tale: An American Mystery* (1995), needs no introduction. Yet he is remembered in both works in extremely different ways. Devoid of all stable ego, his identity a function of disposable documentation and aliases of shifting linguistic configuration (A. J. Hidell, O. H. Lee, H. O. Lee, D. F. Drictal), DeLillo's Lee Oswald is a perfect postmodern subject. His equally shifting political affiliations are determined by whatever nation or organization offers the best hopes of "merg[ing]" with history and so ending the dreadful loneliness from which he suffers (*Libra* 101). In this re-creation of the 1960s through the lens of the 1980s, the Oswald who scripts himself with paper and ninety-eight-cent stamping kit emerges from much the same materials as the lone gunman scripted out of "[p]ocket litter" and the most banal items of consumer culture (Q-tips, Elmer's Glue-All) by those disaffected CIA Bay of Pigs veterans whose plan to stage a "spectacular miss" on the life of the president to prevent any reconciliation between Kennedy and Castro forms the alternating chapters of the novel (50, 51).

At the same time, Lee Oswald's yearning to "merge" with history coexists with a desire to be a great actor on the stage of history. It is this desire that, as DeLillo argues in his essay "American Blood" (1983), makes Oswald the forerunner of all those media-obsessed young men (Arthur Bremer, John Hinckley, James Earl Ray) who, aware of the representation of their actions while performing them, sought celebrity status at the point of a gun. In *Libra*, it makes Oswald typical of *every* American, joined by the medium of television that – as DeLillo hints as early as *Americana* (1971), and decades before the advent of reality TV – encourages even the most ordinary person to believe in his or her extraordinary potential. This is certainly the premise from which the characters who later jump at the chance to testify before the Warren Commission operate, as the final portrait of Marguerite Oswald makes clear. Reminding the commissioners that, as "the mother in the case" (449), she is "all over the world" (450, 451) – unlike those other mothers who, since the time of Mary, mother of Jesus, "disappear from the record" once their sons are "crucified" (453) – Marguerite proceeds to tempt them with the many stories (plural) she has to offer prior to setting them down in book form and strapping on a camera to make a "photographic record" of her son's life (450). Once again, though, the son in question is far ahead of the curve.

Reminded, over and over, that he is just a "zero in the system" (106, 151, 357) – Soviet communism no less than American capitalism – regardless of what documents he offers to "provide substance" (357), Oswald switches from words to pictures to assure his place in posterity. Having once imagined himself sitting in the waiting room of *Life* or *Look,* ready to hawk those actual written texts DeLillo either quotes (the "Historic Diary") or cites ("The Kollective," "The New Era"), and through which the severely dyslexic Oswald has tried to "get a grip on the runaway world" (211), he now poses in his backyard with rifle, revolver, and radical literature, and prepares to enter "the frame of official memory" on the cover of *Time* magazine (279).

Only to find himself, after the assassination of the first media-manufactured president – a "rambling affair that succeeded in the short term due mainly to chance" (441), according to the retired CIA analyst hired to write its "secret history" (15) – the "victim of a total frame" in more than the way he means when the police first apprehend him (418). Tagged by the media with that middle name that, as he learns when confronted in Russia with the imprisoned U-2 pilot Francis Gary Powers, is the mark of notoriety, Lee Oswald cannot recognize the person referred to as Lee Harvey Oswald. Reduced to two dimensions by the black box that is network TV, he ends up encased in what is, in effect, the smallest of the small rooms in which he has been trapped throughout his impoverished life. As a result, when he is finally slain, the shot that kills him is portrayed as coming as much from a camera as it does from Jack Ruby's gun, as evidenced by the description of the replayed scene of his death in which Oswald "comment[s] on the documentary footage even as it is being shot" prior to his own being "shot, and shot, and shot" (447).

Mailer, who over the course of his career alternately deemed Kennedy a "box-office actor," "hipster," and "existential hero" (*Presidential* 38, 44; *Cannibals* 170), rejects outright any such reduction of the Kennedy assassination to "post-modern media fling where everything is equal to everything else" and Oswald to mere "non-entity" who happened to have "felled a giant in the midst of his limousines, his legions, his throng, and his security" (*Oswald's* 198). To accept such a stance is to admit that "we live in a universe that is absurd," an intolerable concept in that it "corrodes our species" (198). His approach, by contrast, is to explore Oswald as a potentially tragic figure, one "to whom, grudgingly, we must give a bit of stature when we take into account the modesty of his origins" (606) – specifically, a Dreiserian tragic figure, as Mailer reveals in the book's last lines when stating that the title he would have preferred for his work is "An American Tragedy" (791). In this transformative endeavor, Mailer is aided by a plethora of sources: previously published accounts of Oswald's life; heretofore unexamined KGB files; new interviews with Oswald's wife and former Soviet Union acquaintances; twenty-six volumes of Warren Commission hearings and exhibits ("a dead whale decomposing on a beach" as an inquiry, but "a Comstock Lode of novelistic material" [351]). Each of the two volumes that Mailer fashions from this material admits to its flaws. The thirty-year-old memories unearthed in "Oswald in Minsk with Marina" that prove astonishingly clear – KGB injunctions to remain silent having caused them, in effect, to be "sealed" up against time rather than eroded by time (350) – still remain subject to errors in translation and individual exaggeration. The previously printed matter informing "Oswald in America" still displays the limitations to which all evidentiary texts are prone: self-serving reporting (Robert Oswald's memoir); contradictory reporting (George de Mohrenschildt's Warren Commission description of Oswald as a "semieducated hillbilly" and unpublished manuscript delineation of Oswald as "outstanding" and "very educated" [439, 437]); aesthetically dubious reporting (Patricia Johnson McMillan's romanticized dialogue fabricated for *Marina and Lee*). But having earlier acclaimed the novel as more deeply probing than the written history in *The Armies of the Night* (1968) and having pitched the *"true life story"* of Gary Gilmore in *The Executioner's Song* (1979) "as if it were a novel" (1022), Mailer has no interest in restricting himself to facts devoid of speculation, particularly when dealing with a figure such as Oswald about whom the facts are so murky. He therefore characterizes his stance as "novelistic" (682), and offers his work as "a special species of non-fiction that can be put under the rubric of *mystery*" (353).

In his efforts to penetrate that mystery, Mailer returns Oswald to a late 1950s milieu in which, politically, American Communists are "as dangerous to the security of the United States as the last American buffalo" (422), but, psychologically, "some enormous majority of Americans still believed that men and women had highly separate roles and that the first obligation incumbent on a male was to behave like one" (370). Viewed with respect to those separate spheres family values emphasized (over and above conspiracy theories) by the Warren Commission – and confirmed by the KGB bugs that record the newlyweds' nonstop bickering – Oswald's home life with Marina is a study in banality: he nags her about not cooking, laundering, ironing, dusting, and washing the floors; she counters with complaints about his laziness, fearfulness, and flatulence. Viewed with respect to the era's sexual mores, in which masculinity, virility, and self-worth are inextricably linked, Oswald's home life is an absolute disaster. Marina marries "a real American" (87) – a novelty to provincial Russians for whom all things Western, from Glenn Miller to Deanna Durbin to Elvis Presley, are exotic – only to discover that the man who likes to parade around the apartment naked and admire himself in mirrors is "a problem" in bed (185), a "[n]ot complete man," as she later asserts to a member of the émigré community in Fort Worth (433). Oswald begins expressing his sense of inadequacy with his fists, to the point where "his murderous impulses could only be gathered if he was without sexual release" (551).

It is not the first time that Oswald has felt so threatened, according to Mailer; in the Marine Corps, in which "[y]our ability with an M-1 was equal to your virility," Oswald barely qualifies, and to be "weak among men was to perceive oneself as a woman" (381). Yet it is the start of Oswald behaving in a way that conforms to Mailer's long-held view of violence as the product of sexual urges frustrated, a belief that extends as far back as the discovery of General Cummings in *The Naked and the Dead* (1948) that the curve that denotes the shape of a woman's breast also denotes the shape of a missile's path. In the case of Oswald, a man Mailer suspects of having been a closet homosexual, there is no other way for him to behave, living as he does in a period in which "homosexuality was still seen as one of those omnibus infections of the spirit that could lead to God knows what further aberration" (379). Increasingly desperate to prove himself a man, and "ready to go to great lengths to combat and/or conceal" those homosexual desires that terrify him (379), he redirects his rage from the figure of his wife to the public figure, Kennedy, who is at the moment "the finest specimen of the American species available" and "the kind of man any woman (most certainly Marina) would find more attractive than himself" (665), and shoots.

Set in 2011, Stephen King's *11/22/63* (2011) is predicated on the far-reaching consequences of that shooting, the kind of *"watershed moment"* that can force the river of history to overflow its banks (57), and the alternative history that might have resulted had Oswald been slain before he could pull the trigger: no late-1960s assassinations (Robert Kennedy not killed while running for president in 1968 because his brother is not killed in 1963), no race riots (Martin Luther King not killed at the Lorraine Motel), no Vietnam War (millions not killed because Lyndon B. Johnson and Richard Nixon are not in positions to escalate it). Or so Jake Epping is convinced, in this time-travel novel, by the owner of a diner in Lisbon Falls, Maine, who discovers a portal to the past – specifically, to September 9, 1958 – in his pantry. As Al Templeton explains, journeying down this rabbit hole to change history has no downside: each trip, no matter how long the traveler stays in the past, takes up just two minutes in the present; each trip, because a reset of the previous trip, comes attached with a damage-control safety device. And, as Jake discovers during both the test runs and final run that he makes, returning to the

1950s and early 1960s – vividly brought to life by way of period details (Ban-Lon slacks, Vitalis hair tonic, Yodora antiperspirant) – has much to commend it. Air smells sweet (the prevalence of chain-smoking notwithstanding), food tastes good (movie popcorn has real butter), everything is incredibly cheap (69 cents a pound for lobster, 19.9 cents a gallon for gasoline), and nobody worries about cholesterol, global warming, or suicide bombers flying planes into skyscrapers. Any anxieties concerning nuclear warfare Jake can easily dismiss because, by the time he goes to college, the Cuban Missile Crisis has become "just another intersection of names and dates to memorize for the next prelim" (515).

King recognizes, of course, that this past is hardly ideal. In midcentury America, a path lined by poison ivy leads to a board over a stream that constitutes segregated bathroom facilities. In Dallas, children celebrate the Fourth of July by throwing firecrackers at stray dogs and chickens. But in locating the heart of the novel in the "anti-Dallas" of Jodie (331), a small Texas town that his traveler displaced from home era and hometown comes to call home, and making that central figure an "ordinary" man trying to improve the world "if God won't make it better" (607), King depicts history as not the product of great men (Kennedy makes three brief appearances, all electronically mediated) or political decision-making (the chance to sit at "the doorway to history" in Washington, D.C., has no allure for the book's high school librarian-heroine [485]). The recounted events that prove most emotionally evocative – "what A+ writing is supposed to do," according to the English teacher, Jake, whose buried manuscript the text is finally revealed to be (5) – involve the bit players of history. Triumph is a football player bringing the crowd to tears at a high school production of *Of Mice and Men*. Tragedy is a janitor crippled as a child by his father, a woman disfigured by her estranged husband, people abused at the hands of unstable men whom Oswald, a man both "[c]olorless" and a "boor" (464, 475), comes to incarnate when sighting along his rifle in the Texas School Book Depository prior to becoming "the daemonic ghost that would haunt America" (744).

That such a "little fame-junkie" can find himself "in just the right place to get lucky" – the view of the Kennedy assassination King provides in the Afterword when explaining why he subscribes to Occam's Razor and adopts the simplest explanation (845) – is more proof of how easily, as the novel's refrain asserts, "life turns on a dime" (5, 14, 71, 212, 398). Jake, however, believes otherwise. Seduced, much like Oswald, into thinking that with an act of violence he can "become a major player not just in American history but in the history of the *world*" (59), he assumes that changing history is a matter of human agency, the difficulty depending on the degree to which history is "obdurate" or "harmonic," a "big machine full of sharp teeth" or a "perfectly balanced mechanism of shouts and echoes" (556, 616). Terrified that behind that balanced mechanism is mere chaos, a "universe of horror and loss" against which "mortals dance in defiance of the dark" (616), Jake looks at all the couples that swing-dance to the same song – teenagers in a picnic area, chaperones at a high school hop, performers in a jamboree – as evidence that the individual events of history, as variations on the same theme, are "*all of a piece*" (615). It is not until the end of the book that he discovers that the harmonies in which he takes such comfort are the result of strings produced by the residue of his own actions, and the symphonic "devil's music" they combine to make is far more catastrophic than any one piece of history he has sought to alter (745). Race riots still erupt, nuclear reactors still explode, earthquakes threaten to tear apart the planet, a janitor not crippled by his father is paralyzed by a helicopter crash in Vietnam, and a woman who survives the attack of a jealous husband is killed while saving the life of the president.

Anxieties and Influences

The celebration of those "frictions of fiction" that informs the portrayal of Charles Dickens in Frederick Busch's *The Mutual Friend* (1978) derives from a view of authors in collaborative dialogue with – not, as Donald Barthelme's *The Dead Father* (1975) suggests, patricidal relation to – one another, and a conception of "texts influenc[ing] writers, in which writers then make texts" so as to produce "art [that] is, because it is passionate and religious, about *the other one*, not self" (*When* xv). It is that paternal bond that Busch explores through the two American protagonists of his second work of historical fiction, *The Night Inspector* (1999): Herman Melville (1819–1891), a "family man with too much family and too few funds to pay for family" (55), who is working nights as deputy inspector at the Port of New York Customs House two years after the end of the Civil War; and William Bartholomew, the book's narrator, who has acted as a "legislator of the night's morality" in his own right while serving as a Union sniper (37). To the writer obsessed by the desire to "strike through" the "pasteboard masks" of things visible to see whether behind them lies an "unknown but still reasoning thing," a thing of "inscrutable malice," or no thing at all (*Moby-Dick* 139), the veteran who literally wears a pasteboard mask to cover his facial wound proves an "object of speculations" impossible to resist (92). To the financial speculator who views the Civil War as waged by "interests of money" and himself as a "coin imprinted with Abe's earnestness"

(8), the employee responsible for the legal unloading of cargoes during the "national beginning of a new lunge" is equally compelling (40). This becomes especially the case after Bartholomew is convinced by a Creole prostitute to help in the rescue of children being smuggled out of Florida whose dark skin is still negotiable. Not that Bartholomew really thinks the "new world [that] was business" will be much different from the old (32). In the global economy in which he exchanges drachmas for rubles for pounds, a Dutch ship still carries the slave-trade commodities of molasses and rum, only now that flesh trade no longer operates along the lines of racial binaries. Jews serve as "Negroes" to northern industrialists (191). Immigrant children prove that "[s]omeone paid some money for everything" (84). And, as the horrifying climax of the book illustrates, black children get stuffed into barrels and shipped for sale by a Creole woman the product of slavery herself, a white survivor of Gettysburg, and a black financier who deems their accidental poisoning a matter of "profit and loss" and not "a loss of actual life" (248).

In this novel devoted as much to the making of literary history as American history, however, writers are also commodities, whose reputations fluctuate according to what the market can bear. Having earlier "invested his efforts" in both US and British distribution (46), Melville has tanked; *The Confidence-Man* (1857) is deemed an "abortion" (56), *Battle-Pieces* (1866) "anything but poetry" (61). Dickens, by contrast, gives good return on the dollar – making thousands of them for himself during his 1867–1868 US speaking tour and earning a hefty profit for Batholomew, who has bought shares in the British author as a "partial investment" (271). In this novel, moreover, just about every major character is a storyteller of some sort. Bartholomew tells tales of his exploits as a sniper. The Creole Jessie constructs stories of her mother's time on Pukapuka and her father's captivity in the Indian encampments from tattoos on her own body. The aspiring author Samuel Mordecai re-creates the events leading up to the death of Melville's eldest son from entries in a log he presents as composed by the father. All entertain no illusions that what they narrate is true, if by truth one means incontrovertible fact. As Jessie informs Bartholomew, "I told you the stories, Billy. Stories aren't always the truth" (244). Yet not all are equally astute in the art of critical reading. The one time when Bartholomew, who reads *Moby-Dick* (1851) as a cautionary tale of poor investment strategy, should interpret tales in the limited terms of economic transactions that he favors is the time that this man without a face takes what he is told at face value. He gets lost in the pleasures of the text imprinted on his Scheherazade's body, so much so that even after the catastrophe he has unwittingly helped to orchestrate has been revealed, he still admits, "I enjoyed them" (244).

Dickens, another man saddled with the burdens of a family to support, understands full well the rewards to be reaped from telling stories that others enjoy; in New York, he shrewdly "bind[s] the audience to himself in a mutual affection" by regaling it with *A Christmas Carol*, the tale in which "the small child did not die" (273, 275), his own experience of dead or brutalized children (himself included) notwithstanding. Melville, however, sees the poisoned "pips of humanity, abandoned by man and woman and God" in New York's harbor as confirming the "harsh truths" of the whaling novel he wrote with no thoughts of enjoyment or money (267, 93). It is to those verities that Sam refers when reminding Bartholomew, "Invention also speaks a certain truth," the kind that, as evidenced by Bartholomew's own war stories, depends on the teller "subtly alter[ing] what another might term *fact*" (180), and, as Melville later illustrates with respect to Shakespeare's creation of Lear, presenting those terrible truths through characters that serve as authorial masks. That, as Bartholomew learns when falsifying documents for the mission that involves him – if only in his own mind and despite its miserable failure – in a "brotherhood surpassing the interests of money" (9), is "how fiction is constructed – of felonies and forgeries . . . against the laws, at night" (207).

And that, as Busch displays, is how fiction is continually reconstructed and revolutionized. The stuttering amanuensis George Dolby, in a "mere parody of he who did it best of all since Shakespeare" (*Mutual* 209), finally speaks through the voices of friends and family abused personally but transformed fictionally by Dickens to create the Dickens that haunts the pages of *The Mutual Friend*; the silent ward attendant, Moon, picks up those pages after Dolby expires and, in an act of Indian defiance against "Her Majesty's bleeding last Empire" (211), rewrites them. The *isolato* William Bartholomew, who states he has "no wish to be a character in a book" (*Night* 114), ends up not just the narrator of the book that Samuel Mordecai reveals "has taken a different turning" after his reading of Melville's *Battle-Pieces* but the hero of Mordecai's *Inspector of the Night* (146), the invented work from which Busch fashions *The Night Inspector*.

The appropriation of *Moby-Dick* and, especially, "Benito Cereno" (1855) along with Frederick Douglass's "The Heroic Slave" (1853) in Charles Johnson's *Middle Passage* (1990) attests to a similar view of the literary text as a palimpsest, the result of what Johnson in *Being and Race* (1988) deems layering and ventriloquizing, and the African American text in particular as not limited to those forms that historically have been employed to portray the African American experience. Committed instead to cross-cultural fertilization – based on his belief that "'[r]ace' dissolves when we trace the gene back to A.D. 700" (*Being* 43) – Johnson sees the "solitary black writer" as actually surrounded by "a very integrated crowd" and, when confronted with "Caliban's dilemma," producing what is "inevitably a compromise between the one and the many, African and European, the present and the past" (40). Within this integrationist view, the slave narrative, which traces the movement from bondage to freedom, is "distant cousin" to the Puritan narrative, which moves from sin to salvation, both of which are, for all their distinctive American pedigrees, the "offspring" of "the first philosophical black writer: Saint Augustine," whose *Confessions* charts the movement from ignorance to wisdom, nonbeing to being (*Oxherding* 118–19).

This, as it turns out, is exactly the journey that Johnson's narrator makes in *Middle Passage*, ostensibly the account written by Rutherford Calhoun between June 14 and August 20, 1830, that miraculously survives both the storm and slave uprising that wreck the *Republic*, a ship transporting slaves from Africa to New Orleans that, as per Melvillian signature, is physically unstable and commanded by a man who embodies "the entire twisted will of Puritanism" (51). Yet unlike Melville, who backdated the year of the actual slave rebellion from 1805 to 1799 when rewriting Amasa Delano's *Narrative of Voyages and Travels in the Northern and Southern Hemispheres* (1817) as "Benito Cereno" so as to comment on the issue of democratic freedoms during a period in which they were the subject of heated debate (Sundquist, "Benito" 94–98), Johnson establishes the contemporary relevance of his tale by way of a distinctly late twentieth-century patois. Punctuated by references to "handjobs" in haylofts and "uncircumcised schlong[s]" (2, 41), and allusions to figures as diverse as Chaucer, Proudhon, Tintoretto, and Leibniz, that patois is as anachronistic as it is artificial. Additionally, in populating the *Republic* with the sons of Englishmen who come to America in the belly of a steamer and sailors employed in the hold as "chattel" (87), Johnson portrays the issue of slavery not in terms of racial binaries: the African American Rutherford is black to the white crewmen, but a Cooked Barbarian among white Raw Barbarians to the captured African Allmuseri. Rather, Johnson portrays slavery in terms of a "larger game of property so vast it trivialized [the] struggles on board" (150), within which "[y]ellow men were buying up half of America," the nation whose "manifest destiny" had been "to Americanize the entire planet" (145, 30). By having his narrator write an account of liberation in the log meant to record the trafficking in humans defined as property, Johnson subverts the documents that ratify property ownership (Rushdy 217). Perhaps more important, by choosing for his narrator a man who begins the book a newly freed bondsman and voluntarily decides in its final pages to bind himself to another human being in marriage,

Johnson considers slavery as a function of mind, which is to say ownership of the self, as well as ownership of the body.

In order to recover that self, though, Rutherford first must relinquish the self – in much the same way that the Buddhism Johnson practices is predicated upon a renunciation of ego – and see the self not in the manner of Captain Falcon, a man *"fixed* and inflexible in his being" (144), who views slavery as the inevitable product of those subject/object dualisms innate to human consciousness, but as a "mosaic of many countries, a patchwork of others and objects stretching backward to perhaps the beginning of time" (162–63). Yet Rutherford also must do more than replace the fixity of the Melvillian Falcon with the fluidity of the fictional Allmuseri, devoted to "process and Heraclitean change" (124), whose vocabulary consists almost entirely of verbs and is nearly devoid of nouns or "static substances" (77). In the wake of the slave mutiny aboard the *Republic*, the Allmuseri change from oppressed to oppressor, much as the uprising they initiate produces a "change not in the roles on ship but a revolution in its very premises" (126). Forced to realize during the book's climactic storm that, within the "chaosmos" that each person navigates, survival depends on developing a "flood mentality" (183, 186), which means "devot[ing] yourself to the welfare of everyone" in order to reach shore (187), Rutherford ends the novel seeking both the Illinois land and the lady "grounded, physically and metaphysically, in the land" that he has originally fled as providing "solid ground" on which to settle (5, 204). Having accepted himself as a "cultural mongrel" (187), Rutherford embraces the "cauldron of mongrels" that is America as his rightful *"home"* (179).

Populated by changeling children, historical theme-park androids, and aliens from other planets, Michael Cunningham's *Specimen Days* (2005) portrays America as a similar mélange, consistent with the vision of the nation formulated by Walt Whitman (1819–1892), the book's presiding spirit, whose *Leaves of Grass* (1855–1891/92) is quoted throughout the text. Comprised of three novellas that project – in a manner reminiscent of Whitman's own rewritings – the same triangular set of characters into a nineteenth-century ghost story ("In the Machine"), a contemporary police thriller ("The Children's Crusade"), and a postapocalyptic science-fiction story ("Like Beauty"), the text is a literary mélange as well. In contrast to Cunningham's earlier act of homage in *The Hours* (1998), however, which is informed not only by the sensibility of Virginia Woolf but the actual presence of Woolf as one of three women – of different places and periods (a London suburb in 1923, Los Angeles in 1949, New York City in the late 1990s) – torn between accepting the temporal present of a home well made as "enough" or attempting the transcendent through artifacts that outlive the artisan and moments (notably, a kiss) that radiate outward in time, this later work limits Whitman's presence to a brief cameo appearance. Set almost entirely in Manhattan, it also renders moot the question of whether it is "[b]etter to die raving mad in London than evaporate in Richmond" that so torments Woolf in the 1998 novel (*Hours* 71). For when the dead, as the book's post-9/11 perspective makes clear, are literally "all around us," both "in the air and the water" in a way that Whitman could never have conceived (*Specimen* 67), the only voices that can sing the body electric with no adjustment to present circumstances belong to a misshapen boy with a "habit of speaking in fits" (4), a *simulo* programmed to spout "involuntary fits of poetry" (266), and an insane child bomber coached by a woman who believes that "[i]f we can return to a time like Whitman's, maybe we can love the world again" and takes the name of the poet as her own accordingly (188).

The time she means, of course, is the time of the 1855 *Leaves of Grass*, the literal leaves of which paper every surface of the East Village flat she turns into a home for the waifs she rescues, not the later editions, in which Whitman embraced the promise of postwar technology in poems like "Passage to India" and "Song of the Exposition." The time Cunningham takes as his analogue belongs to the 1882 autobiographical collage, in which lists of Civil War horrors (copied from *Memoranda During the War* [1875]) cast a shadow upon the familiar lists of natural phenomena celebrated in the section devoted to Whitman's time at Timber Creek, the decade's gap between the two periods evidence, as David S. Reynolds has argued (523), of Whitman's inability to deal with the vexed social and political issues that followed the war he deemed "the distinguishing event of my time" (Whitman, *Specimen* 7).

Whitman, as compensation, returned again and again to the idealized "average," "typical," and "regular" American for whom the Union was preserved: "specimens amid the hospital, and even the dead on the field" whose heroic "latent personal character" bypassed divisions between North and South (80); "young men and working-people" – firemen, ferry men, policemen – that comprised "the whole splendid average of native stock, city and country" (134–35); "average western" men like Lincoln and Grant and "splendid average" writers like Longfellow that distinguished, respectively, an American leadership and literature grounded in the "great average bulk, unprecedentedly great" (154, 194); finally, the city of New York, whose "great seething oceanic populations" formed "the rule and average" and, as such, provided "the directest proof yet of successful Democracy" (117). The exemplary specimens in Cunningham's book, published just four years after the distinguishing event of his own time, are, by contrast, either the "average citizen[s]" that damaged children hug prior to detonating or the "ordinary American citizens" whose failure to take a cue from Al Qaeda's terrorist tactics leaves authorities both relieved and bewildered (*Specimen* 98, 125). Within a US recently reminded of "something much of the rest of the world had known for centuries," that "we all humped along unharmed because no one had decided to kill us that day" (105), it hardly matters that Lucas, the child protagonist of "In the Machine," is a "citizen of no place, come from County Kerry but planted in New York" (12), or that the men who labor in the factory with him have "relinquished their citizenship" in the nation and "immigrated to the [industrial] works" that most defines the union to which they belong (29), or that the *simulos* in "Like Beauty" are in effect stateless for being the "stolen property" of the now-defunct company that originally manufactured them (245). The only citizenship at all relevant is "citizens[hip] in the world of the not dead" (92).

No American writer whose sensibility was shaped during the precarious years of the Cold War would presume that such citizenship is unique to the twenty-first century – one thinks of Norman Mailer proposing the existential model of "The White Negro" (1957) in response to the "psychic havoc" wreaked by the atom bomb and the concentration camps (300), or Thomas Pynchon suggesting in *Gravity's Rainbow* that all our lives are led under a projectile's parabola – and Cunningham does not suggest as much. If he differs from earlier twentieth-century writers, it is in his refusal to counter dangers from without with the refugee's midcentury retreat indoors – to the room of Saul Bellow's *Dangling Man* (1944), the boardinghouse of Mailer's *Barbary Shore* (1951) – or the creation of a home below ground as in Ralph Ellison's *Invisible Man* (1952). Home in *Specimen Days* offers no protection: in the first novella, Lucas's brother Simon gets eaten alive by a machine that makes housings; in the third, the alien Catareen chooses to die in Denver rather than return to Nadia, the "nowhere she seemed to call home" from which she has been deported (269).

Like Whitman, who ends his *Specimen Days* by venturing outward into nature, the "health-element and beauty-element" he found underlying the "whole politics, sanity, religion and art of the New World" (200), Cunningham ends his work with the citizens of the new century voyaging outdoors. Unlike Whitman, who found confirmation in his own 1879 trip West, the figure in Cunningham's book who is the latest of many to "harbor unreasonable hopes" and set a course for the Pacific, with "no way of knowing" what they will find when, and if, they get there (305), embarks upon a journey that leaves him moving "against the current," as Fitzgerald so famously wrote, "borne back ceaselessly into the past" for seeking a dream that is "already behind him" (*Great* 182). The "hysterics and visionaries and petty criminals" who depart instead on a thirty-eight-year voyage to the fourth planet from the sun revive another paradigmatically American journey – the very one charted by the characters in the novels discussed at the start of this chapter – the "zealots and oddballs and ne'er-do-wells" who board the *Mayflower* and, before that, the *Niña, Pinta,* and *Santa María,* who set out "to colonize a new world because the known world wasn't much interested in their furtive and quirky passions" (293). But in journeying *to* a planet they call Paumanok, they reverse the path of Whitman "strik[ing] up for a New World" *from* the "fish-shape Paumanok" of Long Island (*Leaves* 16, 15). And in venturing toward *a* "new world" rather than *the* "New World" (285), these latest pilgrims may indeed be new pilgrims, not the "composite race" that offered Whitman "splendid proof of our country" (*Specimen* 137), but a ragtag group defined not by nation, or race, or even species, whose representative specimen is the half-Nadian and half-human infant that is its youngest member.

Chapter 2

Regional Realism

This was the beginning of what I have come to think of as the permanent
end of my childhood and adolescence. The Vietnamization of my
domestic life. . . . What had been an exception was now possibly the rule.

– Russell Banks, The Sweet Hereafter (1991)

The "goddamn *accident*" that leads Billy Ansel to the above suspicions is not
the accident that sets the plot of Russell Banks's novel in motion, the one in
which fourteen children die after their school bus breaks through a guardrail
and plunges into a sandpit filled with frozen water (53). The incident to which
this Vietnam veteran refers, in fact, does not even take place in the upstate
New York town in which the book is set, "one of those towns that's on the way
to somewhere else" (21), defined by trailer parks and demolition derbies, but
in sunny Jamaica, where Billy and his family have gone on vacation and
where, returning in their Ford Escort from a trip to buy groceries, Billy
discovers that one of his four-year-old twins is missing. Unable to believe
that "such a thing could happen to you in America or even while on vacation
from America" or that the horrors of Vietnam's "then and there" could
impact the "here and now," and unwilling to recognize that he has been less
distracted by the unfamiliar heat than impaired by the ganja he has been
smoking every day of the trip, Billy reasons: "if I admitted that my daughter
had been kidnapped or had fallen from the car or had simply been lost in
a foreign country, then the whole world for the rest of my life would be
Vietnam" (51). So Billy, having been entrusted by his wife with getting the
family "safely, smoothly back" from their shopping (50), continues to drive
back to the rented house that they call "home" (51) – even after his son
informs him that his twin sister has been left behind in the store.

In the fiction of regional realism, Billy Ansel is not the only character to
maintain such a delusional belief in the sheltering power of home. In Bobbie
Ann Mason's *In Country* (1985), Emmett Smith returns from Vietnam to
a Kentucky town without even a mall to commend it and embarks upon
a mission to fix a crack in his house's foundation, convinced as he is that one

structural weakness leads to another, despite the proof provided by the collapsed marriages of the veterans around him that their homes are beyond repair. It is only after the niece with whom he shares his house recklessly takes off to experience life "in country" in the swamps of a local pond that Emmett realizes that no amount of insulation can protect her from the dangers of life outside it. Likewise, it is only after Billy Ansel witnesses both his children die in the icy waters of Sam Dent, victims of another "accident" to which adult negligence has contributed (a driver distracted by her own troubles trying to make up a few minutes in a bus without snow chains in January), that his suspicions about home not being a haven and the exception being the rule become certainties, proof of what he terms "the final contrary" (78). As the attorney who arrives in the town to file a lawsuit on behalf of the grieving parents, a father himself who has lost a child to drug addiction, understands, "the people of Sam Dent are not unique. We've all lost our children. It's like all the children of America are dead to us" (99).

Such extrapolation from the personal to the social occurs frequently in this kind of realist fiction – whether deemed "dirty realism" (Bill Buford), "neo-realism" (Kristiaan Versluys), or "spectacle realism" (Joseph Dewey) – in which fractured familial relations signal cracked national foundations (Joyce Carol Oates's *We Were the Mulvaneys* [1996], Richard Russo's *Empire Falls* [2001]), and lost or injured children evince a more extended failure to safeguard and protect (Anne Tyler's *The Accidental Tourist* [1985], Richard Ford's *The Sportswriter* [1986], Jeffrey Eugenides's *The Virgin Suicides* [1993], Rick Moody's *The Ice Storm* [1994], Frederick Busch's *Girls* [1997], John Burnham Schwartz's *Reservation Road* [1998], A. M. Homes's *Music for Torching* [1999], Lorrie Moore's *A Gate at the Stairs* [2009]). It also goes a long way toward refuting the claims of critics who have diagnosed the failure of contemporary American fiction as a failure to engage in the complex realities of contemporary American life, of which two of the best known may serve as exemplars. Citing 1960 as his *annus horribilis* and Philip Roth as his Judas Iscariot, Tom Wolfe traced a direct line from Roth's 1961 capitulation to an absurd American reality that trumped the novelist's imaginative powers ("Writing American Fiction") to a landscape filled, in 1989, with Puppet-Masters and Neo-Fabulists, on the one hand, and Minimalists and K-Mart Realists, on the other hand. All shirked the challenge of "Stalking the Billion-Footed Beast," which is to say the panoramic city novel that would portray "the individual in intimate and inextricable relation to the society around him" (50). Citing Wolfe's essay seven years later, if only to remark upon its author's "uncanny ignorance" of the many fine socially engaged novels published between 1960 and 1989, Jonathan Franzen still conceded that "American experience has become so sprawling and diffracted that no single 'social novel,' à la Dickens or Stendhal, can ever hope to mirror it" (*How* 67, 80), and wondered, as the title to the reprinted version of his essay asked, "why bother?"

The problem with such laments is not just that they were not especially new. Franzen's query, for instance, repeats one posed by Norman Mailer in 1963 – "Who can create a vast canvas when the imagination must submit itself to a plethora of detail in each joint of society?" – in response to his own feeling that "[t]he Tolstoyan novel begins to be impossible" (*Cannibals* 129). The greater problem is that the laments often were predicated upon a number of premises that were as debatable aesthetically as they were inapplicable demographically: a dichotomy between postmodernism and realism; a model derived from the nineteenth-century European novel; a belief that diversity is synonymous with city; and a conception of realism in which, as Lionel Trilling groused in 1946, "reality is always material reality" and the most trustworthy mind is that which "most resembles this reality by most nearly reproducing the sensations it affords" (10, 11). Yet, as Eric J. Sundquist has argued, "American realism virtually has no school" ("Country" 4), in part because "'the real' in America, like the country itself, has always had a notoriously short life" (6–7), and in part because the boundlessness of the country led to the persistence of romance even in the fiction composed during the late nineteenth- and early twentieth-century realist heyday (10). Far from conforming to any one school, the realist fiction written a century later is likewise a hybrid of many schools, a "mixture of modes," as Winfried Fluck notes, "in which the relations between various narrative strategies are newly negotiated" (79).

If that fiction seems overly devoted to the minutiae of material reality, it reflects its authors' awareness that individuals typically experience the world around them by way of the trivial more than the monumental – the ink stain on a pantsuit and warp in a Paul Simon album that Elena Hood imagines driving her to nervous collapse in *The Ice Storm* and "beside which even Cambodia paled" (Moody 67). And, to be sure, many of those quotidian details – even when imbued with the promise of representative if not revelatory status – signal nothing beyond themselves: "broken glass is broken glass," states an Ann Beattie character in response to her daughter's query about what the tale of two shards she has just been told "mean[s]" (*Burning* 204). Yet contemporary realist writers also understand that broken glass also can be more than broken glass. John Updike can thus praise William Dean Howells for his "fidelity to the mild, middling truth of average American life" and attention to immediate detail (*Odd* 183) and also quote Walt Whitman for recognizing "the true use for the imaginative faculty" as the offering of "ultimate vivification to facts, to science, and to common lives, endowing them with glows and glories and final illustriousness which belong to every real thing, and to real things only" (*Hugging* 117).

Set in those suburbs that have become, as Keith Wilhite asserts, "the end-game and final outpost of US regionalism" (618), the place where public and private, local and global, now meet, the first novels in the discussions that follow take as their subject the suburban household as portrayed by Jonathan Franzen, Rick Moody, and Tom Perrotta and extrapolate from familial to national. What are the implications to a homeland when the family that is, in Franzen's words, "the house's soul" no longer occupies the home (*Corrections* 269)? What happens when relationships with "*the potential to be toxic*," as Moody writes, turn out to be quite literally lethal, as occurs in *Purple America* (1997), in which both nuclear family and Connecticut nuclear facility are about to implode from the effects of leaking wastes (138)? The second are composed by writers linked to particular places – sometimes cities (Baltimore for Tyler, Albany for William Kennedy), sometimes states (Texas for Larry McMurtry, West Virginia for Jayne Ann Phillips), sometimes regions (the Southwest and Mexico for Cormac McCarthy, the generalized Midwest for Moore) – in this case, the Northeast for male writers like Frederick Busch, Richard Russo, and Russell Banks concerned with imperiled masculinity and the Midwest for female writers like Jane Smiley, Marilynne Robinson, and Louise Erdrich concerned with fecundity and genealogy. Finally, the third portray regions with respect to a single character over the course of multiple works: the arch-American consumer Harry Angstrom of John Updike's "Rabbit" tetralogy, whose "typical American heart" has become so "tired and stiff and full of crud" by the final volume as to emblematize the "frozen far heart" of the "grand old republic" (*Rest* 166, 442); and the "arch-ordinary American" Frank Bascombe of Richard Ford's series (*Independence* 141–42), who views communities, including the one framed in 1776, as "contingent groups trying to improve on an illusion of permanence" and the selling of real estate as the "True American profession" (386, 440).

Suburban Sprawls

St. Jude, the Midwestern suburb to which the Lambert children are called back for one last Christmas in Jonathan Franzen's *The Corrections* (2001), is introduced as a town in which a "religion of things [is] coming to an end" (3), and not just the celebrated "optimistic egalitarianism" or "prairie optimism" for which the region has long been known (178, 540). Fluid demographics (people exiting for the more stylish coasts, crème brûlée entering the gastronomic imagination) and unfettered economics (money returning home from overseas, megafirm headquarters relocating from cities) are dissolving the borders on which suburban life was historically predicated. In much the same way, post–Cold War politics – as the globe-trotting parts of the book attest – have made black-market Lithuania and free-market America indistinguishable insofar as concentration of wealth and division between private and public sectors are concerned.

Lacking a "*positive* definition" for a country that, prior to 1989, identified itself by way of contrast with Soviet Russia, the Lithuanian answers the question of "how do I be a patriot now?" by creating the new "for-profit nation-state" and hawking its sand and gravel to naïve investors (447, 439). Repulsed by the idea of Europeans owning stock in American conglomerates, Enid Lambert retreats to a "paroxysmal love of *place* – of the Midwest in general and suburban St. Jude in particular" – that is for her "the only true patriotism" (118). And so, their protests to the contrary, do her three children, each of whom reproduces the hierarchical structure of their St. Jude family home in one form or another: Gary in the Seminole Street home where he lives with his own three children, Denise in the restaurants where she turns crews into surrogate families, Chip in the college classrooms where he goads students to sit up straight. Not surprisingly, when they finally converge on St. Jude for Christmas, all effortlessly assume their familial childhood roles, to the extent of occupying the same seats around the dinner table.

In Franzen's view, however, the most recent assaults on suburbia only expose the vexed contradictions that underlie the entire suburban venture: an isolationist agenda at odds with imperialist longings that have had St. Jude "swallowing" fifty small towns "in its endless sprawl" years earlier (375); a division between inside and outside that locates the "extremely cool," which is to say the "extraordinary," elsewhere and leaves the citizens of America's heartland to perform "the thankless work of being comparatively *uncool*" (197). Consistent with this diagnosis, the house that is the Lamberts' largest asset proves, upon close inspection, to be structurally unstable – with finger-wide cracks in the foundation, retaining walls that list, and mold throughout the basement – leaving Enid to envision herself in a building with no walls and only tissues to keep out inclement weather. Equally consistent, in a house that, in Franzen's anthropomorphized depiction, "felt more like a body ... than like a building" (541), set in a suburb portrayed as "gerontocratic" (3), the body that is disintegrating in the most tragic way belongs to the dying father whose Parkinson's disease is somatic in origin and gradual in onset. Unfortunately, his only hope lies with a drug that promises a "basic gut cerebral rehab" ("[l]eave the shell and roof, replace the walls and plumbing") based on an electropolymerization process concocted by Alfred in his own decaying basement (97).

More than just one link in the chain of associations derived from the novel's title – that range from stock market to screenwriting, prison reform to parental child-rearing – Corecktall is the nexus in which the other strands of the novel converge. A "global positioning system," as its makers claim (192), it epitomizes all those state-of-the-art (and as-yet-unapproved) drugs from abroad that find their way into the most local of US enclaves (a supply of one arriving on Enid's St. Jude doorstep by way of a good neighbor blessed with an Austrian son-in-law) and that are devoted to the same two things: the maximizing of personal pleasure and the maximizing of conspicuous consumption. The Aslan® prescribed to Enid while on board Nordic Pleasurelines blocks all thoughts of morbid shame and, at just four dollars a pill and with twenty blends soon to choose from, provides more bang for the buck than any Starbucks beverage – as befits a drug named after the "Great Lion" of C. S. Lewis but recalling the ascendant lion earlier hailed by a Market Street evangelist as a sign that "now's the time to shop" (223). Conversely, the Mexican A caplet that Chip does not take after a weekend of popping the pills like Pez results in sexual mortification likened to "a market inundated by a wave of panic selling" (57). As such, the drugs *do* promote the ultimate "liberal *vision*" proclaimed by their manufacturers (209), which is, to cite the governing metaphor of the 2010 work in which two "super-guilty sort of liberals" serve as Franzen's center, *Freedom* (7).

Carved into college buildings, celebrated in rock lyrics, and informing everything from unlimited population growth to the behavior of sociopathic cats in this later work set mainly in 2004, freedom *is* a "pain in the ass sometimes," as the son of Walter and Patty Berglund admits, in that it grants each person the "right to think whatever you want" even if those wants collide (*Freedom* 268). In the US, however, the inalienable right to personal freedom is presented by Franzen as one to which Americans cling even more tenaciously when the other right they view as inalienable, the right to make money, is threatened. The Bush conservative, undeterred by hypocrisy, responds by cynically invoking the golden – in every sense of the term – opportunity provided by 9/11 to "radically expand the sphere of freedom" to Iraq and "get a nation of free people to let go of their bad logic and sign on with better logic" (267, 268). The liberal, wanting to do "good" but hobbled by being "nice," either withdraws – like Al Gore, "too nice a guy to fight dirty in Florida" (217) – or opts for willful blindness. Walter thus continues in his work to set up a preserve for a North American songbird even after he learns that the Texas oilman funding his efforts has been planning all along to use the West Virginia land purchased for the extraction of natural gas. After that cover is exposed, along with the fact that the jobs created for the two hundred families displaced are in a plant built to make body armor for the war in Iraq, he, too, retreats to his own version of Walden Pond in a lake near Grand Rapids.

In *The Corrections*, Alfred Lambert retreats from nothing, not even a small boy slumped for hours over an uneaten plate of liver and rutabaga, his intransigence both a rebuke to the laissez-faire parenting of *Freedom* and a reminder that "there were limits to correction" (263), an ambivalence that, in the end, reflects the sensibility of an author who describes himself as both Midwesterner and Manhattanite (*How* 259). For Alfred – neither cosmopolitan liberal nor suburban stalwart but native-born Kansan – also believes that civilization depends upon restraint, that reality is not relative, that individuality is a function of privacy, values of "decency" his son Gary derides as "bullshit" (173). As the turd that appears in a hallucinatory nightmare explains, they interfere with that constitutional right to "[l]ife, liberty, [and] the pussuit of hotpussyness" that drives the majority of which the turd is a representative (285), and make for a minority of which Alfred – the one character who refuses the lure of insider trading and who, as is finally revealed, has quit a job that would have secured his financial future in order to protect his daughter's privacy from scandal – is the sole survivor.

An inalienable right to happiness underlies the adulterous pursuits in the more modestly scaled suburban fiction of Rick Moody and Tom Perrotta. "Being right and being happy are on opposite ends" of the dance that is human life, intones the hip new rector of Moody's *The Ice Storm* (1994) when reminding his flock that "having a right is different from *being* right" (162). In fact, "[b]eing right is the last refuge of scoundrels" in that it restricts the pursuit of what *est* terms "options" (162–63), advice that parishioners looking to maximize their "options" during a 1973 key party are more than happy to take (55). Believing herself an exception to, but afraid she may be as ordinary as, the other tired mothers of Tom Perrotta's *Little Children* (2004), Sarah impulsively kisses a stay-at-home dad on the playground one day and, having "tasted happiness for the first time in her adult life" (355), embarks upon an affair, taking as her model Flaubert's Madame Bovary, who, in Sarah's revisionist reading, simply refuses to "accept unhappiness" and errs only in selecting "losers" for soul mates (195, 196). Unfortunately for Sarah and Todd, who mainly seeks distraction from a house in which "[e]verybody [is] happy but me" (214), the husband upon whose child care their plan to run away and *"finally be happy"* depends suddenly decamps for California to experience for himself *"what life feels like for happy people"* (298, 309). In this he is but one of a demographically mixed set of web-surfing fans who journey to meet the actual woman behind the virtual Slutty Kay of their fantasies and then compete in a group photo "to see who could look the happiest" (314).

In Moody's novel, no one looks even remotely happy, and not only because of the years it takes for the Summer of Love to migrate to New Canaan, Connecticut, the "most congenial and superficially calm of suburbs" in the "wealthiest state in the Northeast" in the "most affluent country on earth" (*Ice* 3), and Republican as far back as Garfield. Just one more betrayal in the age of Watergate when "[t]he idea of betrayal was in the air" (55), adultery leaves Benjamin Hood slinking out the back door of his mistress's house "[l]ike a Plumber, an official burglar" (29), as unfulfilled – both emotionally and physically – as he is in his own house, surrounded by the family he views as a "bad idea he got" during a time when "there were no other ideas" (14). Indeed, far from being an alternative to marriage, likened to "settling [a] debt" (14), infidelity, in the book's yoking of politics and economics, adheres to a similar set of principles, specifically free-market monetarist principles. Thus at the key party in which Milton Friedman is the holy name most mentioned, wives are traded like "commodit[ies]" (55), selections proceed as "flawlessly as a bank line" (168), and partners size each other up as they would "a new hi-fi or a new dishwater" (171), with any extras – like the offer to stay in a spare bedroom after the deal is sealed – a bonus thrown in for substandard service. "I owe you one, I want to pay up" (179), explains a chagrined Jim Williams, before whose house an American flag usually hangs "limply" and around whose neighborhood power lines all over are beginning to fall (42).

The actual fall that destroys the Williams and Hood households comes after a live wire that dances like a "charmed snake" touches the guardrail with steel cable on which a son decides to sit during the storm of the book's title (211), the death at which he longs for "the consolations of some imagined and perfect family" forcing upon the book's imperfect families knowledge of their parental neglect (214). More than "[o]ne of the unsupervised kids of New Canaan" (209), however, Mike Williams is one of a nationwide "community of lost teenagers" (189). As Paul Hood, whose retrospective account the narrative is midway revealed to be, states, "Abandonment was in the parlors of America" (186). Alone among the book's characters in recognizing that nothing will assuage a loneliness portrayed as pandemic, he knows even as a sixteen-year-old that masturbating against the buttocks of a passed-out classmate will "not bring him the good feeling he wanted" but only make him – in Moody's acronymic echo of the Committee to Re-Elect the President – a "creep" (189). Knowing in advance that all they can hope for is "the cheapest approximation of exalted feeling" (55), the adults around him keep "trail[ing] after ecstasy" and, when caught with their pants down, they, like the Watergate burglars, "denied it, rationalized it, [and] dressed it all up in talk" (247).

In Perrotta's novel, by contrast, the only direct link between local and national affairs comes by way of a brief reference to Gary Condit, which functions in much the same way as the opening references to Clarence Thomas, Anita Hill, and Gennifer Flowers in *Election* (1998), in which a race for high school president is used to address questions raised by the 1992 race for US president, and passing references to Jerry Falwell and Pat Robertson in *The Abstinence Teacher* (2007), in which the battle over a sex-ed-turned-Wise-Choices curriculum serves as a "demographic fun house" for an entire nation taken over by the Christian Right (330). To explore the thin line that separates American deviance and American decency, *Little Children* employs a subplot involving a sex offender who has returned to live in the "sleepy suburban community" of Bellington, Massachusetts (95), after his release from prison and the attempts of the upstanding citizenry to divorce itself from him by any means possible, from mass exodus to ritual expulsion.

Yet as a "bad man," the words with which Sarah describes him to her young daughter (136), Ronnie McGorvey recalls the introduction of Sarah as a "bad mommy" (3). More to the point, as a grown man with no job and no responsibilities, nicknamed the "Prince" by a friend of the mother with whom he lives (68), McGorvey exposes all too uncomfortably the reality behind the life led by the "Prom King" Todd, a grown man who lives off the earnings of his wife, and whose willingness to do so as far back as a college course in the Sociology of the American Family has made him the professor's poster boy for the domestic arrangements of the future. The threat of McGorvey, then, has less to do with the antithesis he poses than it does with the mirror he presents to the Bellington community, composed of people who view their personal behavior as stemming from urges over which "[t]hey didn't really have a choice" (129) and with which it is "ridiculous to be at war" (109) – no different from Todd's three-year-old after the discovery of his penis grants him "a sort of standing invitation that he found impossible to resist" (41), but far more dangerous in that their actions have consequences that extend beyond the football games and frat pranks and fifty-yard-line make-out sessions in which they engage. Hardly an innocent man, McGorvey is indeed guilty, as the end of the book makes clear, not just of the charge of indecent exposure for which he has been sent to prison but of murdering a nine-year-old girl from a neighboring town. But, as the book's interrogation of decency and deviance suggests, so, in their own ways, are Todd, whose surreptitious looking at preteen skateboarders is tantamount to stalking, and the disgraced ex-cop Larry Moon, whose efforts to protect the town's children from a "creep" end in neighbors phoning the police about the "creep" whose acts of vigilante justice are terrifying their children (267). "This used to be a nice town," says May McGorvey after she sees the word "*EVIL*" spray-painted at the foot of her driveway. "It was never that nice," replies her friend. "It just liked to pretend it was" (73).

Geographies and Genealogies

Unlike the settings of suburban fiction, which often differ only in degrees of affluence, the settings that form the backdrops to the fiction of imperiled masculinity function as distinct characters unto themselves. In these novels, moreover, the story of man's ongoing relationship with the environment is, as Robert Rebein recognizes, a story that is "inseparable from the larger narrative of American history" (38). Perhaps nowhere is the entrapment of both more evident than in the fiction that takes place in the upstate regions of the Northeast, in which a bleak economy and brutal climate remind characters daily of their own insignificance. As Frederick Busch suggests in the portrait of townspeople digging up a frozen field in a futile search for a missing child's body in *Girls* (1997), "If you watched us from above, you would have seen the small men and women making themselves move slowly and carefully. There was the huge field out behind the barn. There were the little creatures hauling some of the millions of tons of snow" (277).

Such extrapolation from climate to cosmos is not unique to contemporary fiction, of course. Hemingway's *A Farewell to Arms* (1929), for instance, opens with rain bringing cholera that kills seven thousand World War I combatants and ends with Frederic Henry walking in the rain after his son and lover have died in childbirth. But the combination proves especially emasculating in fiction composed by novelists rewriting the classic American hero as middle-aged man. When Jack, Busch's laconic "rent-a-cop," returns in *North* (2005) to the upstate New York wilderness he has fled five years earlier (66), he is a man who views himself as "climbing slowly down the ladder of police work" (9), from Vietnam MP to campus cop to Carolina resort security guard. He also is a man without a home or family, whose pathetic record as a rescuer – of which the young man he is hired to find is but the latest victim in a series that began with Jack's infant daughter – is directly a function of his self-enforced separateness, of being an "American cowboy," much like Cooper's Leatherstocking (295), just "Jack with Nobody," as the elderly lady who runs the local diner notes (198). Never could he have saved his ex-wife from driving into the "deep white shit" of a blizzard armed with Percodan and Powers Irish whiskey because he is, in the words of the friend who informs Jack of her death, a "man without a phone number" (266).

For characters attributed family histories tantamount to destinies, the prospects are even worse. Miles Roby, the forty-two-year-old manager of the one eatery not part of a fast-food chain in Richard Russo's *Empire Falls* (2001), knows he has not been "an entirely unwilling participant in his own foiled destiny" (103), even if dropping out of college to return to a Maine town decimated by the closing of its textile mill and shirt factory has been necessitated by his mother's terminal illness. Yet as the descendant of a family alleged to spring from the same tree as the Robideauxs, Miles is both indentured servant to and surrogate son of Francine Robideaux Whiting, the widowed matriarch who has sold the industries to a multinational corporation concerned only with tax write-offs and who still owns half the town's real estate in the millennial year in which the novel takes place. Indeed, in assuming these roles with an employer who habitually refers to him as "dear boy," Miles has become successor to the (not so) dearly departed husband, Charles Beaumont, infantalized by Francine as "Charlie," who is himself the last in a line of Whiting males "curse[d]" by wives who make their lives miserable and to whom they remain bound after their plans to kill them go awry (5). Knowing that what he wants is just two weeks a year on Martha's Vineyard, something he "can desire without ever being expected to strive for" (224), then, does not afford Miles the kind of "will-*power*" that, in Francine's view, comes with knowledge of one's desires, in the absence of which will "remains impotent," a "limp dick, as it were" (61). For, as the book's description of C. B. Whiting's return from ten years "living more or less happily" in Mexico attests (475), no one can resist the summons home – especially when it comes from a woman. Determined "to fulfill his destiny as a Whiting male, or, more precisely, to be the first in his male line to get that destiny right" (475), Charlie responds by directing his "impotent rage" against himself with a bullet to the brain (478) – but only after he arrives back in Empire Falls in compliance with his wife's wishes.

That Miles responds by embracing fatherhood as "his best destiny" (469), returning from the island to which he has fled with the daughter traumatized by high school violence to a town that "accommodated just about everyone" (21), a place in which "kindness" can be considered "sexy" and the "nicest, saddest man" is also "the sort of man you could love without completely losing your self-respect" (126, 127), reflects the book's generous spirit. And Russo, in fact, extends that generosity to almost everyone in his large cast of characters – from sixty-year-old Walt Comeau trying to pass for fifty in tight T-shirts to the "blighted, but not entire barren" Francine Whiting (482). That being said, Russo never allows his readers to forget the limits of human agency. "[S]imple kindness" is not enough to "fix" whatever it is that years of parental abuse have "broken" in John Voss, the abandoned teenager who shoots up his high school art class (424). Diet and exercise cannot dispel a lifetime's worth of disappointment for Miles's ex-wife, who mistakes "losing weight" for "changing" and fails to see that StairMastering her way to slimness is, as her mother quips, just "shoveling shit against the tide" (196). The wisdom of this remark is confirmed quite literally in the book's last pages, when the Knox River – always prone to flooding and more so after the Whitings, in an attempt to correct one of "God's basic design flaw[s]," cut a new channel to stop trash from washing up on their estate (12) – overflows its banks after the snow melts. Submerging half the newly revived downtown under water, it also sweeps away the matriarch who has brokered that deal to the nearby community that had been receiving waste from Whiting industries for generations.

Such flooding would be unlikely to occur in the upstate New Hampshire of Russell Banks for the simple reason that the snow there never seems to melt, leaving residents both isolated and increasingly prone to the kind of violence that, when it erupts beyond the wife-beating so common as to be endemic, is biblical in its wrath and righteousness. In the case of Banks's white males, however, that propensity is as much genealogical as environmental, part of a tradition passed down from father to son. Aged out of the sports and military that once served as identifiers of and outlets for the best and worst of manhood, respectively, they turn to work, the "something" that, in Busch's terms, "[g]rown-ups have to do" (*North* 54). But unlike Busch's "Jack with Nobody," who knows that "there were always jobs because there was always plenty of disorder" to regulate (149), Banks's working men are constantly frustrated in their attempts to provide and protect, their desire to be "good" men no match for a determinism that, finally, is only exacerbated by place, as the comparison between the man who leaves and the man who stays illustrates.

Size does matter in *Continental Drift* (1985), in which the sense of manhood that comes from work derives entirely from the paycheck that accompanies it. Enraged by his measly $137.44 take-home after eight years at Abenaki Oil Company, Bob Dubois smashes all the windows of his car and, lured by the "old life-as-ladder metaphor" that "everyone in America seems to believe in" (14), uproots his family to Florida, where he plans to make "a fucking killing" (74). More than just discovering that working in his brother's liquor store is no better than working as an oil burner repairman – worse, in fact, in that the seventy-two-hour week is longer and home is now a trailer instead of a house – Bob is confronted in Florida with an entirely new racial demographic that makes him question why he ever left a place "where all the people were white and spoke the same kind of English and wanted the same things from life" and where "[h]e wouldn't worry if his prick was too small because he was a white man" (142, 143). Yet once he descends a rung lower on that life-as-ladder, seduced by another get-rich-quick scheme, Bob discovers that, relative to the wealthy men who hire him to take them fishing, he is barely different from the Haitians with whom his story is juxtaposed, another part of the substructure that supports Miami's tourist industry and living with his family at the end of a dirt road "like niggers in a shack in the middle of nowhere" (271). Further reduced after his wife takes a job as a waitress, the man introduced as an "ordinary-looking young man" (6) realizes while diapering his infant son that the boy's "ordinary, circumcised penis" is just a "doctored tube coming out of his digestive tract, that's all," endowed with "no mystery, no power" (385–86).

And when a last-ditch attempt to make a windfall by ferrying illegal immigrants into Florida results in the deaths of fifteen Haitians forced to jump overboard at gunpoint to avoid capture by the Coast Guard, any possibility of this "ordinary man" ever becoming a "decent man" dies as well (408) – and not only because the moral arithmetic by which Bob later tries to justify his act as doing "something bad ... in order to do something good," a "trad[ing]" of lives that will allow him to return his family to New Hampshire and build a "new life out of the scattered, cast-off pieces of their old lives," is so dubious (405). Far from aiding those "searching for America" much like himself and his father before him as he initially thinks (348), agreeing to join a friend "[r]unning coke from Colombia and niggers from Haiti" for whatever the market will bear involves Bob in a global economy that long antedates him (316). It is that participation that turns the story introduced as *"an American story of the late twentieth century"* into the tale of *"a proper middle-class American's shame for his nation's history"* (2), and that story, in turn, into an "ordinary variation of an ancient story on this part of the planet, so ordinary that even Bob Dubois knows it": the tale of a "white man claiming to act as [a] friend and savior" to a "helpless, history-weakened people" and refusing help to those "begging for what's an absolute right" as they sink beneath the roiling waters (372).

Having taken "[r]ight's right" as his code of conduct in *Affliction* (1989), Wade Whitehouse, by contrast, takes his measure of himself as a man by the degree to which he does help the people of Lawford that, as town police officer, he has sworn to protect (110, 129, 244). But when a speeding BMW cuts around a school bus stopped to unload children the same morning a man is shot to death on the first day of deer-hunting season, the coincidence propels Wade into the realms of obsession and conspiracy and ends with a double homicide – the kind of violence that Americans like to think of as "an isolated explosion of homicidal rage in a small American town" but that, in Banks's portrayal, only exposes how precariously balanced even the most "*normal* man" is (354).

Wade, of course, is both normal and anomalous. A man with "an aptitude for being polecat mean" and "pissed" to have been sent by the army to Korea instead of Vietnam (77), Wade is also a man who has opted out of the "ancient male rite" of deer hunting while living in a town filled with men pumped by the idea of "kill[ing] something with horns" (11, 38) – or, if necessary, paying somebody else to shoot an animal for them. Likewise, he is a man who has twice married the same woman because he thinks a "demanding intelligent woman" can prevent him from becoming one with the men that "cultivat[e] their violence for another to admire and shrink from, . . . and then encourag[e] their sons to follow" (207, 300). The most dangerous of such men is his own father, a man so burning with rage as to appear to "burst into flame" (97), yet a man from whom Wade can no more permanently divorce himself than he can Lawford, in part because "he loved the town, and he could not imagine loving any other" (84), and in part because the propensity to violence is portrayed as an "afflict[ion]" (277).

Desperate "[t]o be a good man," Wade heroically does all he can to extract that rottenness at its core – much like the "afflicting" tooth that he finally yanks out with a pair of pliers in an attempt to "break through the pain and confusion of his life to something like clarity and control" (320). He embarks upon a custody battle he deems his "right" to reclaim the child whose loss is emblematic of his own lost pride and self-respect (162). He fashions a makeshift family for her out of the drunken grandfather who allowed his own wife to freeze to death and a divorced waitress he tries to turn into happy homemaker. But the battle he fights is doomed from the start. It is from that drunken father, after all, that Wade learns the phrase "[r]ight's right" (186). Once he is fired from his job as town cop – a position that has never been more than part-time, paying one-tenth of his total income – and replaced by the surrogate son Wade holds responsible for the deer-hunting shooting, there is nothing to prevent him from imploding. After he accidentally injures his daughter in a scuffle – a scene his father observes with glee because in striking a female child, however unintentionally, Wade exceeds the old man in doing the one thing this wife- and child-beating parent never did – Wade is forced to accept the inevitable, the acts of patricide and homicide that follow a final attempt to rid the community of evil prior to ridding it of the evil that is himself with his disappearance.

Genealogy plays a crucial role in the fiction of the Midwest written by women, although genealogy in their works acts not in concert with an inhospitable environment but in the poisoning of the natural environment. Jane Smiley thus distinguishes between land and farm in *A Thousand Acres* (1991), her reimagining of *King Lear* through the lens of domestic realism. The fertility of the land in Iowa's Zebulon County is a function of its moisture, water in the soil that causes prairie settlers to envision "a sea or an ocean of grass" and that Ginny Cook (Goneril), the book's narrator, conceives as laying over the soil for millennia and as lodging in her own DNA (16). The value of the one thousand contiguous acres that make up her father's farm – worth over three million dollars in 1979 – is a function of subduing the land, of draining it with man-made tile lines so that it can support the heavy machinery that will increase production and profits, and of consolidating separate parcels through typically hostile acts of acquisition. Larry Cook (Lear), a farmer who "was never dwarfed by the landscape" and steadily enlarges his holdings by exploiting his neighbors' losses for his own gain, is respected throughout the county (20). Jimmy Carter, the peanut farmer president who subordinates what he "*want[s]* to do" to what he "*should*" do when it comes to "the big pieces of equipment he's got access to [that] are weapons," is reviled (71).

In a novel that opens with an epigraph from Meridel Le Sueur, "The body repeats the landscape" (n. pag.), however, the perverse nature of those "wants" is made apparent through the perverse sexual practices in which they have been expressed for generations. The original land deal that cements the holdings of the first Cook to arrive in America involves the marriage of a sixteen-year-old girl to the thirty-three-year-old John Cook. The "lust for every new method designed to swell productivity" and "covet[ing]" of acres (45, 132) that forms the "I want, I take" credo that drives his grandson is the same urge that enables Larry to take his own daughters (212), possessions "to do with as he pleased, like the pond or the houses or the hogs or the crops," with impunity (191). Significantly, such power of the patriarchal paradigm – what makes Larry a "monolith" that exceeds his six-foot-three frame (115), a mythic figure who extols the virtues of home in the tradition of American self-made men – is not strictly a function of gender. Jess Clark, the neighbor's draft-dodging son without "the guts to serve his country" who returns to Iowa with plans to introduce organic farming (219), imagines his father trying to "fix" him to the land in the way that Bob the Beef steer was "fixed" (127).

Conversely, Rose (Regan), the self-described "grabby" Cook daughter already defeminized by a mastectomy (62, 304), plays Monopoly by "steadily accumulating money, buying properties only with a certain percentage of it and hoarding the rest" (78), asserts her right to "*want* what was Daddy's" as recompense for his abuse (303), and transforms herself with the land she inherits after his death into a "land baroness," as Ginny's estranged husband puts it, "your dad all over" (341, 340).

The only thing that Ginny wants – to the extent that this good Midwesterner who "go[es] along to get along" and good Midwestern woman who adopts a strategy of "limp inertia" when dealing with her father can express a desire for anything (260, 280) – is a child. But after five miscarriages, she discovers that the same toxic chemicals her father has used to promote plant growth have entered, in what Smiley terms a "closed loop" (168), the well water and resulted in her own inability to sustain any growth. Or, to put it another way, the growths that the women of Zebulon County are most likely to sustain are cancerous ones that attack them at the sites of their womanhood and kill them at young ages: Rose succumbing at thirty-seven to the breast cancer that attacks her at thirty-four, Jess Clark's mother succumbing to the same illness at forty-three, the same age that Ginny and Rose's grandmother dies. In this toxicity, the Cook farm is hardly unique. As Ginny knows, a farm "abounds with poisons" (310). Yet even after the Cook farm conceived as family bequest goes bankrupt, and must be sold to pay off debts incurred by overextension and unchecked ambition, the toxins at the heart of its enterprise continue to extend beyond the Iowa heartland. While Ginny can escape Iowa for Minnesota at the book's end, she cannot escape the "molecules of topsoil and atrazine and paraquat and anhydrous ammonia and diesel fuel and plant dust" that are as firmly lodged in her DNA as those "molecules of memory" of the incest she has tried to suppress (369). Nor can she escape knowledge of the poison that is lodged in her own heart. As she realizes while pouring tainted food that she has jarred years earlier in a moment of jealous rage at her sister down the disposal of her St. Paul apartment, fifteen minutes of flushing toxins with water relies on a "sewage treatment plant that I had never seen," about which she has "misgivings" (367).

The poison that permeates the Midwest in Marilynne Robinson's *Gilead* (2004) and *Home* (2008) is racism, which not only destroys but defiles a region in which the best of American traditions historically commingled. For the Midwest, as Robinson argues in her essays, is the place to which abolitionists came to deploy their resources when met with virulent opposition in the East, which is to say "people from New England and New York who were Puritans by culture and descent and who saw their movement into the Middle West from the 1830s onward as a reenactment and in effect a vindication of the Puritan settlement in America in the seventeenth century" (*Death* 136–37). Not, in the view of this devout Christian author, that the theology descended from Jean Cauvin – the name Robinson uses to free him from the legacy of intolerance ascribed to the Anglicized John Calvin – requires any vindication. As she asserts, anyone who takes the trouble to peruse his actual writings will find support for the divine presence revealed in the human body, the Fall of Man resulting in an outpouring of God's grace on earth, and the seeds of American popular government, separation of church and state, and universal schooling (*Death* 183–84, 205–06).

God is still very much imminent in the landscape of Gilead, Iowa, a setting infused with "brilliance" (*Gilead* 67) – oak trees that "astonish" (57), prairie dawns that flood with "radian[ce]" (246). So writes John Ames, a Congregationalist minister who views God as a "Middle Westerner of New England extraction" (124), in the letter he begins to his six-year-old son that ends by updating those early American spiritual autobiographies devoted to exemplary lives in a more quotidian sense than the hagiographic accounts of statesmen (Leise 352). Failing health has only made him more attuned, as he turns seventy-seven, to the beauty and joy of those things "ordinary in kind but exceptional in degree" (28), from the casual laughter of garage mechanics to the pitch of a baseball, evidence to him that "[w]herever you turn your eyes the world can shine like transfiguration" and all that is needed is "a little willingness to see" (245). To the thirty-eight-year-old Glory Boughton, who, like Sylvie in *Housekeeping* (1980), is forced by circumstance and gender to return to act as family caregiver in *Home*, these are the very things that always have constituted the "ordinary, dutiful choring that made up most of every life" (61), even if she often fails to appreciate fully the value of chicken and dumplings as a salve to grief.

The state of Iowa itself is another matter, though, in these twinned novels of fathers and sons – biological, surrogate, divine – that depict the return of the prodigal son, a man named after Ames but born to the Presbyterian Robert Boughton who is his friend and ministerial alter ego, from different perspectives. (A prequel, *Lila* [2014], traces the arrival of the vagrant woman who becomes Ames's wife and gives birth to their son.) When Glory's brother Jack comes home to Gilead in 1956 after twenty years of dissolute living, he arrives with a specific purpose in mind: to see if the state that Ulysses S. Grant acclaimed "the shining star of radicalism" (*Gilead* 176), its very topsoil so deep as to provide better tunnels for fugitive slaves than New England, and a town that was one of hundreds in the Midwest to which John Brown could retreat, can accommodate the African American woman and mixed-race son who comprise his family. What he finds, however, is a destitute town that has no African Americans currently living in it, a fact to which the men of faith that should be the community's moral arbiters are completely indifferent. To Ames, grandson of a fiery abolitionist who left Maine for Kansas to aid the Free Soilers after receiving a vision of Jesus in shackles, the fire in the black church that prompted the last remaining congregants to leave for Chicago is a "little nuisance fire" that "happened many years ago" (231), as much a part of the past as those passions of his grandfather that "now just look awkward and provincial and ridiculous" (234). To Boughton, deprived of any familial link to that "fanaticism" because his ancestors left Scotland in 1870 (*Home* 204), the desire of Autherine Lucy to attend the University of Alabama is a pointless "commotion" (156), and the televised sight of riot police turning fire hoses and dogs on black protesters during the Montgomery Bus Boycott one of those forgettable "things [that] come and go" – like the murder of Emmett Till the year before that he vaguely remembers as an execution of a man for attacking a white woman – and of less consequence than the gravy he goes to praise as "wonderful" (184).

The destitution of Gilead, then, is first and foremost a destitution of the human heart: literally in the case of Ames, whose heart is failing; metaphorically in the case of Boughton, whose "good house" with "gracious heart" looks "abandoned" and "heartbroken" to Glory upon her arrival (*Home* 4), having become an "oppressive tabernacle" of "probity and kind intent" (102), the limits of which are exposed by the failed rescue missions undertaken in both novels. When the Boughtons attempt to rescue the illegitimate daughter Jack has left behind from the impoverished conditions in which she is being raised, the mother is not "moved or swayed by any kindness they could contrive" (233); the child dies from an infection that a little penicillin could have cured. When Jack visits Ames in the hopes that he might use his influence to make it possible for his family to settle in Gilead, Ames is "very kind" but, as Jack relates, cannot do anything more because his "heart is failing" (308).

And it is precisely because these two fathers fail to enact the duties placed upon them by their heavenly father that it is left for Glory, a woman who takes the shoe as her marker when playing Monopoly and eats dry toast to avoid the sound that buttering makes, to become, in Robinson's inversion, steward of "my father's house" (325), as she does with her inheritance of that house upon his death. Whereas Ames, in ending his letter with a prayer that his son will "find a way to be useful" (*Gilead* 247), can only echo his grandfather's admonition that "[t]o be useful was the best thing the old men ever hoped for themselves" (49), Glory, at the end of *Home*, invites Jack's African

American family into her house when the two arrive on her doorstep. The gesture comes too late, of course. Jack, having learned how greatly the "shining star" of Iowa has dimmed (*Gilead* 220; *Home* 210), has already departed, and so must Della and her son, who cannot cross that threshold because they must return to their own house in Missouri before nightfall due to "the way things are now" (321). All of which leaves Glory – in the book's wonderfully nuanced conclusion – to "live out her life in a place all the rest of them called home, a place they would mean to return to more often than they did" (308), a place better as idea than actuality, and presided over by a woman named for a theological abstraction.

The original home to which Louise Erdrich traces each individual's beginnings is "formed out of the body's interior landscape" in which "our mothers' bodies are the boundaries and personal geography," following which "it is the earth with which we form the same dependent relationship" ("Where" 24). This statement, published shortly after *Love Medicine* (1984) initiated what would become a tribal tetralogy, also pertains to the fiction devoted to the new cast of characters introduced in her more recent works set in the North Dakota plains. In *A Plague of Doves* (2008), it is by "blend[ing] into the earth as they made their way along the edges of fields" that the two fleeing children who grow up to become the grandparents of Evelina Harp, one of the book's narrators, "slipped [the] knots" of Catholic ritual and "cut the harnesses" that relatives have already tightened (13, 12). In *The Round House* (2012), it is by seeking shelter from a blizzard in the carcass of a female buffalo who adopts him that a young boy receives instructions to build the sacred place of Ojibwe worship of the book's title: a "round house [that] will be my body, the poles my ribs, the fire my heart," as well as the "body of your mother" (214), a "place to keep [the] people together and to ask for mercy from the Creator" (315).

These relationships from Native American culture that bypass all boundaries – male/female, human/animal, material world/spirit world – are just as real to Erdrich as the blocks of commodity cheese and canned tomatoes that stock her characters' kitchen cupboards. Coexisting with the fluid landscape *of* the earth, however, are those boundaries imposed *on* the earth by "drawing a line and defending it" – with arms, with law – and by which humans think they have "mastered something" or "manage[d] to form a country, a reservation," a delusional belief in that whatever is so formed the earth eventually "swallows and absorbs" (*Plague* 115). A line drawn by Clemenceau and Wilson permits Fidelis Waldvogel to wake up in Germany instead of France after he returns home from World War I in *The Master Butchers Singing Club* (2003), and this same idiosyncrasy infuses that northern Midwest region where Fidelis mistakenly assumes he will find "the great dying finished, and the blood already soaked into the ground" (290). On the contrary, in Erdrich's conflation of local and global, Indian treaties with the government are "like treaties with foreign nations" (*Round* 2) – a line creates the town of Pluto out of land inside reservation boundaries that keep shifting "according to government whim and Indian agent head counts and something called allotment" (202) – and the landscape itself provides a "record of old brutality that hadn't yet bled itself out" (211). Indeed, because of the mixtures of aboriginal, Catholic, Indian, French Canadian, and German blood that come from intermarriage, "[n]othing that happens, *nothing*, is not connected here by blood" (*Plague* 115), to the extent of producing what Evelina terms a genealogical "blood history" that she first envisions as "spider webs of lines and intersecting circles" (86), and later a tangled rope impossible to unravel because of the way that so many "have mixed in the spring of our existence both guilt and victim" (243).

The original rope in the braided narratives that form *A Plague of Doves* is the rope with which, in Erdrich's fictionalized version of an 1897 lynching in Emmons County, three Indian men and a boy are hanged outside Pluto in 1911 in retaliation for the murder of a white family of five – an event in which Evelina's grandfather, who has mentioned while drunk the men's discovery of the slaughter, is implicated. The event that opens *The Round House*, the brutal rape and attempted murder of Evelina's aunt, Geraldine Coutts, in 1988, is the indirect result of that 1911 crime in that it is perpetrated by a white man whose great-uncle was part of the lynching party, a man who, driven by the same "gimme-gimme" desire that prompts all men who "do something nasty to a woman" (223, 222), violates one Indian woman because of what she knows about the statutory rape of another by a neighboring state's governor. Yet the lust that makes people unable "to keep our hands off one another" is portrayed by Erdrich as the same lust for land against which tribal law is impotent and US law complicit (*Plague* 116). For the hate crime against Geraldine is also payback for a 1976 ruling made by her tribal judge husband concerning a grocery owned by the rapist's family located on purchased allotment land surrounded by tribal trust land. And it cannot be prosecuted because it occurs near the round house where three different classes of land – tribal trust, state, and fee – meet, and therefore on land of uncertain jurisdiction.

Like the roots of the small trees that attack the foundation of the Coutts house in the book's opening paragraphs, the laws that govern jurisdiction have roots in court decisions and legislation that, as Judge Antone Bazil Coutts instructs his thirteen-year-old son, Joe, extend as far back as the founding of the nation: *Oliphant v. Suquamish* (1978), *Tee-Hit-Ton Indians v. United States* (1955), *Lone Wolf v. Hitchcock* (1903), the Major Crimes Act of 1885, Ex Parte Crow Dog (1883), *Johnson v. McIntosh* (1823). It is against the boundaries set by those rulings that he and the other tribal judges press while presiding over the cases of stolen hot dogs and fifteen-cent washers that Joe finds so inconsequential. Recognizing that "thing[s] can grow so powerful even when planted in the wrong place" (*Round* 293), Erdrich replaces an uncritically accepting view of nature with a more contextualized view of nature: a white dove as Holy Spirit but a plague of white doves as biblical scourge; a family tree of "complicated branching and interbranching" but children conceived in violence as fruit of a poisonous tree whose lineage can "shake the branches" of other trees (149). When Joe, then, hunts down his mother's attacker, a sadist so "[b]eyond the limits" (92) – not just of his father's law but, as a wiindigoo or evil spirit, all human law – he replaces the case law of his father with the sleeptalking stories of his grandfather to obtain neither vigilante justice nor "best-we-can-do justice" but, for once, "ideal justice" (306). Yet by predicating that ideal justice on doing the "wrong thing" that the taking of any life is (306), he sentences himself – in Erdrich's nod to Faulkner's Compson family saga – "to endure" forever the knowledge of his act (317).

All-Americans

From the beginning of his career, the desire to transcribe "middleness with all its grits, bumps, and anonymities" that informed John Updike's portrayal of southeastern Pennsylvania (*Assorted* 186) – in fiction that translated Shillington into Olinger and Reading into Brewer – has been complicated by his belief that "a page of printed prose should bring to its mimesis something extra, a kind of supernatural as it were, . . . a fine excess that corresponds with the intricacy and opacity of the real world" (*Odd* 869–70). Such a conception of layered realism, wherein what is visible suggests what is invisible, both equally constitutive of what is "real," allowed Updike to assign to the most ordinary things the "sacred status that in former times was granted to mysteries" and produce what he termed "distinctive 'American realism'" (*Hugging* 117), in which, democratically, "[e]verything can be as interesting as every other thing," a milk carton as much as a rose, a trolley car as much as a tree (*Picked-Up* 518).

In the four novels that follow the travails of Harry "Rabbit" Angstrom from 1959 to 1989 (a novella, "Rabbit Remembered" [2000], revisits the Angstrom family ten years after his death), "everything" is replaced by a character conceived as "everyman," or, more to the point, every American man. A "big pale uncircumcised hunk of the American dream," as Updike writes in *Rabbit at Rest* (1990), Harry has led a life circumscribed by the Cold War (57). He also, by this final volume of the tetralogy, has suffered a drowned child, a dead mistress, a destroyed home, a dope-addicted son, and a newly liberated wife, not to mention the additional indignities of a bad heart and faltering libido. On the one hand, he hates the way that economics have replaced bipolar politics and standing armies as the adjudicators of power. Asserting that "[t]he only difference between the two old superpowers is they sell their trees to Japan in different directions" (352), he mourns the Cold War that "gave you a reason to get up in the morning" (353). On the other hand, the absences that pierce his heart most deeply he expresses with respect to less monumental things: Where have all the Chiclets gone? "Have they really gone the way of penny candy?" (97); "Whatever happened to the old-fashioned plain hamburger? Gone wherever the Chiclet went" (100).

In the last two Rabbit novels, the things in question are increasingly those items of consumer culture that have made Harry, underneath the Uncle Sam costume he wears in a Fourth of July parade, "a fearsome bulk with eyes that see and hands that grab and teeth that bite, a body eating enough at one meal to feed three Ethiopians for a day, a shameless consumer of gasoline, electricity, newspapers, hydrocarbons, carbohydrates" (*Rest* 381). In the last two novels, moreover, those items are typically manufactured overseas and purchased not out of need but because they are "beyond what you need" (417). As such, the ERA OF COROLLA proclaimed by the banner on his father-in-law's car lot that Harry inherits in *Rabbit Is Rich* (1981) heralds an era in which American industries of all sorts have succumbed to the money of foreign investors, just as the Double Stuf Oreos and Fruit Newtons that Harry consumes in the most literal sense throughout *Rabbit at Rest* recall all those prototypical American foods, many of which are produced by other nations, from the Burger King Whoppers and Ball Park Franks owned by Britain to the Carnation evaporated milk controlled by Switzerland's Nestlé.

Yet as the real also becomes increasingly constituted by that which this Toyota franchise owner sees most frequently, namely metal – sex with his wife an act of "fucking money" with gold Krugerrands acting as aphrodisiacs (*Rich* 175) – the decline of America that the tetralogy chronicles is measured not just by the facts of where the items consumed originate but by how far beyond the literal the items in question resonate. For while Harry has never been much of an intellectual, he is introduced in *Rabbit, Run* (1960) as a man who instinctively "feel[s] that there is an unseen world" with which "more of his actions than anyone suspects constitute transactions" (195), a soaring golf ball affirming that elusive "*it*," that "something" that "somewhere behind all this" Harry is meant to find (113, 107). Perhaps most important, Harry is a man who, in *Rabbit Redux* (1971), can remember picturing a "quilt-colored map of the U.S." emerging from the head of a sleeping God after hearing the phrase "American dream" for the first time (106). Forced to acknowledge by the last volume of the tetralogy that the president with movie magic and his own "dream distance," Ronald Reagan, has been replaced by the Bush that publicists have turned into a "beer commercial" (*Rest* 295, 61), that the statesman who, "like God," might know "nothing or everything" has shrunk to the reality of another who "knows something, but it seems a small something" (295), Harry adjusts his imaginative horizons accordingly. With the freedom that comes with being an American now defined as the freedom to watch whatever television shows he wants, it is no wonder that, while Updike's imagistic prowess grows over the course of the tetralogy, to the extent that television screens suggest air traffic control screens, which suggest heart monitors whose twitching lines suggest worms that suggest the origins of life, Rabbit's steadily declines, to the extent that television screens become places on which to see Vanna White turn around letters on *Wheel of Fortune*.

By this final volume of the tetralogy, however, the television show that has the greatest impact on Harry's consciousness is the "Rabbit Angstrom Show" on which he sees his heart surrounded by specks of plaque that look like Rice Krispies while undergoing an angioplasty following the heart attack he has while Sunfishing with his granddaughter in Florida (*Rest* 271). Having once derived his sense of exceptionalism from imagining "himself the heart of the universe," with "all the world beyond" just "frills on himself, like the lace around a plump satin valentine" (294), Harry learns from his doctor that the myocardial scarring that indicates a dying muscle "happens to all of us" as part of an inescapable aging process (284), that his "typical American heart" is simply a heart (166). And this medical diagnosis, in turn, confirms the historical diagnosis of US origins provided by the book that Harry is shown reading over the last months of his life, Barbara Tuchman's *The First Salute* (1988), which portrays the alignment of friends and foes during the colonial period as a product of the very mercantilist politics that Harry so detests and the American Revolution as "a power struggle of the Old World" that just happens to have been played out on New World battlefields (Tuchman 143). With the fall of the British empire following the fall of the Dutch empire and, before that, the fall of the Spanish empire, the fall of the American empire at some future point of time becomes, by extension, as inevitable as the direct article becomes inapplicable.

Fittingly, that point in Rabbit's saga comes during his last basketball games, final attempts on the part of this former high school athlete to recapture his lost days of glory. "Hey man," taunts one of the racially mixed group of boys Harry challenges to a game of hoops, "you're history!" (*Rest* 491). Fittingly, it is when shooting a worn red, white, and blue basketball that the second heart attack that makes real this observation occurs. If earlier in his life, Harry has refused to believe in America's not being perfect "any more than he believes at heart that he will die" (*Redux* 312), the last pages of Updike's saga call the bluff of what has increasingly become a weakly maintained rationalization. The weary "Enough" that serves as an end to Harry's literary life thus signals a final resignation about the nation no longer having to be at center stage (*Rest* 512). Admitting that with Bush's 1988 election "we're kind of on the sidelines, . . . sort of like a big Canada, and what we do doesn't much matter to anybody else," Harry also intimates that such a position may not be all that bad: "Maybe that's the way it ought to be. It's a kind of relief, I guess, not to be the big cheese" (358).

The cardiac problem that prompts Frank Bascombe to consult a physician at age thirty-eight in *The Sportswriter* (1986) for his "pounding heart" has little to do with age and everything to do with the death of his nine-year-old son from Reye's syndrome (67), the event that has propelled Frank into the state of emotional shutdown that he terms "dreaminess" as the series opens (41). And, in many ways, the emotional trajectory that Richard Ford sketches over the next two volumes – *Independence Day* (1995) and *The Lay of the Land* (2006) – and four linked stories that comprise *Let Me Be Frank with You* (2014) is one wherein the character divorced by his ex-wife for not possessing a "true heart" (*Independence* 254) eventually responds to being shot in the chest by answering the question "[d]o I have a heart at all?" with a guarded affirmative (*Lay* 476). By that point of his saga, however, Frank's having been diagnosed with prostate cancer at fifty-five makes quite literal the feeling of imperiled masculinity that he recognizes much earlier: "Being a man gets harder all the time" (*Sportswriter* 343). For unlike Updike's Rabbit, possessed of an adolescent grace that promotes a sense of his own specialness that, in turn, lends itself to an interrogation of American exceptionalism, Frank, as he goes to great lengths to point out, is a man "born into an ordinary, modern existence in 1945" (*Sportswriter* 24), who moves to a New Jersey town "as straightforward and plumb-literal as a fire hydrant" (103), knowing he is "more at ease in the mainstream" (*Independence* 7, 272). Having settled for a "small life lived acceptably," he exchanges special place for secure space (*Lay* 289).

What changes over the course of works that chart the events of three holiday weekends – Easter 1984, Fourth of July 1988, Thanksgiving 2000 – and the two weeks leading up to Christmas 2012, and collectively trace Frank's movement from self-styled Existence Period to Permanent Period to Next Level to Default Period, is the degree to which the Garden State can accommodate the kind of life Frank has adopted once "the suburbs suddenly go queer and queasy" (*Sportswriter* 352). An acquaintance blows his brains out with a duck gun on the holiday meant to celebrate resurrection. A real estate agent is raped and murdered inside a condo she is showing. A couple is shot to death by undersized Russian twins out to steal their Corvettes. A hospital guard is killed when a bomb is detonated by a Muslim wanting to send a message to a nonobservant doctor. And Frank, prior to being shot in the chest, is mugged with a Pepsi bottle by an Asian boy on a minibike and nearly killed by a supermarket cart that an African American teen driving a Trans-Am smashes into the phone booth in which he is making a call. No longer a place in which "[d]eath's a preposterous intruder" (*Sportswriter* 339), a bordered alternative to the city, the suburbs have become barely different from the city, possessed of their own downtowns for commuter workers, their own homeless populations, and a "new sense of a wild world being just beyond our perimeter" (*Independence* 5) – if even that far. The "suburban sixties *grown out*" have made Haddam, New Jersey, by the third volume, "a place where maybe someone might set a bomb off just to attract its attention" (*Lay* 51, 90).

This failure of the suburbs to safeguard its inhabitants is especially troubling to Frank because it directly impinges upon the mission he has set himself as a sportswriter-turned-realtor (or, as he likes to say, "Residential Specialist"). Having been chastised for his political isolationism "from events on a grand scale" and forced by his friend's shotgun suicide to acknowledge his "responsibility to a somewhat larger world" at the end of *The Sportswriter* (279, 366), Frank returns to New Jersey after beating a quick retreat – first to Florida, then France – and switches careers, convinced that there is nothing more worthy one can "do for wayward strangers than to shelter them" (*Independence* 424), in particular those strangers of suburbia's new demographics to whom he, as landlord and realtor, can offer a "sense of belonging and permanence" these late arrivals might otherwise lack (27). In this way, he can "do for others while looking after Number One" (112). Because Frank also believes that real estate prices are an "index to the national well-being" (5), and that one's home is a "natural extension of what was wanted from life, a sort of minor-league Manifest Destiny" (*Lay* 90), these professional obligations are inextricable from his patriotic duties, making Frank a "citizen with a niche," a "realtor and a pilgrim" catering to the wide "variety of citizen pilgrims" who cross his threshold (*Lay* 466, 482).

Such communitarian sentiments, of course, are fully in keeping with both the New Deal politics by which Frank defines himself (the kind that have him inform his son during a road trip to Cooperstown that the annual Hall of Fame baseball game is played in a 1939 stadium built by the WPA) and the centrist Third Way policies of the Clinton Administration to which Ford subscribes that allowed for the commingling of personal profit and common good. They also are consistent with Tocqueville's notion of "self-interest rightly understood" in *Democracy in America* (1835), a copy of which (along with Emerson's "Self-Reliance" and Carl Becker's *The Declaration of Independence*) Frank dips into during that Fourth of July father-son weekend (Knapp 511). This concept of citizens willingly "sacrific[ing] a portion of their time and property to the welfare of the state" (Tocqueville 130), however, could not be further removed from the politics of Frank's pilgrim clients whose citizenship is a function of courtroom ceremony rather than birthplace and whose history of global movement reduces in value the importance of any particular arrival. Mike Mahoney, Frank's Tibetan employee in *The Lay of the Land* – "as American as I am, only from farther east," Frank notes (192) – contemplates going into the "sprawl business" with a developer in the process of literally buying up (Old) MacDonald's Farm (38). An enticing prospect to the new Republican formerly known as Lobsang Dhargey, who "sees clients as rolls of cash that happen to be able to talk" (411), it is horrifying to Frank, who understands that "[f]lattening pretty cornfields for seven-figure mega-mansions isn't, after all, really *helping* people in the way that assisting them to find a modest home they want – and that's already there – helps them" (198). Not that, in an environment in which houses are as mobile as the people who purchase them, the words "already there" have much meaning. The house on 118 Timbuktu that a South Asian family of Bush (*fils*) support-ers wants to buy and move to another lot is already up on girders, "detached from the sacred ground that makes it what it is – a place of safety and assurance" (413), awaiting transport to a new address prior to the delivery of a house made in Indiana for the clients to whom Frank has earlier sold the property. Yet as Frank, who has moved in this third volume from Haddam to the midline (naturally) Jersey Shore town of Sea-Clift, knows all too well, even those whose domiciles are more firmly planted "hold our ground on the continent's fragile margin at nature's sufferance," their ownership mere custodianship given the "transitory essence of everything" (207). When Hurricane Sandy strikes in 2012, the "climatological shit train" turns Sea-Clift into "Nagasaki-by-the-sea" (*Let* 31, 11).

That "everything," significantly, includes the nation itself, as Frank learns while lecturing his son on the origins of the United States, framing colonial consolidation in the contemporary terms of falling property values and improved trade in an attempt to get the disturbed adolescent to connect his own "fractured past with his hectic present" (*Independence* 259). Forced to recognize that American independence was motivated primarily by American expedience, Frank comes to the realization that, far from being a "fixed, continuous entity" that is "anchored into the rock of permanence," every community is "anchored only to contingency like a bottle on a wave, seeking a quiet eddy" (439). The millennial angst and contested presidential election that make the lay of the land so uncertain in 2000, the hotel that comes tumbling down and hospital bombing that intimate the events of a year later, thus testify to a nation founded, if not on "shitty pilings," like the Doolittle house Frank tries to sell, at the very least on "shifting sand" (*Lay* 280). And so, applying a lesson of the realty profession – "cease sanctifying places" because "[p]laces never cooperate by revering you back" (*Independence* 151) – Frank adds "Place means nothing" to the litany of aphorisms that punctuate his tale (152) – "Forget best … Best's gone" (*Independence* 146), "Anything can be made worse" (*Lay* 201) – which leads to the most desacralizing one of all: "[H]ome's where you pay the mortgage" (*Independence* 449). As he explains at greater length, "Home's a musable concept if you're born to one place, as I was (the syrup-aired southern coast), educated to another (the glaciated mid-continent), come full stop in a third – then spend years finding suitable 'homes' for others. Home may only be where you've memorized the grid pattern, where you can pay with a check" (*Lay* 14). That includes his own Hoving Road home, transformed with its 1980s sale into the Chaim Yankowicz Ecumenical Center, torn down in the 1990s by the Korean Fresh Lighters, and resurrected as a southern plantation by a Kentucky horse breeder who calls the place "Not Furlong."

The same might apply equally to Frank himself, who suspects, upon his initial diagnosis, that he will not outlive his own mortgage, and whom Ford shows bound for the Mayo Clinic in *The Lay of the Land*'s last pages to find out how successful the sixty radioactive iodine seeds encased in titanium BBs have been in nuking his prostate into submission. Yet the plane "going down fast" (485) – with all that such descent implies in a novel published in 2006 – makes a safe landing. And falling – I use the term deliberately – in the "mid-range of patient-passenger profiles," as Frank admits is his "usual" (469), is *un*usual this time in not signaling an opting out of the uncontrollable but a realistic acknowledgment of it, a "practical acceptance of what's what, in real time and down-to-earth," which is, in this lay of the land, "as good as spiritual if you can finagle it" (484).

Chapter 3

The Contemporary Political Novel

"We made the sixties," he says, speaking in a generational "we"
that excludes me. "We made the counterculture. You were twelve
years old." . . .

"Yes, you made it, but as a result it was a thing outside of you. You
could walk away from it. And you did. We couldn't, you see. It was in us.
And when it was no longer out there in the world itself, it left us
stranded, confused, betrayed, masturbating and doomed little outlaws."
                        – Lorrie Moore, *Who Will Run the Frog Hospital?* (1994)

The age difference that separates the married couple of Lorrie Moore's novel is
nine years, enough for Daniel to have experienced the sixties personally and
Berie to have, as she puts it, "inherited" the era and, having "hung [her] own
incipience on [its] politics," been left hanging emotionally when faced with
a subsequent decade in which "[t]here was only Ford pardoning Nixon" (47).
Aware that the activism of the woman born in 1957 has extended no further
than ice-skating to Barry McGuire's "Eve of Destruction," Daniel sees his
wife's hyperbole for what it is. "You can't use the sixties to explain yourself
to yourself," he remonstrates (47); to do so is to be a "person looking for
excuses," a "hoodlum seeking politics" (48).

Strictly speaking, Moore's coming-of-age novel is not a political novel, if by
political novel one means a novel devoted to the representation of politics, as
opposed to a Jamesonian politics of representation that would make every
novel a political novel (Hutchison xvi–xvii). In fact, the casual sprinkling of
proper names that grants Moore's protagonist, if only in her own mind,
a political identity points to the vexed nature of the political novel as
a genre and the American political novel in particular among scholars: the
former a bastard child born of the commingling of impure ideological matter
and aesthetics, the latter a runt of the litter when compared with its European
and Third World counterparts. "The idea of politics can seldom seem so
'natural' a subject to American novelists as to European," wrote Irving Howe
in 1957 when discussing the tendency of American writers to think of politics

as "a special 'problem,' with all the awkwardness and self-consciousness that entails" (*Politics* 161), an assessment reiterated by Robert Boyers almost thirty years later when ascribing the omission of American novels from his post-1945 survey to "the striking disjunction between political intelligence and advanced literary thinking in the United States" (n. pag.). At the same time, the sense of political impasse with which the end of the sixties leaves Moore's protagonist, legitimately or not, informs a large number of contemporary American novels. Written by authors of age in the 1960s as well as authors not born until the 1960s (or after), these works are explicitly devoted to exploring the political legacy of the decade: the Civil Rights movement (Rosellen Brown's *Civil Wars* [1984], Jay Cantor's *Great Neck* [2003]); the counter-culture (Maxine Hong Kingston's *Tripmaster Monkey* [1989], Jennifer Egan's *The Invisible Circus* [1995], T. Coraghessan Boyle's *Drop City* [2003]); and, perhaps most of all, the New Left (Tim O'Brien's *The Nuclear Age* [1985], Neil Gordon's *The Company You Keep* [2003], Sigrid Nunez's *The Last of Her Kind* [2006], David Goodwillie's *American Subversive* [2010], Kurt Andersen's *True Believers* [2012]).

A similar sense of political impasse informs those American novels that responded to a felt "end of ideology" produced by the "exhaustion of political ideas of the fifties," to recall the title of Daniel Bell's 1960 study, and earlier chronicled the demise of the Old Left: Lionel Trilling's *The Middle of the Journey* (1947), Norman Mailer's *Barbary Shore* (1951), Mary McCarthy's *The Groves of Academe* (1952), Ralph Ellison's *Invisible Man* (1952), Clancy Sigal's *Going Away* (1961), and E. L. Doctorow's *The Book of Daniel* (1971), *Ragtime* (1975), and *Loon Lake* (1980), to name but a few. In their cases, however, the failure in question was traced back to a foreign paradigm, the interrogation of which forms the substance of the books' plots. Doctorow's eponymous narrator in *The Book of Daniel* concludes that "no revolution is betrayed, only fulfilled" only after reviewing the history of the Soviet Union and those events – the Moscow Trials, the POUM purges in Republican Spain, the 1939 Nazi-Soviet Pact – that proved "moments of agony to world-wide socialism" (66). Contemporary American political novels, by contrast, have little interest in exploring the demise of a Soviet dream portrayed from the start as authoritarian if not irrelevant. William T. Vollmann's *Europe Central* (2005) opens with Hitler's "ever-wakeful sleepwalker" and Stalin's "soon-to-be-duped realist" getting married prior to raping the "good docile girl" that is Europe (3, 9). Lauren Groff's *Arcadia* (2012) dispatches the toothless codger that carries a hammer-and-sickle flag to an undistinguished death in his wheelchair. Jonathan Lethem's *Dissident Gardens* (2013) reduces Marxism to a "Dialectical Whosis" in its first pages (4). The political movements to which the contemporary novels discussed in this chapter return are depicted with respect to a dual historical perspective that is closer to home – earlier nineteenth-century radicalism (Emerson and Thoreau), on the one hand, and later domestic terrorism (Patricia Hearst and Theodore Kaczynski), on the other hand. Their aim is to determine how the foundational American tenets of the former can lead to the unredeemable violence of the latter.

Consistent with this approach, the chapter begins with a discussion of Philip Roth and Thomas Pynchon, two writers who examine the political by way of the familial and whose portrayals of the Edenic and the anarchic, respectively, illustrate that "moral ultimatism and apolitical politics" that Howe later deemed the distinguishing feature of the American political imagination ("Anarchy" 117). It then turns to a sampling of works by Russell Banks, Paul Auster, Christopher Sorrentino, and Susan Choi that trace the genealogy of American activism and American terrorism with reference to exemplary figures from US history and the alter egos whose tales serve as alternatives to the official accounts – Oswald Garrison Villard's *John Brown* (1910), Patricia Hearst's *Every Secret Thing* (1982) – about to be written. It concludes with a discussion of novels by Dana Spiotta, Rachel Kushner, and Jonathan Lethem that query not just the ethical discrepancy between intentions and actualities but the entire efficacy of political protest in an age of globalization. For when the targets no longer are American companies like Dow Chemical and DuPont making munitions but, as Spiotta depicts, multinationals that make everything from pharmaceuticals to genetically modifying seeds, what – to invoke an old Leninism – *is* to be done? What Kushner and Lethem do is look beyond the spatial borders of the US and the temporal borders of the 1960s – here, there, and everywhere, to recall a Lennon(-McCartney)ism of a different sort – in order to assess whether 'tis nobler simply to opt out or to occupy.

The American Berserk

The three novels that comprise Philip Roth's remarkable American Trilogy – *American Pastoral* (1997), *I Married a Communist* (1998), and *The Human Stain* (2000) – address a half-century of American political history, from the McCarthy era to the late 1960s to Watergate to the Clinton impeachment hearings. Each takes as its touchstone a post–World War II milieu experienced as "the greatest moment of collective inebriation in American history," a moment when "Americans were to start over again, en masse, everyone in it together" (*American* 40). It is in this specific environment that the Jewish Nathan Zuckerman, the narrator through whose authorial consciousness all three works are filtered, thinks he can "partake of the national character" instead of the "Jewish character" (*I Married* 39). Conversely, it is in this same environment that the African American Coleman Silk, who has already remade himself in the navy as a white man, can return from his wartime stint and reinvent himself as a "self-analytic, irreverent American Jew" (*Human* 131). And it is in such a postwar American environment that the "post-Jewish" Seymour "Swede" Levov can marry the "post-Catholic" Dawn Dwyer and move to a New Jersey enclave eleven miles from the nearest train station "to raise little post-toasties" (*American* 73) – only to have that "longed-for American pastoral" blasted to smithereens by his daughter's 1968 bombing of the village post office and replaced by "the fury, the violence, and the desperation of the counterpastoral," the "indigenous American berserk" (86).

Roth has little sympathy for the sixteen-year-old who goes on to kill three more people after accidentally killing a doctor who has dropped off some mail at the general store that has not even been an official US government facility: "Four innocent people, to kill them off – no, this was barbarism, gruesome, depraved, this was evil" (415). Yet aware that the bomb detonated in Old Rimrock is one of many "going off everywhere" during the period (147), a three-page listing of which he provides, Roth has great interest in exploring how the "triumphant days" of wartime's end could have exploded so completely in a mere twenty-five years (88). Equally aware of how many of the perpetrators – not just the fictional Merry Levov, but the factual Mark Rudd, Katherine Boudin, and Jane Alpert of the Weather Underground – are children from middle-class Jewish backgrounds, he knows that modeling themselves after "revolutionaries whose conviction is enacted most ruthlessly" has required "renounc[ing] their roots" (254). The question that remains, however, is which roots. Plagued by a similar need for explanation – "how did Merry get to be who she is?" (138), "[h]ow did all this happen to this perfectly normal child?" (272) – the Swede alternately traces the cause to a chronic stutter, an early interest in science, a suspiciously long kiss of his own, the televised immolation of Buddhist monks that brings into their Arcady Hill Road home "whatever was going haywire over there" (153). What he does not consider is how the paradise bled of all parochialism from which a "perfected" fourth-generation American child was meant to issue has resulted in a child last seen with a torn stocking over her face in an attempt to achieve the "perfection" of a practicing Jain (86, 232). Recognizing that something has happened to "our smart Jewish kids" to make them "crazy," even aware that "[s]omething is *driving* them crazy" (255), the

Swede never realizes that it is in part the severing of all particularizing roots that has left those kids so unmoored, leaving his own kid nothing but his unadulterated love of America to renounce with her all-consuming hate.

As Roth makes clear, this renunciation of all things American that characterizes the New Left stands in stark contrast to the public embrace enacted by those of the Old Left in their attempts to promote Communism as twentieth-century Americanism and an American Communist Party that in 1938 declared its support for the Constitution, the achievements of democracy, and the traditions of Jefferson, Paine, Jackson, and Lincoln. Ira Ringold, the husband whose political affiliation is finally exposed by the 1952 tell-all memoir of his wife in *I Married a Communist*, performs Lincoln's Gettysburg Address and Second Inaugural in front of high school assemblies and impersonates heroic figures from the nation's past on a weekly radio show called *The Free and the Brave*. His mentor woos a young Nathan with pamphlets that cast Communism as facilitating, "in the deepest sense of the word, your responsibility as an American" (237) – sentiments the teen is quite willing to accept, having earlier taken Tom Paine as "the most uncompromising patriot in American history" based on a reading of Howard Fast's 1943 *Citizen Tom Paine* (31). As Roth also makes clear, such invocations of an idealized and egalitarian past had little to do with the actual past in which William Bradford's attempts at collective farming in Plymouth bred "much confusion and discontent" despite the Mayflower Compact (121), John Winthrop's "Modell of Christian Charity" ascribed class differences to God's Providence wherein "some must be rich [and] some poore" (195), and Jefferson's "pursuit of happiness" meant not personal fulfillment but a numerically distributable quantity akin to *félicité publique* (Wills 248–55). Ira's retreat to a two-room shack in Zinc Town that Nathan first traces back to Thoreau's "palliative of the primitive" is later revealed to spring from his need for a hideout after having brutally killed a man with a shovel (*I Married* 72).

In *American Pastoral*, a similar set of falsehoods quite literally underlies the Swede's entire foundation. Unlike the earlier Communist portrayed as mendacious, though, the man introduced by Nathan as the Jewish JFK is simply oblivious. The stone house he imagines as probably "standing there since the country began" and so "impregnable" that it "could never burn to the ground" is in fact the second building to stand on the one hundred acres of America that he buys (190), the one destroyed by fire shortly after the Revolution serving as prelude to the fire next time that engulfs Newark during the 1967 riots. The same holds true for the seemingly harmless item at the foundation of Newark Maid Leatherware, the Levov business that makes the purchase of that home possible. Devoted to protecting the opposable thumb, the glove to the Swede testifies to "the root of humanity," that which "enables us to make tools and build cities and everything else," more important in his view than the brain (131). Yet made of skins first shipped from Africa (a 1790 manifest of which the Swede owns), processed in tanneries barely improved from sweatshops, cut by men who stand so long at tables as to wear their footprints into the floor, and outsourced to Puerto Rico in the 1950s, Czechoslovakia in the 1970s, and the Far East in the 1980s – in short, to wherever "the labor force was abundant and cheap" regardless of political affiliation (26) – the glove in fact epitomizes a centuries-long history of American slavery and oppression.

It is only when the Swede discovers the evil behind this history to have poisoned his own home – after chancing upon his wife and a neighbor sharing an intimate moment by the kitchen sink during a summer-of-Watergate dinner party – that he awakens to an awareness of what Roth will later term "[t]he human stain," that inborn propensity for "cruelty, abuse, [and] error" that makes all professions of Edenic purity such grotesque lies (*Human* 242). "[C]ivilized and predatory," the Swede concludes of the adulterous neighbor whose envied American lineage goes back to 1774, "protecting what he has by birthright and taking surreptitiously what he doesn't have" (382, 383), even if it means "transgress[ing] to the utmost by violating the unity of a family already half destroyed" (366). And this recognition, in turn, forces Roth's "liberal sweetheart of a father" to acknowledge the futility of remaining a "reasonable father" when dealing with a child that is, quite simply, mad (69, 244): to offer unaccompanied trips to New York in exchange for overnight stays with family friends, to tolerate a poster that advocates violent mayhem out of a reluctance to interfere with personal property, ultimately to leave an emaciated daughter squatting in a hovel beside an underpass instead of asserting his parental prerogative and doing "what he should have done and failed to do" all along to protect her from danger (383).

Reviled by the Left, repulsed by the Right, and vice versa, the Swede ends the novel in the exact same position as the protagonists of the two Roth works that follow: politically "[w]hipsawed" (*Human* 316). How else to express the nation's political prospects when the president who "turned a whole country's morale inside out" with Watergate is honored at his 1994 funeral by a bipartisan rogues' gallery of criminals? (*I Married* 279). Yet being "whipsawed" for Roth does not necessarily mean being whipped. As an older Nathan is reminded by the former high school teacher who tells the tale of his brother Ira's tragic blacklisting, there is a crucial difference between the "unpleasant" situation, which might be the "as bad as it can get" situation, and "the situation that is total, which is totalitarianism" (*I Married* 14). When

Roth then returns to World War II in *The Plot against America* (2004) to sketch an alternative history for the nation had the anti-Semitic Charles A. Lindbergh been elected president in 1940, the acts of heroism that prevent the triumph of fascism in America qualify the trilogy's earlier suggestion that "[h]eroism is a human exception" (*I Married* 263). Only in this book – which recalls Jack London's *The Iron Heel* (1908) and Sinclair Lewis's *It Can't Happen Here* (1935) in its governing premise – the most memorable of those acts are inspired not by political ideology but by what can only be termed common decency. An undersized tour guide and cafeteria counterman stand up to a bruiser spewing ethnic venom in Washington, D.C. An Italian immigrant offers his upstairs Jewish neighbors a gun to protect themselves from the threat of pogroms. A family of churchgoing tobacco farmers takes in a hysterical boy whose mother has been beaten and burned by Kentucky Klansmen. A forty-one-year-old father suffering from broken ribs and incipient septicemia drives fifteen hundred miles to return that child to New Jersey for the simple reason that, as Roth's alter ego Philip notes, "My father was a rescuer and orphans were his specialty" (*Plot* 358). As Roth, writing as Roth, states when revealing "The Story Behind" the novel's story, "at the moment when it should have happened," given the virulent hatred of Jews in America that could have resulted in policies like those of Nazi Germany, "it did not happen," the "why" of which remains the subject for another book, "one about how lucky we Americans are" (11).

The American pastoral to which Thomas Pynchon returns in the works that complete his California trilogy is predicated on the Pacific being a lost source of "redemption," a sea first portrayed in *The Crying of Lot 49* (1966) as once "inviolate and integrated" (37). But these two later works explore the ruin of that pastoral with different degrees of success. Set in 1970, *Inherent Vice* (2009) imagines the Southern California paradise that greeted the 1769 Portolá expedition and coastline that sheltered refugees from the lost continent of Lemuria as overrun by real estate developers that would "make Godzilla look like a conservationist" and an ARPAnet system acclaimed the "wave of the future" and soon to flood the land with 24/7 surveillance (7, 366). Yet having cast the book as a hard-boiled detective novel centered around the figure of Larry "Doc" Sportello, the rather soft-boiled gumshoe that, as per the genre's dictates, knows less than anybody else about the set of disappearances and deaths he is investigating, Pynchon's own investigation of how the "little parenthesis of light" that was the "Psychedelic Sixties" eventuated in the Manson murders that "fucked up" a "certain kind of innocence" forever remains limited (254, 38). In the end, all the evidence on display is made the product of the book's titular concept, a phrase that in marine insurance denotes "what you can't avoid" (351), making the tendency of entropy in Pynchon's earlier works the inevitability of this one. Set in 1984, when the ARPAnet "wave of the future" has crested to become a "wave of History" (27), an Orwellian "Info Revolution" that reduces the 1960s revolution to a "fantasy handjob" (74, 27), *Vineland* (1990) offers a more pointed critique.

Names are named – lots of them – in this portrayal of northern borderlands that once offered "A Harbor of Refuge" to vessels in distress overrun by two campaigns aimed as much at despoliation as oppression (316). Cable TV companies attack virgin redwood groves and force a partitioning of the county into zones "which in time became political units in their own right" (319). Federal Campaign Against Marijuana Production troops act "as if they had invaded some helpless land far away" (357), employing "search-and-destroy missions" to force frontier territories to rejoin, "operationally speaking, the third world" (334, 49). Radiating backward (Vietnam) and forward (Nicaragua) in time and recalling those mass exterminations in *Gravity's Rainbow* from the Slothrops' slaughter of trees onward, these most recent incursions are tied to specific men (Ronald Reagan, Ed Meese, George Bush) and specific mandates (Organized Crime Control Act of 1970, Comprehensive Forfeiture Act of 1984, Readiness Exercise 1984), all the offspring of a State gendered as male. Only when it comes time to offer a counterforce of equal specificity and strength, Pynchon demurs. When a cop challenges Zoyd Wheeler to ask himself "Who was saved?" by the sixties (29), the hippie holdover's failure to respond provides Pynchon's own answer: Nobody.

The novel's flashbacks to the late 1960s trace this failure back to a counterculture that, for all its impassioned rhetoric, refuses to engage. The college that rechristens itself The People's Republic of Rock and Roll opts to secede from California and become a nation of its own. The 24fps filmmakers who take "[a] camera is a gun" as their motto go "looking for trouble" only to "quickly g[e]t the record of their witness someplace safe" (197, 195), where the aesthetes can debate their different ideas about light without ever having to consider "[w]herever death may surprise us" (202), a possibility the New Left fantasy does not permit. Indeed, it is not until Reaganomics budget cuts take an ax to the livelihood as a government snitch that Frenesi Gates has made for herself in the book's present, forcing her, in Pynchon's vertical geography, "down ... from all the silver and light she'd known" and "back to the world," that the former New Left filmmaker recognizes the folly of having presumed she ever was "privileged to live outside of Time" (287).

It is for this reason that Pynchon, writing decades after the sixties, rejects the hope of "transcendent meaning" granted Oedipa Maas as an alternative to the earth that is "just America" at the end of the California novel written during the sixties (*Lot 49* 136, 137). The one time a Transcendentalist is quoted in *Vineland*, during the annual picnic at which the old Wobblies and blacklist survivors of Frenesi's family converge, the passage from Emerson's "American Slavery" (1855) that affirms those "[s]ecret retributions" that "are always restoring the level, when disturbed, of the divine justice" and against which "[a]ll the tyrants and proprietors and monopolists of the world ... in vain set their shoulders" is recited by a logger crippled years earlier in an accident arranged by his bosses (369). Frenesi's daughter is thus warned not to rely on "any big transcendent moment" for enlightenment (112). The film collective's "realist wing" (198), DL Chastain, is instructed by her *sensei* to forgo the samurai's code of *bushido* and, like "all the rest of us down here," take steps that appear both "cruel and more worldly" when fighting "incrementalists, who cannot act boldly and feel only contempt for those who can" (127), in effect to engage in guerrilla warfare. And this is exactly what *Against the Day* (2006) depicts all the anarchists who take up arms doing between 1893 and 1923: in Chicago, where memories of the 1886 Haymarket Square bombing still linger; in Russia, where strikers revolt and sailors mutiny against tsarist rule in 1905; in Mexico, where rebels oust Díaz in 1911; and, in the case of Frenesi's maternal ancestors, in the mine fields of Colorado, where for twenty years nothing less than a "war between two full-scale armies" tantamount to a "civil war again" is being waged (177).

The difference is that Plutocrats now send their slaves underground instead of into cotton fields and railroads "r[u]n out over all the old boundaries, redefining the nation into exactly the shape and size of the rail network" (177). As typified by those "four straight lines on paper" that form Colorado (83), a rectangle repeated throughout the checkerboard of Western states created by ordinances that took the Mason–Dixon Line as their starting point, the shape is standard. The size, however, is not. For unlike the octopus envisioned by Frank Norris in 1901, the "living organism, growing by the hour," that comprises Pynchon's railway network is global in scope and still growing (177): Edward Harriman goes to Alaska to see about a link across the Bering Strait that would connect with the Trans-Siberian; Germany and Britain vie for Balkan concessions that would provide a shortcut to India. So are the consequences to life in which these crisscrossings eventuate. In the Cartesian grid of Chicago, where twenty or thirty rail lines converge, a geography of "straight lines and right angles" ends in "unshaped freedom being rationalized into movement," the final turn of which leads cattle onto stockyard killing floors (10). In Europe, where nations are blasting through mountains in order to determine how best to move troops, and the Balkans, where cities approaching the "orthogonal" have replaced winding alleyways with "grid[s] of neat wide streets" (843, 944), a First World War turns the entire landscape into an abattoir.

Pynchon provides a detailed account of the alliances and annexations already in place that cause that powder keg to explode with the 1914 assassination of Franz Ferdinand in Sarajevo. More than just a war between the Great Powers inspired by regional politics, though, or a scramble between nations to secure the mineral wealth underlying the Ottoman Empire, the conflict is portrayed as originating in a need to preserve the power of the nation-state itself. "[S]o promising an idea a generation ago," it "has lost all credibility" by the turn of the century and requires generalized strife, with all the attendant jingoism, to wipe out Anarchism, "the idea that has seized hearts everywhere" (938), most obviously in that American setting that since More's *Utopia* (1516) had played host to such social experiments from abroad.

Writing in the twenty-first century, Pynchon already knows that the "mythical time of American Anarchism" is in the distant past (372), just as the frontier that lent itself to asocial literary fantasies from Cooper onward has already closed: Frederick Jackson Turner announces as much at the 1893 World's Columbian Exposition that opens the book. But when Pynchon turns his attention to the actual blood brothers whose mission to track down their father's murderers loosely joins the book's many narrative strands into a plot, his juxtaposing the urgency *for* activism against an ethics *of* activism reveals the conundrum at the heart of all revolutionary politics regardless of time or place. "One thing to try and keep to an honorable deal with your dead," the eldest Traverse brother thinks, in a variation of one of the book's refrains, "another to just go spreading death any way you can" (850). Not that any of the Traverse brothers makes much more of an immediate move to honor anything than their descendant Frenesi will years later: Reef becomes an itinerant gambler, Frank an engineer, and Kit a mathematician whose Yale degree is bought and paid for by Scarsdale Vibe, the Plutocrat behind his father's death. Yet when they finally do act, the brothers are portrayed as operating from misplaced motives. Haunted by their father Webb's "bone-deep voice of retribution" (316), they pursue the personal instead of that which is "tactic[al] in the bigger fight" (852), and thus obtain not the justice of accounts balanced but the temporary satisfaction of revenge – if even that much, as the anticlimactic ends sketched for their father's killers confirm.

Sloat Fresno is shot without knowing his gunman's identity. Scarsdale Vibe is plugged by a right-hand man who claims first dibs before a Traverse brother can get a round off. Deuce Kindred is last seen married to a Traverse sister and providing security for the California film industry.

It is this human predilection for revenge that produces the history of "revolution and re-revolution" in Mexico where a Madero revolution is followed by a Huerta coup (988), the "history of back-and-forth killing" in the Balkans that has an entire population of ghosts "surfac[ing] wherever there's a fight with the same shape to it" (1003). In the end, it is this human predilection that dooms all attempts to replace the idea of the nation-state with alternative arrangements, whether denoted in terms of "planetary one-ness" (942), or Hamiltonian Quaternions, or the "supranational idea" of "transcend[ing] the old political space, the map-space of two dimensions, by climbing into the third" (1083). When one of the remaining Traverse clan proposes starting "our own little republic" while "up in the last corner of the U.S. map," she is quickly reminded: "Fine idea while the opium supply lasts, but sooner or later plain old personal meanness gets in the way" (1076). Yet having cast off the politics of the many, Pynchon returns to the politics of the few, replacing the alternative community of "single male authority . . . and a membership willing to comply" with the ménage à trois of three that ventures into the "unmapped country" beyond heteronormativity (934, 942). And, like Roth, he counters personal meanness that gets in the way with acts of personal kindness that show the way. Swiss citizens, "[s]uspecting that their country was the scene of a great experiment in the possibilities of compassion in the depths of war," hand out schnapps and chocolates to POWS being exchanged by the nations responsible for the war (1026). An Ellis Island customs officer, "some crypto-Anarchist who'd drifted into government work but could still recognize and help out a fellow outlaw," erases from an immigrant's back the chalked designation that would have sent him back to that hellhole (1074–75). In the words of the book's metaphor of checks and balances, "as long as a person was willing to forgo credit, there were very few limits on the good it became possible to do" (976).

American Activism, American Terrorism

For American novelists who view late 1960s activism as an extension of the earlier 1960s Civil Rights movement, and the war in Vietnam as part of an ongoing campaign against people of color, the figure of John Brown (1800–1859) is the American activist writ large – comparable in Russell

Banks's *Cloudsplitter* (1998) to the giant mountain that looms over the family's Adirondack home and from whose translated Indian name, Tahawus, the book takes its title. A deeply flawed figure even before the evolution of his band from "anti-slavery activists" merely inspired by Emerson's depiction of "[t]imes of heroism" as "generally times of terror" to "guerilla fighters and militiamen" who ultimately declare themselves "terrorists" (313, 621), this John Brown is riddled with contradictions. A father who sires twenty children, he remains an unforgiving autocrat to a family "sometimes scorched by his flame" but "seldom warmed by it" (104). A son of New England Puritans who hopes to build a "true American city on a hill" based on racial harmony (143), he enters black communities on horseback so as to "make a proper show" from an elevated position (176). An opponent of agricultural slave labor, he adopts a "luxurious detachment" when exposed to Manchester's industrial slave labor (366). A Christian who believes himself chosen by God for "election" (413), he shamelessly casts himself as star on the stage of world history, arranging for his letters to be copied and giving interviews before he has done anything to warrant notice. It is not surprising, then, that this self-styled American Garibaldi later comes to believe his own press, embracing "Osawatomie Brown" as his public *nom de guerre*, or that he later sees himself as in direct communication with the God for whom he is sometimes permitted to speak.

   Yet Brown is also, in Banks's delineation, unique among abolitionists of the time in three crucial ways. He recognizes the economics of slavery and uses his Underground Railway (or, as he calls it, Subterranean Passway) work to make the costs of holding on to slaves prohibitively expensive. He recognizes that many Northerners, whose opposition to extending slavery into the western territories is a matter of restricting labor practices that would give the South an economic advantage, are as anti-black as they are anti-slavery. Perhaps most important, he recognizes that race is "the central and inescapable fact of American life and character" (421), and understands that until a society "poisoned at the root" by racial differences becomes a true democracy, "every American, white as much as black, red, or yellow, lives not in his skin but on it," making every American a "colored" person (423).

   What this Mayflower American is remarkably naïve about are the particular conditions of nineteenth-century America and the nature of American race consciousness that will doom his venture even before the disastrous 1859 raid on Harpers Ferry. Viewing himself as successor to "great Negroes" like Cinque, Toussaint L'Ouverture, and the Roman slave Spartacus (75), and convinced that in the end it is "right principles and simple economics" that will prove triumphant (735), he mounts what he terms an "African

Campaign" on a federal arsenal with twenty followers. Such a raid, he believes, will inspire a "spreading black wave of mutinous slaves, nearly two million strong," to form the "largest army ever seen in this land" (704), which will be joined by thousands of non-slaveholding whites "who will come running to our side" to assist in "burn[ing] the ancient sin and scourge of slavery entirely away" (705). Yet as Frederick Douglass reminds Brown when explaining his own refusal to join Brown in suicide, "It's *race* that will settle it," and not in his favor, "[r]ace and simple arithmetic" in a United States that is not Haiti or Jamaica and in which, "[s]imply put, there are more of you . . . than of us" (735). Undeterred, Brown mounts an attack in which the first person killed is a Virginia freedman who, in response to Brown's ultimatum to join his army or be treated as an enemy, is shot while running away from enforced conscription.

It is not the evangelical father, however, who most typifies those activists-turned-terrorists portrayed by other contemporary writers, but the godless son, Owen, whose attempt to present history operating "from the ground up" instead of "from the top down" forms the "Secret History of John Brown" that is the book's narrative (677, 678). Unlike the older man who views slavery as a sin to be expunged, this "fallen man" alternates between wishing blacks did not exist and engaging in homoerotic fantasies about the married black man he fears has replaced him in his father's affections (693) – a conflict he finally resolves by handing the man a fully cocked pistol that "accidental[ly]" goes off (529). Unlike the father so overdetermined by biblical figures (Aaron, Job, Christ) and national liberation figures (Mazzini, Napoleon, Nat Turner) as to appear divine Father (upper-case) in his own right, this third son defines himself by way of just one sacrificial figure – Isaac to his father's Abraham – a role that, as he correctly notes, feels "emblematic to me – as if an Age of Heroism had acceded to an Age of Cowardice" (740). Indeed, it is precisely because he fears himself invisible as compared to his father that he takes so readily to the killing that he imagines turning "the outcast, the grunting, inarticulate, crippled Owen Brown" into "twice the man my father was" (640), and his life into a "storm that would alter the face of the planet" (678). Yet the fact that this Melvillian *isolato*'s tale of survival is the result of having watched the raid on Harpers Ferry from the top of a tall oak tree makes him just "a man of another time: a man of the future," specifically, "[a] modern man" (740).

In Paul Auster's *Leviathan* (1992), Benjamin Sachs is that modern man, a writer who looks like John Brown, takes Thoreau as his model, and finds in blowing up replicas of the Statue of Liberty the "unifying principle" that "bring[s] all the broken pieces" of himself together into a "whole" for the first time (256). Or, at least, so Peter Aaron concludes near the end of the account he begins on July 4, 1990, shortly after learning of a man killed in Wisconsin while assembling a bomb, a literary race against time in which he competes with the FBI agents investigating the case to see who will have authority over Sachs's story. Such authority is no writerly vanity in a novel whose Emersonian epigraph – "Every actual State is corrupt" – comes from the essay on "Politics" (1844) whose opening description of the State as "not aboriginal" turns government into as much an artificial construct as any work of the imagination (427, 422). The difference between Aaron and Sachs, in this novel that replaces the Oedipal drama of Banks's book with the fraternal drama of twins, doubles, and alter egos, stems from the degree of satisfaction that the authority of authorship grants those subject not just to the Hobbesian sovereignty of human design but to a universe that resists human agency of any sort.

Aaron – like many of Auster's surrogates – accepts as given the music of chance, to recall the title of Auster's 1990 novel, even if its sounds are often discordant. As such, the path he traces for Sachs from the civil disobedience of Thoreau – that lands him in prison in lieu of Vietnam – to the gunshot anarchism of Alexander Berkman is suffused with contingency, happenstance, coincidence, and bad timing. Sachs, in contrast, who looks to "read the world as though it were a work of the imagination" (27), structures his one completed work of fiction, *The New Colossus*, as a "jigsaw puzzle of historical facts" that joins together otherwise unrelated actual figures living between 1876 and 1890 and intertextual figures (42). But seeking to uncover a "complex pattern embedded in the real" based on connections that "become steadily more fantastic" only results in a narrative of increasingly "unstable character" (27, 44). And this is exactly what happens to the character of Sachs himself after he renounces the writing of literature as having turned him into a "shadow" and decides to "step into the real world" and "do something" (137), even though he has no idea at the time of what that "something" is or that the actions he finally does take evince not the omens he assumes but the chance he abhors. He takes a baseball bat to a man he unexpectedly runs into after the man, for no apparent reason, shoots the friendly youth who has offered Sachs a lift after he gets lost in the Vermont woods. He comes upon the shooter's dissertation on the anarchist who believed there was a "moral justification for certain forms of political violence" and that terrorism, "[i]f used correctly," could enlighten "the public about the nature of institutional power" (252). He stumbles into a used bookstore and finds a copy of his own book with its distorted Statue of Liberty cover illustration (much like the monstrous frontispiece figure by Abraham Bosse of Hobbes's 1651 text).

From "the original bomb child" who happens to have been born on the date that the US bombed Hiroshima emerges the Phantom of Liberty (25).

Far from providing Sachs with an authentic identity, however, this folkloric persona is one more shadow self that gets more and more insubstantial as Sachs, in his act of penance for killing Reed Dimaggio, fashions it from more and more ghostly presences. For the "crazed idealist" (and possible government agent) Dimaggio, who "dream[s] of changing the world" through radical environmentalism but kills an innocent boy offering roadside assistance (191), has in turn assumed the mask of his dissertation subject, Berkman, a man who spent the last years of his life as a ghostwriter prior to turning his own gun on himself. It is no coincidence, then, that the first encounter with violence that eventuates in Sachs becoming a man of violence himself results from his getting lost in the Vermont woods without a compass "to orient his position" (167), an image that Aaron takes from Sachs's own imagining of Ellery Channing giving Emma Lazarus the pocket compass of his deceased friend Thoreau in *The New Colossus*, an emblem of America's having "lost its way" with the death of "the one man who could read the compass for us" (43). With no moral referents outside his own conscience to guide him, a conscience born of "guilt in the face of his own desires" that he mistakes for "the conscience of the world" (147, 250), Sachs remains lost – at times dangerous (as when he threatens to kidnap a child being raised in a manner of which he disapproves), more often merely ineffective. Reduced to spouting platitudes about "practicing what you preach" and "faith in the future" that are as empty as they are easily appropriated (243, 244) – by novelty shops that sell Phantom of Liberty T-shirts, by strippers that incorporate the Phantom as part of their acts – the biblical prophet turns into a pop culture phenomenon, subject, like all such phenomena, to a built-in expiration date. By 1989 and the end of the Cold War, he is a "solitary speck in the American night" (266). When he finally blows himself up while in the process of assembling what turns out to be his last bomb, the lack of fingerprints that makes identification of the mangled body impossible attests to a man who has long before surrendered all sense of a self and any imprint he might have left on the world.

Possessed of no self at all is the figure of Patricia Campbell Hearst, whose 1974 kidnapping by (and later enlistment with) the Symbionese Liberation Army lends itself to a variety of stories, as commentators have noted – early American captivity narrative (Castiglia 87–105), Flaubertian sentimental education (Didion, *After* 96) – updated to contemporary times. Christopher Sorrentino's *Trance* (2005) introduces Alice Daniels Galton as the public face of a ragtag bunch of seven middle-class whites (an MA in urban education, a former senior class president, a doctor's son, and a stuffed-animal-loving Jersey girl, among others) led by an escaped black convict. She is the one always forced to identify herself to the owners of vehicles "borrowed" (not "appropriated," and never "stolen") and whose abduction has brought "fame and notoriety and the power to make extortionate demands" to an organization viewed by the Left as at best a joke and at worst a front for the CIA (32). As well it should be. For the group that takes racial "symbiosis" as its political agenda but kills a progressive African American school superintendent in Oakland as its first public act is perennially plagued by an inability to attract any actual people of color to its cause. Those in the East Fifty-fourth Street house in which the cadre buys shelter – and quickly trashes with empty beer bottles, half-eaten food, and crates of bullets stacked on a dinette instead of the floor – are more concerned with getting a neighborhood supermarket than fomenting a revolution. But when that South Central house goes up in flames in an LAPD-FBI shootout captured on live TV, the resultant spectacle grants a group that most excels at "preempting the regularly scheduled programming" (247) not just the opportunity, as Jay Cantor argues, to "watch themselves being burnt up on television in Los Angeles, even as they were being physically burnt up" (*Space* 90). The entire scene typifies the representational element in all acts of terror, governmental or radical, that replace the genocidal killing of all with the killing of some before an audience of others, control of which depends upon that audience having borne witness (*Space* 76).

The problem for the three fugitives who watch their friends' martyrdom while holed up in a motel near Disneyland is that in order to transform their own acts of petty theft (sweat socks, bath towels) and botched bank robberies (one of which ends in the killing of a mother of four depositing church funds) into more for posterity they must rely on the far less sexy medium of print. Specifically, they must rely on the "radical sportswriter" Guy Mock (modeled on Jack Scott), who lures them with promises of six-figure book deals (122), to satisfy that desire that, in Sorrentino's view, animates every radical in the US who spends at least "a minute or two wondering who'd play him in the movie" (408), indeed, what "every kid snug under the blankets with his secret wishes wanted, the cover of *Rolling Stone*" (450). Mock, however, knows that any pitch he makes to publishers depends entirely on turning the tale of Alice (now Tania) Galton into a morality play, and Galton is a pitiful symbol of the Left's threat of what "could happen to anybody's kid" (247). "[B]asically a homebody" by her own admission (201), she basically exchanges domestic confinement with her fiancé for confinement in the SLA's closet, and, after her arrest, confinement in a federal prison. Her name changes notwithstanding (Alice to Tania to Pearl to Amy), she continues to imagine herself in variations of the same scenario even after her alleged political conversion: getting a job in a New York ad agency or publishing house and "keeping the SLA business confined to the weekend" (201); working as a community activist in Boston, where she will "garden in a backyard plot, assemble a collection of recipes on three-by-five cards, walk the dog, eventually have a child" (500).

To the extent that she represents anything beyond herself, she represents the degree to which "the normal exerted its pull" (498), as do those other SLA members who speak of bombs going off in the manner of entrepreneurs talking of "new franchises opening" (323), and the married pair caught while following their daily jogging routine, "natural satellites of the culture" that "hauled them back every time," who subscribe to *TV Guide* (498). It is only that orbit, as the book's sly coda suggests, that separates them from the middle-aged "nutburger" Sara Jane Moore (269), so desperate to attach herself to a cause ("Doesn't matter what" [407]) as to work as radical food distribution program bookkeeper and FBI informant with no sense of divided loyalties. Cast adrift from both by the book's last pages, she sees an ad for improved frozen waffles as a sign that she must overthrow the established order and, so inspired, decides to take aim at the US president when Gerald Ford happens to be passing through San Francisco the next day.

The *American Woman* (2003) at the center of Susan Choi's book is not the Patricia Hearst surrogate, Pauline, just as the *Person of Interest* (2008) of her next book is not the Theodore Kaczynski–like "Brain Bomber" who attacks other mathematicians with explosive devices, but the Asian characters that function as their "mirror[s]" (*Person* 336). In the earlier text, that person is Jenny Shimada, a fictionalized version of Wendy Yoshimura, the woman who cared for the three surviving SLA members in Pennsylvania after the LA fire. A West Coast bomb maker living in upstate New York and entering her third year of life underground as the novel opens, Jenny defines herself by two criteria: the "moral certainty" that enables her to believe that "her generation was surely the luckiest, best, and most blessed" (*American* 177); and the conviction that the only race to which she has any affiliation is the human race. This is despite the fact that the certainty that verges on sanctimony, a "moral absolutism" that stems from a lifelong desire to be "morally perfect" (216), rests on very shaky ground. Jenny assumes that "high intentions gave her the right to use violence; the same violence she abhorred in her government" (352), even though she cannot remember when she consciously "*decided*" to leave her first bomb in a government building (224), and has only been spared having to judge good intentions against "how things turned out" by the element of "dumb luck" (352, 283). This is also despite the fact that Jenny's entire family history – a Nisei father interned in Manzanar during

World War II and imprisoned as a "no-no boy" for draft evasion, a man too American in the Japan to which he exiles himself and his child and too Japanese in the America to which they return five years later – is the product of vexed race relations. Indeed, those on the Left constantly invoke those relations when reminding Jenny of the advantages of having a "Third World perspective" when battling a nation that drops "[b]alls of fire" on "[l]ittle children who look just like you" (140, 230).

All that certainty ends when a grocery store stick-up that leaves the owner dead forces Jenny and Pauline to take to the road in a union born of necessity – surprisingly, given Jenny's realization that Pauline has lied to her about a threat to her life should she fail to gain Jenny's consent to drive a switch car. Yet this turbulent trip in the company of a "gold-haired debutante" recalls a much earlier trip that Jenny has made in the company of other "gold-skinned and gold-haired" children of privilege she meets on the way to Japan (100, 343), into whose luxurious lounge Jenny has been able to sneak because of a ticket mix-up that grants the Shimadas seats in the First Class compartment. Entranced by those children she helps to entertain during the long flight, and with whom she swears eternal penpalship before they deplane in Hawaii, she is even more fascinated by everything about the kidnapped heiress in flight – from her ancestry to her "towering American pedigree" (343) – whom she is asked to babysit years later.

The story behind that pedigree, as portrayed by Choi, is the story of the American West, of Pauline being the descendant of people "who'd gotten [t]here first," people "who'd stuck it out" and "[k]illed enough, grabbed enough," and "[n]ever looked back" (285). True to that tale, Pauline quickly cuts her losses upon her arrest, betraying a person a day with each day's newspaper. Jenny's, in contrast, is the story of a "Westerner born with his back to the Pacific," a man who dreams of journeying east to raise his child as "a citizen of the world, a Universal Human," because he associates New York with "the final achievement of American belonging, sheared free of ethnicity," and ends up going "backwards, to the wrong East, Japan" (338). True to that more complicated narrative, Jenny grows up fighting for justice when what she really wants is "less justice than vengeance" – for remaining a "ridiculous, small, not-taken-seriously, average American girl" (350) – all the while seeking in the Left the company of those "self-confident children of the white upper class" with whom she still yearns to play (343).

Except the rules of play have never been the same for each, the SLA's penchant for the game of "ego reconstruction" notwithstanding. When Jenny bleaches Pauline's hair blond, she looks at the redhead with brown roots as "transforming again"; when Jenny looks at herself, she sees the "same self" in the mirror, a woman amenable to no amount of whitening, able at most to exchange a Japanese surname for a Chinese alias while living underground (248). Choi's depiction of the two women's sentences just confirms that difference: "Pauline would 'get the book thrown at her' yet somehow be redeemed, or rather shown to require no redemption, while Jenny would 'get off easy,' for somebody like her" (355). Yet the minimum sentence that concludes a trial treated by the press as of no more consequence than "lint" is made possible by those Japanese, Filipino, Korean, and Chinese individuals whose daily attendance in the courtroom, and not "any unusual worth" of Jenny herself, the judge cites in his recommendation (323, 359). Devoid of any such worth, Pauline last appears at her televised wedding, an "unrecognizable girl" swallowed by a "huge puff of gauze" (364). Determined to gain a sense of worth, Jenny makes a journey in the company of her father to Manzanar, moving neither east nor west but south in order to find her true north.

Here, There, and Everywhere

Set in Washington State between 1998 and 2000, but flashing back to trace Mary Whittaker's life underground after a 1972 bombing of an industrialist's summer house goes awry, Dana Spiotta's *Eat the Document* (2006) works by way of juxtaposition and contrast. This results in a novel that moves beyond the failure of New Left politics to the futility of any political action. In Mary's case, in fact, the promise of the 1960s has died before the book even opens with her hiding in a motel near Lincoln, Nebraska, fabricating a new identity after that botched bombing leaves a housekeeper dead. And it dies again and again as Mary crisscrosses the country in the book's alternating sections: in a bar in upstate New York, where rednecks are grooving and getting down much like freaks; in a Pontiac driven by a pot-smoking girl, where she is beaten and raped in the back seat; in the outskirts of LA, where "harder, meaner drugs" have "taken the aura of the counterculture and extracted every decent aspiration" (200). By the time Mary reinvents herself one last time as Louise Barrot, all that remains of the 1960s is the music of the Beach Boys, which her teenage son likens to "a meditation or a prayer" (22), and the memory of having once met a drunk and past-his-sell-by-date Dennis Wilson in a Venice Beach dive, proof to her that even in the age of Reagan "America was still a place where you could dance with a barefoot rock star in a nowhere bar in the middle of a weekday afternoon" (88).

America as it approaches the millennium lacks anything that lends itself to such nostalgia, however. The misfits who gather at Prairie Fire Books call themselves "*testers*" rather than "activists" based on the fact that they plan not "demonstrations" but "*tests*" – Busby Berkeley dances performed in business attire, website virtual sit-ins – exercises in style that never get executed, as befits groups with names like Strategic Aggravation Players and Neo Tea-Dumpers Front (36). As Nash Davis, the middle-aged store manager committed to "Antiology, or the study of all things anti" (36), informs a skeptical newcomer, "The point isn't to win" but to "make persuasive and powerful the beauty of their opposition" (65). In part, such adherence to aesthetics derives from Nash's earlier history as a New Left filmmaker whose "pursuit of art" at the expense of rousing polemics has been so vilified by his then-girlfriend Mary as to prompt him to offer up a list of summer homes of corporate board members as penance (227). Yet it also reflects his very accurate awareness of the differences between the 1970s and 1990s: "It used to be you had to make munitions to piss people off. Now it was enough to be large, global and successful. That made it a more radical, systematic critique, Nash thought. And more futile, naturally" (43).

Typifying the decentered apparatus of Empire that operates through "hybrid identities" (Hardt and Negri xii), and aims at managing social life in its entirety, is Spiotta's fictional Allegecom, involved as it is with the manufacture of "everything from pharmaceuticals (through its offshoot Pherotek) to genetically modifying seeds with coordinated, matching pesticides (through its biotech arm, Versagro)," which include the Agent Orange pesticide sprayed during the Vietnam War (157). The 1993 launch of Alphadelphia, the "First Self-Sustaining Techtopia in America," just extends that reach to the manufacture of communities (157), the running of which is easily maintained by the psychopharmaceuticals that make up the Nepenthex system and ever-improved supplements that the company also happens to produce. Whereas Mary and her political cohorts of the 1970s have had specific addresses at which to leave their explosive devices, the testers of the 1990s only have moving targets invisible to pin down – divisions and sub-divisions with separate identities and distinct liabilities, some of which are "defunct, disappeared," and thus impossible to sue (159) – but fully capable of appropriating and thereby neutralizing any perceived threat. The site for Ergonomica, the first "radiant posturbia" that Allegecom plans to franchise with the motto "Local community, global convenience" (238, 239), is located in the upstate New York region with a long history of utopian socialist experiments and takes as its *raison d'être* the notion that "[a] commune and a corporate community are not all that different" (238).

That the defining figures of the 1960s and 1970s have already been reduced to pictures on decks of playing cards priced at $19.95 ("New Left Series" for

David Dellinger and Abbie Hoffman, "Outlaw" for Baader-Meinhof and the Red Brigades) is because they have left themselves open to such appropriation, as Mary comes to realize with the advantage of a quarter-century's worth of hindsight. Unable any longer to hide behind the fugitive's fallback line of good intentions once she acknowledges she has "even doubted the intentions, the motivations" (224), Mary begins to consider the ways in which the "failure of language belied deeper failings in the counterculture" (101): names to obfuscate, acronyms to exclude all but the initiated, aliases to preempt the possibility of real engagement, ultimately silence to preclude the taking of responsibility. It is this kind of responsibility that Mary's son, Jason, queries when working on a paper on Alger Hiss and citing the refusal of Hiss to admit to his acts as signaling a lack of worth in the actions themselves. It is no wonder, then, that the film collective for which Nash has made films under his given name of Bobby Desoto has taken SAFE as its acronym, or that what begins as "Secret Attack Fear Effort" can morph so easily into "Soft Art Film Elastic" or "Soft Art Film Efflux" and reemerge in the 1990s as "Scratch Artists for Effacement" or "Scavengers Against Flat Effrontery" – groups that hold meetings "as needed and when necessary" (64), which is to say never. Nor is it surprising that the impotence of the groups he facilitates at Prairie Fire can be measured by the fact that they never meet more than one time under the same name and that they rely on promiscuously recycling words that begin with "re" ("resist," "reclaim," "rebel") or adjusting the letter "k" in words so as to induce psychic "dislokations" (62). It is only after a billboard for Allegecom's latest cancer-causing drugs is defaced with a skull and cross-bones at the end of the book that the challenge posed in cutout letters – "WHO IS RESPONSIBLE?" – gains any traction (284). No longer a pointless gesture of simply ripping down the billboard, an "illegible act" that – repeated – only has resulted in the mounting of a bigger sign (206), the graffiti artist's act affixes a tag to the work and in so doing reclaims the word SAFE as a signature of responsibility.

The artists in Rachel Kushner's *The Flamethrowers* (2013) lend their names to no political acts for the simple reason that they either are attributed no proper names or subscribe to a nonrepresentational aesthetics they see as divorced from politics. The only revolutions that concern Reno, who gains her name from a one-night stand as she floats around New York's 1970s art scene, are those revolutions per minute that produce the Land Art–inspired skid-mark pieces she plans with her motorcycle. The same applies, however, to those Red Brigades into whose orbit the passive twenty-three-year-old from Nevada later drifts, whose appellation denotes simply the "most visible" group of many in Italy that "come together only after an action, to give those who committed the action a name," after which they "disband, disappear" (121). Unable to attach their own names even to the scores they write on the pinball machines they play to kill time between what are in effect performances, complete with painted faces and scrawled graffiti, they strike, kidnap, and kill, but with scant lasting impact on the fictional Valera Company that embodies the abuses of capitalist enterprise, other than to reinforce how thin the line is between *popolo* and *popolaccio*, multitude and mob (283).

If the stakes seem somewhat higher during the 1950s "in-between era" portrayed in *Telex from Cuba* (2008) – namely, that time between the arrival of conquistadors from Spain and Marxists from Russia (257) – it is because the organization that employs the American expatriates living in the gated community of Preston's La Avenida is the real company of United Fruit. Owning nearly all the arable land that forms Oriente Province, United Fruit is little concerned with the island's history of political upheaval; having "worked with every government, installed or elected, it didn't matter, since 1898," its executives blithely assume they will "work with Castro" even after being evacuated to Haiti following the 1959 New Year's overthrow of Batista, where they wait for things to "eventually return to normal" (299). So think all those other Americans – magnates ensconced in Havana plantations, more recent arrivals come to run the US government's Nicaro nickel plant – that have turned Cuba into a replacement frontier, a "loser's paradise" for those looking for better-paying jobs, safety from extradition, and exemption from tax and labor laws (87). As a United Fruit executive's son born on the island that is the only home he knows says, "A fresh start in a place like Cuba meant you could be wanted by the law at home, and it wouldn't matter because you were under a different set of laws. Not Cuba's laws. You were under the company's laws" (89).

Unlike the Valera Company, built on the backs of Polish and Amazon Indian slave labor, which expands from motorcycles to tires to petrochemicals to superhighways to become "practically a public utility" in Italy and supply the Brazilian government with enough funds to build its new capital city of Brasilia (*Flamethrowers* 266), United Fruit in the 1950s is not yet a company whose reach extends beyond the Caribbean. It is nonetheless a company whose practices duplicate those of nations with a long history of imperialism, practices that have as much to do with hierarchy, race, and social class as they do with money. The Spanish conquistadors who gorge on parrots until there are none left eat not to fill up or sample a local "delicacy" or enjoy a specific "taste" (*Telex* 152), but to exact "punishment and justice" on a species that can talk back (153). The United Fruit manager who urges his young son to view lobster as a "delicacy" introduces the dish as having nothing to do with "taste" and everything to do with "having things that other people couldn't have" (170). This results in a pecking order from which none on the island are excluded. Those living on the exclusive La Avenida, backwater functionaries to the American ambassador used to dealing with financiers in New York and Boston, view the blue-collar Cajun overseers who work for them as white trash. Cubans who work as house servants view darker Jamaicans who work as cane cutters, and before them the darkest-of-all Haitians, with contempt. And because those with less mimic the behavior of those with more, the Cuban movement that purports to sweep away all divisions with a revolution inspired by "attitude and passion, not ideas and ideology," is doomed (290) – and well before the inevitable "executions" (as distinct from opportunistic "assassinations") take the "*pachanga*," or "spirit of fun," out of it (233, 234). The Castro brother who torches his own father's cane fields is also a man who has married a society girl, invaded Cuba on a yacht with a built-in liquor cabinet, and maintained clean fingernails while in the Sierra Maestra with his troops because it is understood that neither he nor the former Nazi collaborator he appoints as his tactician do "chores" (243).

In this propensity, Fidel is hardly unique. Having framed the novel with reference to "the paradox of zones and borders on a surface that was fluid" (319), Kushner punctuates her tale of Castro's revolution with tales of other revolutions – past and present – betrayed by mimicry of the master. In 1790s Haiti, freed slaves start calling themselves "chevalier" and "viceroy" (29). In 1840s Cuba, slaves that lead revolts against the Spanish assume the titles "kings" and "queens" (187). In neighboring nations in the 1950s, Duvalier and Trujillo adopt the magisterial third person in lieu of the first. Such patterns, in a strange way, only confirm the assumptions of those Americans who, in their "naive and imperialist love" of Cuba (291), host country club dances while the surrounding country is literally and figuratively burning, smug in their belief that the difference between "viol*ence*" and "viol*ent*" is the same as that between "incid*ent*" and "*intent*" (257). United Fruit survives Castro to become United Brands and then Chiquita. The Cubans – deemed "gorilla[s]" by the Americans who hire them (116) – in contrast, end up much like Poncho, the actual simian owned by a United Fruit couple. Unable to bite, scratch, or act aggressively in any way because his teeth, fingernails, and testicles have been removed, and last seen dressed in the double-breasted jacket of a Pan-American Club bartender, Poncho throws himself headfirst off a ship in an attempt "[t]o *get* someplace, into some other life, away from being [a] pet monkey," as if "suicide were a form of travel, like air travel or sea travel" (281).

The closest to a neutered figure in Jonathan Lethem's *Dissident Gardens* (2013) is the storybook character, Ferdinand the Bull, who likes to sniff at flowers and, when faced with the call to arms of the red cape, *"preferred not to"* (285). Such Bartleby-esque reluctance is fully in keeping with a novel that opens with the Communist Rose Angrush Zimmer being put on trial in her own kitchen for the crime of "excess zeal in the cause of Negro equality" (sleeping with a black cop) just months before Khrushchev's 1956 speech to the Twentieth Soviet Congress shatters faith in all things scarlet (5). But Rose's inability to relinquish a cape already in tatters signals the political conundrum with which all three generations of the novel's characters contend: those who embrace Marxism in the 1930s and are left "frozen like M[iss] Havisham" when the Dialectic of History crushes them in the 1950s (213); those who adopt the "cloud politics" of the 1960s that "floated in the air, unmoored in theory or party" (156); and those who enter the book floating in the ocean during the second decade of the new century for whom "[t]he sixties formed a seaweed gauze through which they all paddled, browsing for opening enough to surface and breathe free" (311). More than just victims of bad timing who "should have been at the inception, forging a bloody Communism," or "participat[ing] in its eventual triumph" rather than "stranded" in the "endless disaster between" (254) – not to mention the "century's great comedy" after the end of the Cold War (272) – these orphans abandoned by history expose the pitfalls of subsuming the self to any force of history, dialectical as much as familial. As such, the personal struggle to cut or claim ties to a "point of origin" that consumes the two most powerful forces in the book (182), the "Red Queen" Rose and her "maven of MacDougal Street" daughter, Miriam, extends beyond the political struggle between an Old and New Left as much at odds with as offshoots of each other (33, 217). It encapsulates the entire legacy of those "dead utopian Gardens" from which their respective dreams spring (182).

As Lethem makes clear, the various gardens that lend themselves to his wonderfully nuanced title have indeed gone to seed in one way or another. The Werkhofinstitut Rosa Luxemburg, nicknamed "Gärten der Dissidenz" (227), to which Rose's feckless husband, Albert, is exiled by the Communist Party pumps out revisionist history that pitches Nazi war crimes as no worse than Allied crimes and spins the bombing of Guernica as a "military episode" limited to bridges and arterial roads (232). The "official Socialist Utopian Village" of Sunnyside Gardens into which Rose and Albert move – in another instance of bad timing – the day news of the 1939 Hitler-Stalin Pact wrecks the Popular Front's alliances devolves into a ruins for "homeless old people gossiping about Florida and death" (14, 266). That being said, Lethem's riffs on the political novel's invocation of the pastoral bend the genre's conventions in a specifically urban direction, the same direction in which his earlier *Motherless Brooklyn* (1999) and *The Fortress of Solitude* (2003) point. The errand into the actual wilderness on which the Communist Party sends Rose and Albert as prospective "Jersey Homesteaders" bespeaks an "impoverishment of the imagination" (134), a reversal of the path taken by that sixteenth US president who "had put log cabins behind him, in favor of cities, of civilization" (142). The errand into the Nicaraguan wilderness on which Miriam and her husband, Tommy, later send themselves as do-gooder ethnomusicologists ends with their ashes being scattered in a Lower East Side community garden after a botanist (and possible CIA plant) working in the Estero Real Natural Reserve hands them over to a guerrilla chief waiting out the Sandinista revolution until the inevitable next revolution comes along.

Rejecting chickens for skylines, and reasoning that "Utopia was better when equipped with a subway stop" (144), Rose thus replaces her husband's 1930s "Communism is twentieth-century Americanism" advocacy with her own "Sunnysideism is Late-Twentieth-Century Communism" community activism (140, 254). And, for all her desperate attempts to extricate herself from that Queens "suburb of disappointment" and a mother who responds by putting both their heads into an oven (26), Miriam follows suit. "The Dutch, they had this footpath, leading to the farms and woods. There was a bower here, like a giant arbor," she states when explaining to the newly arrived immigrant Tommy how the downtown street that used to be where New York ended came to be called the "Bowery" and accounting for those indigents that fill the street as historically awaiting "[e]ntry to the gardens" (174). In the version of the legend that she and Tommy go on to enact, however, the homeless are fed without ever having to leave behind concrete.

Therefore, even if the Irishman's fears that he has "arrived to this great party too late" turn out to be justified once an electrified Bob Dylan starts pouring over the airwaves in 1965 (173), his desire to reinvent a Geoghan boy of Belfast as a Greenwich Village folksinger is satisfied by New York's "great mad city" that confers "the sweet gift of anonymity on hordes tormented by a surplus of identity, by a surplus of wounds and legacies" (161). In this capacity, New York differs dramatically from Toronto's "New World where Her Majesty still squinted at you from the currency" in which Tommy makes his first pit stop on his way from Europe (159). In fact, in its capacity to take in those who are orphans and those who orphan themselves, New York serves as emblem for the nation at large, citizenship in which unites all the book's ideologues regardless of particular affiliation. "My identity [i]s New Yorker, and leftist," writes Miriam to the father whose expulsion from the Edenic metropolis returns him to the Germany of his birth. "An anti-American American" (241). This point she makes even more explicit during a disastrous TV quiz show appearance when defending the city against J. B. Priestley's "Babylon piled on Imperial Rome" charge and proposing – while completely stoned – a category on "dumb shit the Brits say about America" (118, 128). Such identification proves especially true of the book's two "Last Communist[s]," who embrace things prototypically American either as substitutes for the God that failed them or as reincarnations of that God in different form (98). Rose erects a shrine to Lincoln out of Carl Sandburg's six-volume biography and appropriates to herself the education of her African American lover's son as "what Abraham Lincoln wanted from her all along" (151). Her second cousin Lenin conceives the Sunnyside Proletarians as an "[u]rban Socialistic" baseball team that would "demolish the monopoly teams" (79), and function as a "place for the truth to hide in plain sight" (102).

Writing in the twenty-first century, Lethem is well aware of how dangerously short-sighted such patriotism can be. Rose insists that Miriam learn "proper English" (120) – to the extent of sending her for elocution lessons – for a variety of reasons that combine: a second-generation Jew's distaste for Yiddish as a diasporic language, a "grain of the Communist one-worlder" (121), a desire to raise a child proud of being "an *American* and a *New Yorker*" (29). And Miriam, who joins her mother's "horror of second tongues" with her own need "not-to-be-Rose" and "to-be-Rose-trying-not-to-be-Rose-who-speaks-Yiddish," refuses to learn Spanish, opting for her school requirement to study the Vichy collaborationist's French instead (121). But the insularity of extolling English as a *lingua franca* finds its correlative in the inwardness of a dementia that later leaves Rose, a woman of voracious appetites, obsessed with those innermost bodily functions that have reduced her to a "block of solid human waste" (341). And the refusal to familiarize herself with a language she has heard her entire life leaves Miriam, who as a teen imagines her power equal to that of the Empire State Building, completely powerless when she is unable to understand the language spoken in Nicaragua by the men who are planning to kill her.

When Lethem, then, closes the novel with reference to the Occupy movement, he ends with a movement that arises as neither extension of nor opposition to any antecedents, a movement unique in having little political genealogy beyond the Arab Spring and 1999 World Trade Organization Seattle protests. Indeed, as a movement with no official leaders or fixed demands, sustained by rotating facilitators and horizontal loose connections fostered by modern technology, it embodies the "new type of resistance" comprised by a global "multitude" that Hart and Negri called for to combat the transnational corporations that had eclipsed nation-states but for which, in 2000, they had no models to offer (308, 400). To this movement Lethem brings the two orphaned characters so weighed down by their respective political legacies as to opt out of activism entirely. Cicero Lookins, son of Rose's dead lover, knows as early as thirteen that he wants to unmask the "veil of sustaining fiction[s] that drove the world" (65), and grows up to unmake all ideologies from the safety of a small Maine college's ivory tower. Sergius Gogan, son of Rose's daughter, dons the garb of Ferdinand when even younger (while his parents dress up as Sandinistas for Halloween), and returns as an adult to teach at the Quaker boarding school that takes him in after they die, where he first sees a print of Edward Hicks's *The Peaceable Kingdom* with its lamb lying down with all the other beasts.

It is only when Sergius sees the three small tents that form Occupy Cumbow while on a trip to interview Cicero about Sunnyside Gardens that he begins to understand – when the last camps are about to be dismantled, ironically – that the movement that has no cells and is located "wherever you are" may constitute a political "way of being," of "[j]ust living differently," that suits him (360). As well it should. The care for the homeless and the mentally ill – of which, as an Occupy groupie states, there are "a *lot*" (359) – that arguably is Occupy's most important work recalls the feeding of Bowery derelicts in which his parents' courtship begins and those interpersonal "secret sympathies" that are not "ideological nor even really ideals" from which his grandmother's politics originate (272). Yet it is not until Sergius is himself flagged by an incongruous time signature on a surveillance video when trying to leave Maine that he fully comes to realize that lambs that lie down with beasts get devoured and bulls that refuse to fight get slaughtered in the arenas into which they are led. "*You've apprehended an American Communist*," he wants to scream at the Transportation Security Administration officer who detains him with questions about whether the woman who has accompanied Sergius to Portland's tiny Jetport (and whose Occupying a bathroom while having sex with him is the reason for the time-stamp snafu) is – in Lethem's loaded phrasing – a "fellow traveler" (365), even though Sergius "hadn't the first idea what these two words really meant even apart, let alone when you ran them together" (365–66). Instead, he replaces Bartleby's preferred "not to" for the more thunderous Melvillian "NO!" and refuses to provide the woman's name or identify for the officious gatekeeper exactly what kind of agitator his post–9/11 sharp eyes have "caught" (366). Sergius doesn't really know himself, of course. What he accepts, however, enables the book to exchange fellow traveler for forward voyager. *"[E]very cell is infiltrated in the end,"* concludes Miriam in despair as she awaits what she knows is her inevitable fate (329). "A cell of one, beating like a heart," thinks Sergius (366), arrived "at last at this nowhere in which he became visible before the law" that is his destiny.

Chapter 4

The Novel and 9/11

"I got a call from an agent," Paul said. . . . "It's going to be a while before anyone writes directly at it, but there's lots of what he called *subtext*. . . . He says everything goes through this cycle of opportunity: first inspiration stories, kids and animals, shit like that; then the backdrop stories, he called it the home-front . . . and then the big money – thrillers. . . . After thrillers come anniversaries: five years, ten, and the real money –" Paul dragged it out, took a long drink of coffee. "Nostalgia."

– Jess Walter, *The Zero* (2006)

A hero upon his return to Ground Zero in the days after 9/11, Paul Guterak is more than willing to turn over his experiences as a first responder to the highest bidder, especially after the agent who approaches him likens his story to a "good stock" that will go "public" with the nostalgia boom. "Bet your ass I'll sell my experiences," Guterak declares. "I sure as hell don't want 'em anymore" (150). His partner, by contrast, demurs when offered the chance to get his own appraised. Not that anyone could fashion much of a story from the experiences that Brian Remy opts to "hold onto" in Jess Walter's novel (151), let alone a cohesive written account. Suffering from memory gaps that prevent him from establishing a "string of events, the causes of certain effects" (43), and plagued by chronic eye problems that a burst blood vessel on 9/11 has exacerbated, the traumatized ex-cop can neither re-view nor remember. All he knows – vaguely – is that he "may have done some . . . really bad things" in his new job (117).

As part of the cover for that job in counterterrorism, moreover, Remy is already involved in a major project of reconstruction, the attempt of the new Documentation Department of the new Office of Liberty and Recovery to *"gather up the paper and put it all back"* (19) – the same paper that constitutes "everything that wasn't smoke" in the book's opening depiction of the attacks on the World Trade Center (3). Successful recovery of that *"record of our commerce, the proof of our place in the world,"* signals the beginning of a return to "normal," the form that nostalgic desire takes in the days immediately afterward (19, 7); failure confirms that *"the forces aligned against us have already won*" (19). By the end of the book, the condition of Remy's body suggests which outcome Walter deems more likely. The "thin, tattered tissue" of his retinas that metonymically – and barely, according to his doctor – distinguishes Remy as a "human being that wasn't a cadaver" conveys his prognosis, and by extension that of the nation he emblematizes, in terms of the flimsiest of paper products (266). That insubstantiality, in turn, is linked to a visual impairment that is now willful as well as physiological. When asked by a nurse whether he wants to open his eyes, Remy, who has awakened to his own complicity in the botched sting operation that has led to the train station bombing that lands him in the hospital, chooses to squeeze his eyes shut as tightly as possible.

The amount of paper devoted to addressing the subject of 9/11 in fiction is anything but flimsy. *New York* magazine, as part of its ten-year anniversary issue, compiled a two-page flow chart of artistic responses divided (and subdivided) by approach: "The Way We Were" (Nicholas Rinaldi's *Between Two Rivers* [2004], Paul Auster's *The Brooklyn Follies* [2006]); "9/11: How It Looked" (Benjamin Kunkel's *Indecision* [2005], Siri Hustvedt's *The Sorrows of an American* [2008]); "Troubled Times" (William Gibson's *Pattern Recognition* [2003], Lawrence Block's *Small Town* [2003], Philip Roth's *Everyman* [2006]); "Prophecies, Time Travel, and Alternate Histories" (Stephen King's *The Dark Tower VI: Song of Susannah* [2004], Michael Cunningham's *Specimen Days* [2005]); to name but a few of the literary first responders cited in a broadly conceived survey ("Encyclopedia" 52–53). Not surprisingly, the critical response to these endeavors also has taken up a considerable amount of paper, beginning with questions about the ability of fiction, as Don DeLillo wrote just three months after the attacks, to represent an event that has "no purchase on the mercies of analogy or simile" ("In the Ruins" 39), to the ethics of representing in fiction an event that, as Thane Rosenbaum wrote three years later, still demanded silence because "murder is not a work of art, but rather a moral crime" (134), to the use of an adjectival name-date already vexed – and not only because of its American idiomatic linkages – to denote any fiction produced. "The figure 9/11 is not a place (although New York City plays that role in the national imaginary), nor yet even a time, since what is missing is the designation of the year, 2001," David Simpson notes when commenting upon the "manipulable iconicity" of a signifier that "can draw to itself, with a minimum resistance, almost anything that comes its way" (16).

Much the same can be said about the body of work that has been alternately termed "Ground Zero Fiction" (Alfred Hornung, Birgit Däwes), "Literature after 9/11" (Ann Keniston and Jeanne Follansbee Quinn), or simply the "9/12 novel" (Jess Walter). Some texts use the September attacks as backdrop (the setting against which Joseph O'Neill's depressed financial analyst wanders in *Netherland* [2008]); others as mere bait (the blank page that enables Jay McInerney's adulterous lovers to meet cute in *The Good Life* [2006]). Some treat the events as confirmation (the twin towers in Thomas Pynchon's *Bleeding Edge* [2013] part of a long history of shady real estate deals and their collapse part and parcel of the dot-com collapse); others as convenient plot point (enabling the faked death that allows the Emersonian wannabe in Claire Messud's *The Emperor's Children* [2006] to start over in Florida after burning his bridges in New York). Very few, however, approach the subject head-on in all its horror. "[T]he best 9/11 novels are diffident linguistically," writes Kristiaan Versluys in the first full-length study devoted to the genre. "As an event, 9/11 is limned as a silhouette, expressible only through allegory and indirection" (*Out* 14). Anita Shreve's *A Wedding in December* (2005) thus re-creates in a subplot the December 6, 1917, collision of two ships carrying war matériel in Halifax Harbor and the resulting explosion that killed 2,000 people and wounded 9,000, many of whom had gone to their windows to witness the "spectacle" and lingered there out of curiosity and "a kind of compelling beauty" (22). Yet such sideways approaches to 9/11 have also led to the charge most often leveled against those works that employ the domestic – the troubled marriage that signals patriarchal decline, the home invaded that marks the homeland violated – as their particular means of indirection. In "simply assimilat[ing] the unfamiliar into familiar structures," as Richard Gray argues, "[t]he crisis is, in every sense of the word, domesticated" (30). Viewed from this perspective, the couple that flees their downtown loft for the safety of a house in the Hamptons in Helen Schulman's *A Day at the Beach* (2007) makes an unnecessary trip, having not just domesticated but aestheticized 9/11 as an event. The aging dancer Suzannah, who chooses not to think about the fruits she eats having been picked by migrant slave workers, observes it "already framed and turned into an artifact" on the television she watches while the attacks are taking place outside her window (57). Her choreographer husband Gerhard, who thinks of the Beatles' *Rubber Soul* when imagining "hinge[s] in the culture" and "breach[es] in a continuum" (23), finds in it the inspiration for the ending of his ballet that has thus far eluded him.

Underlying these debates is the question of the degree to which what took place on September 11, 2001, comprised the kind of historical watershed that Dominick LaCapra terms a "limit event" (7), so characterized by "unrepresentable excess" as to defy imaginative transformation (92). The various endings proclaimed within the news media – irony (Andrew Coyne, Roger

Rosenblatt), innocence (Pankaj Mishra), exceptionalism (Ariel Dorfman), postmodernism (Edward Rothstein, Julia Keller, Tina Beattie) – suggested that it was, even if what was asserted as having ended was more imagined than actual. Recognizing the dangers of a permanent "state of exception" to which exceptional measures taken in response to a crisis deemed singular can lead, Giorgio Agamben cautioned against such a stance in 2003, citing as evidence the October 26, 2001, Patriot Act and the November 13 executive order that authorized indefinite detention and trial by military commission of noncitizens suspected of terrorist activity (2–3). Marc Redfield went so far as to find the "spectacular horror of 9/11" appearing "strangely wan and distant on the horizon" four years later, "nearly buried under the mounting wreckage" of events in Iraq and Afghanistan (56). And yet the ongoing wreckage that comprises the lengthiest conflict in US history has resulted in very little fiction devoted to its portrayal: the visceral experience of war in Kevin Powers's *The Yellow Birds* (2012) and Phil Klay's *Redeployment* (2014); the official language of war for public consumption in David Abrams's *Fobbit* (2012); the war brought home to Dallas and upstate New York, respectively, in Ben Fountain's *Billy Lynn's Long Halftime Walk* (2012) and Joyce Carol Oates's *Carthage* (2014). This paucity becomes even more glaring when contrasted with the outpouring of fiction devoted to the Vietnam War that continues to be written years after its 1975 end, as evidenced by Tim O'Brien's *The Things They Carried* (1990) and *In the Lake of the Woods* (1994), Robert Olen Butler's *A Good Scent from a Strange Mountain* (1992), Mary Gardner's *Boat People* (1995), John M. Del Vecchio's *Carry Me Home* (1995), Lan Cao's *Monkey Bridge* (1997), Wayne Karlin's *Prisoners* (1998), Denis Johnson's *Tree of Smoke* (2007), Tatjana Soli's *The Lotus Eaters* (2010), Karl Marlantes's *Matterhorn* (2010), Ward Just's *American Romantic* (2014), Marian Palaia's *The Given World* (2015), Viet Thanh Nguyen's *The Sympathizer* (2015), and David Means's *Hystopia* (2016). It is to 9/11 instead, the "'mother' of all events," as Jean Baudrillard famously remarked, "the pure event uniting within itself all the events that have never taken place" (4), to which the literary imagination keeps returning.

The novels in the discussions that follow grapple with the complexities of 9/11 and its aftermath in a variety of ways. Beginning with works by Jonathan Safran Foer, Don DeLillo, and Ken Kalfus that take the image of the falling man, arguably the most circulated image of 9/11, as their starting point, the first set considers the degree to which 9/11 functions as cause or confirmation of trauma. Do the "figures in windows a thousand feet up, dropping into free space" evince "the world now," as DeLillo writes (*Falling* 4, 3), or do they expose a world in which life has always been precarious, as a passage later quoted from Kierkegaard implies? Presuming, as Emmanuel Levinas (167) and Judith Butler (134) argue, that an awareness of that precariousness requires an understanding of the precariousness of the Other, the second set turns to novels concerned with the portrayal of the Islamic Other, both those written by Muslim authors (in particular, Laila Halaby and Mohsin Hamid) and those written by non-Muslim authors (John Updike and Andre Dubus III) who run the risk of ethnic ventriloquism. The chapter then returns to the challenge of representing 9/11, focusing on works whose artist-protagonists serve as surrogates for their authors: works by Lynne Sharon Schwartz and Paul Auster that explore the limits of language in an environment plagued by a governmental mutilation of language; graphic works by Jay Cantor and James Romberger, Sid Jacobson and Ernie Colón, and Art Spiegelman that presume from the outset that words alone are insufficient to convey the enormity of such an event; and a final work by Amy Waldman that considers how best to memorialize that event.

Falling Men and Haunted Women

Oskar Schell, the nine-year-old protagonist of Jonathan Safran Foer's *Extremely Loud & Incredibly Close* (2005), is a textbook case of post–9/11 trauma after his father gets trapped in Windows on the World where he has gone for a business meeting that Tuesday morning. Unable even to identify 9/11 as anything but "the worst day" (11), much less move beyond melancholia to mourning as his insufficiently grief-stricken mother seems to have, he suffers from nightmares, entertains apocalyptic scenarios, experiences panic attacks, and regularly bruises himself over a year later. Some of these symptoms, like Oskar's fears that the earth is falling through the universe and suspicions about "how relatively insignificant life is" (86), predate 2001, the product of a brain that always has needed "quiet[ing]" (12). Others, like his contriving skyscrapers that move up and down and birdseed shirts that provide humans with winged escape, are the direct result of the events of that September. Convinced that Thomas Schell has died the "most horrible death that anyone ever could invent" (201), but without a body to indicate exactly how, Oskar proceeds to invent a variety of ways his father might have perished – thoughts that Oskar is so desperate to halt that he enlarges Internet photos of jumpers from the twin towers in the hopes of recognizing one. When he accidentally breaks a vase in his father's closet that contains a key in an envelope marked "Black," he embarks upon an eight-month quest to locate the 472 people in New York City with the surname, one of whom he is certain possesses the lock into which the key fits, which in turn will emotionally reconnect him with his lost parent.

Such pursuits obviously make Oskar the literary sibling of the Jonathan Safran Foer who journeys to Ukraine in *Everything Is Illuminated* (2002) to find the woman whose family saved his grandfather from the Nazis during the Holocaust, the event to which 9/11 is often compared. Oskar, however, is not the only character in Foer's second novel to be plagued by a loved one who has disappeared (as references to Chandra Levy, the missing Washington, D.C., intern prove) or to be experiencing a ruptured familial bond (something nearly every character in the book suffers). More important, Oskar is not the only character traumatized by loss incurred as a result of what can be construed as a terrorist act: his paternal grandparents are survivors of the 1945 bombing of Dresden, the event that leaves one afflicted with aphasia over the loss of his fiancée and unborn child and the other still tormented by nightmares over having "lost everything" – including the sister who was that fiancée – more than fifty-five years later (80, 313). In fact, as the history through which the Black born on the first day of the twentieth century has lived attests, 9/11 is hardly an unusual event in a world "filled with a lot of horrible people" (156) – so many that this war correspondent who has reported on conflicts "like the Spanish Civil War, and the genocide in East Timor, and bad stuff that happened in Africa" has not left his apartment in twenty-four years (154). What is most "horrible," then, about the event in which Oskar's father dies is neither its body count nor the particular circumstances contributing to it – Foer makes no reference to the geopolitics of 9/11 – but the suddenness of it. Yet that unexpectedness is the very quality that characterizes the two particular events cited by Foer in which the country victimized in 2001 has earlier acted as perpetrator. Those living in Dresden in 1945 do not hurry to shelters when air-raid sirens sound because they cannot imagine why anyone would want to bomb their city, only to learn afterward that "[e]verything in the history of the world can be proven wrong in one moment" (232). Those living in Hiroshima six months later, on whom Oskar reports to his class, go to their homes or offices while waiting for warnings to be lifted, only to have 100,000 of them die in "a flash" (187).

Absent any consideration of 9/11 as unique in its traumatic impact, the novel focuses on the representation of trauma itself and the means by which it can be healed. In particular, it explores the role played by narrative in dealing with memories that manifest themselves as recurring sensations and images – as evidenced by the disjointed photos and illustrations of Oskar's *Stuff That Happened to Me* scrapbook – because they cannot be integrated into a completed story of the past or ongoing life story (Caruth 153; Herman 37). "I believe in the story!" states the war correspondent A. R. Black after telling Oskar the tale of the community of Russian artists who feed one another after Stalin sends thugs to break their arms (164). Oskar's father likewise has "believe[d]" in the story of the Sixth Borough that recedes until it floats away to Antarctica (217), a cautionary tale of the perils of isolation whose moral is underscored by the acts that keep Oskar's grandparents in a state of emotional limbo and without a listener required for the narrative that promotes healing (Laub 57). One writes letters to the son he abandons before his birth, explaining "Why I'm Not Where You Are" in missives that, with one exception, are never received. The other composes two thousand pages of "My Life" on a typewriter without a ribbon.

When Oskar finally locates the Black who possesses the solution he seeks, what frees him to compose his own story comes not from the safe-deposit box lock to which the key he has worn over his heart like a Band-Aid is revealed as belonging – a key that Oskar's father mistakenly acquires in a vase he has purchased at an estate sale. Rather, it comes from Oskar and Black exchanging stories about their relationships with their deceased fathers. Oskar prompts William Black not "to make a long story short" in response to the other's inclination to do so when talking about the father who bequeaths him the safe-deposit box (296, 297); Black allows Oskar to tell him the "thing that I've never told anyone" (301) – his failure to pick up the telephone for his father's last call. When Oskar, then, reverses the order of events from the morning of 9/11 to the evening of 9/10 in the story he narrates on the book's last pages, and illustrates by way of a flipbook of similarly reversed images in which a man falls up through the sky instead of crashing to the concrete, the story that ends with "We would have been safe" is neither fairy tale nor wish-fulfillment (326). The conditional "would've" he uses in his reverse re-creation attests to the limited powers of the story. At the same time, Oscar's learning the identity of the lock's owner – the clue that ends his quest – from a woman living in the house in which Edna St. Vincent Millay once resided, a woman "with a face like Mom's" who facilitates a reconciliation with the mother he feels has abandoned him (91), suggests the value of the tale turned into literature.

The circularity that structures Don DeLillo's *Falling Man* (2007) – which ends with Keith Neudecker being where he is at the book's opening, witnessing a white shirt falling from the sky after his escape from the World Trade Center – signals a far less sanguine view of the role that traditional forms of art can play in the alleviation of trauma. Keith's retired art historian mother-in-law, who responds to 9/11 by retreating to her armchair to read "my

Europeans," is dying (34); the "old masters" at the Metropolitan Museum of Art, to which she returns for proof of "what was unfailing," have become the trophy pieces in which her art dealer lover specializes (11). Such commodification, of course, has long informed DeLillo's fiction, as evidenced by the tomes on the bookstore shelves of *Mao II* (1991) that scream "*Buy me*" (20). So, too, can 9/11 be viewed as having long been prefigured in that body of work. The "counter-archaeolog[ists]" of the future in *Great Jones Street* (1973) climb "vast dunes of industrial rubble and mutilated steel" (209). The travelers to the Mani in *The Names* (1982) find "two clusters of tower houses" that resemble a "modern skyline" in ruins (185). The waste managers of *Underworld* (1997) delineate the ever-growing Fresh Kills landfill – where the remains of those who worked in the twin towers would, four year later, be taken – as a "poetic balance" to the World Trade Center (184).

Confronted in *Falling Man* with the actualization of these earlier intimations, Keith and the estranged wife to whom he returns after his narrow escape respond to 9/11 in gender-specific ways. Having survived attacks genealogically linked to the 1960s–1970s radicalism of Kommune 1, Baader-Meinhof, and the Red Brigades but repeatedly figured as the product of male aggression – "nineteen men come here to kill us" (64), "the thing that happens among men" (112), "the force of men's intent" (134) – Keith thinks of the "gentle fist" rehab extensions he performs for an injured wrist as the "true countermeasures to the damage he'd suffered in the tower" (40). So committed is he to the regimen that he continues the exercises after the wrist has healed and supplements them with the "offsetting discipline" of "serious gymwork" designed to keep him "from shambling into the house hating everybody" (143). Yet such post–9/11 aggression merely rechannels the pre–9/11 behavior displayed by Keith and his buddies – all involved in investment and banking – during those weekly five-card-stud poker games that emblematize their hypercapitalist pursuits, in which "hoisting their balls" and drinking only alcohol of darker "manlier tones" form part of their acts of shredding one another's "gauzy manhood" (96, 98, 97). For Keith, as his mother-in-law has early recognized, is an "archetype" (59). Not a New Yorker but "an American," he is a man who once owned a pit bull, "an American breed, developed originally to fight and kill" (44) – both of which the US is doing in Iraq and Afghanistan at the end of the novel three years later.

His wife, Lianne, is no less an American when it comes to twisting her hand into the face of the neighbor who plays music "located in Islamic tradition" – which she indiscriminately translates as "Middle Eastern, North African, Bedouin" and can only hear as "noise" (67, 68) – too loud for her taste. But in the fascination that Lianne develops for the performance artist known as Falling Man, who with hidden harness restages the famous (and quickly censored) Richard Drew photograph of a man plunging headfirst to his death, "forever in free fall" and "subject only to the earth's gravitational field," from the World Trade Center (221), Lianne is able to work through the trauma of 9/11 in a way denied her husband. This she achieves not by way of its representation but its re-creation – unmediated, in motion, and in all its horror – to which she bears witness (Duvall, "Witnessing" 162). Because this post–9/11 obsession with free fall merely extends the impulse behind her work with those Alzheimer's patients condemned to an inevitable "falling, growing fainter" (94), conducted in the weekly storyline sessions that serve as counterpoint to Keith's weekly poker games, Lianne also is able to confront the "slow and certain decline" she fears she has inherited from the father who has shot himself after determining that "the deal was sealed" with his own diagnosis (125, 41).

That sealed deal is, in DeLillo's delineation, part and parcel of the human condition, the basis for the quotation from Kierkegaard – "*The whole of existence frightens me*" (118) – that has haunted Lianne since college. Unlike Keith, then, defined by absence – ascribed no more depth than an urge to rock climb can contain, appalled by the "clear and distinct definition" of three-dimensionality that turning forty is meant to provide (157) – who eventually returns to the company of "[m]en in stylized yawns with arms raised, men staring into dead space," whose "precious losers' blood" he yearns to make bleed in the hell that is Las Vegas (228, 230), Lianne is granted presence. Afforded the presence of her body and "everything it carried, inside and out, identity and memory and human heat" (236), and the presence of mind to know that "[s]he wanted to be safe in the world and [her husband] did not" (216), Lianne accepts the fact that she and her son are "ready to be alone, in reliable calm," and to consider perhaps the "hovering possible presence of God," however much it means placing her faith in a voice that says, "I am not here" (236).

The feuding spouses in Ken Kalfus's *A Disorder Peculiar to the Country* (2006) are too preoccupied with their acrimonious divorce proceedings to have any interest in things spiritual. For them, 9/11 is a source of exhilaration, not personal examination. Thinking that her husband is dead in his upper-floor World Trade Center office instead of just late to work, Joyce Harriman experiences "a giddiness, an elation" (3), and, even after learning of his survival, fantasizes about "terror sex" with firemen and the thrills of living in a city filled with checkpoints and FBI agents (22). Thinking that his wife has been on board United 93 instead of in her office after a business meeting in Berkeley is canceled, Marshall skips down the street, despite having just dragged a man out of the towers whose head is subsequently ripped apart by falling debris. If DeLillo's book ends with "all life ha[ving] become public" in the three years "since that day in September" (*Falling* 182), Kalfus's satire, which takes place between that September day and June 2003, opens on the opposite premise. Catastrophic public events are measured only in terms of their impact on the personal lives of the characters, each of whom turns 9/11 into a tale of personal travail (rushing nude from a shower in Florida becoming one man's tale of "what had happened to him on September 11" [*Disorder* 77]) and renewal (descending into the pit of Ground Zero bringing one woman "closer to her real self" [22]).

This narcissism that Kalfus sees as peculiar to the country is most evident in the ways in which the Harrimans appropriate 9/11 to portray their own collapsing union. Joyce imagines its specter as rising up before her, "a tower one hundred stories high," when questioned by the FBI about her husband (45); Marshall conceives of the "entire structure of their lives" as brought "down on their heads" by his wife's pettiness (6). Such foundational instability, significantly, characterizes the union prior to 9/11, bankrupt as the couple is even before they turn the Brooklyn Heights co-op they cannot afford but are unwilling to vacate into a war zone, leaving Joyce to wonder at one point whether their situation had been "predetermined" by their "inborn flaws" (53). With 9/11 giving the two new roles in which to cast themselves, however, such moments of introspection are fleeting. Convinced of her own victimhood, Joyce responds to the US bombing of Afghanistan by dining at local Afghan restaurants, strapping a lapis bracelet around her ankle to feel "exotic and gritty-real" (62), and applying a chocolate-colored facial masque to appear a "cast-off child of another country" (120). Acknowledging his actions as "a bit deranged that autumn" (36) – wandering aimlessly around New York, reeling at the sound of loud noises, returning to the image of a head exploding on the World Trade Center plaza – as a result of what he has experienced on 9/11, Marshall conflates his own trauma with that of the nation and decides he can "do whatever he wanted now, absolutely anything, he was a crazy fucking divorcing superpower" (106).

As *American* narcissists, though, the two are equally oblivious to anything beyond their isolationist sight lines. "Now you know what it's like to live in history," remarks the doctor from whom Marshall seeks treatment for a post-9/11 rash and sympathy for all he has suffered (58), as the man's daughter injured by a land mine during the family's year-long journey from the Middle East to America limps around bringing them cups of tea. More than a lone example, such reminders surround the Harrimans: their Jewish babysitter, nearly killed by a Scud attack in Israel after emigrating there from

Tashkent, takes to her bed for a week after 9/11, certain that "world history was hot on her trail" once more (181). Yet so much energy do the Harrimans expend dismissing not just Israeli history but "other places' just-as-complicated histories" that they remain blind to the history going on in their own household (99): a daughter who draws pictures of the family jumping from the twin towers, a son who shoots toy planes from rubber bands. When they finally tell the children about their impending divorce, the four-year-old, who has noticed the signs but failed to process them correctly, realizes that "[t]hey had been plotting it" for quite some time (144), turning Joyce and Marshall from victim and superpower, respectively, into terrorists collectively, with Viola and Victor their collateral damage.

Hobbled in much the same way by the arrogance that such tunnel vision encourages, the US is portrayed, on the one hand, as repeatedly caught off-guard after disastrously being caught off-guard on 9/11: a stock market slide becomes an avalanche after traders ignore a reversal that begins two years earlier, *Columbia* explodes after NASA experts ignore repeated warnings about damage to the shuttle's foam insulation. Compensating, on the other hand, for the consequences of its own neglect, the nation responds with misguided reassertions of will. Nowhere does Kalfus depict this more clearly than at the Long Island party to which Marshall is taken by his son's preschool teacher, during which a young African American teen – in the book's deliberate allusion to the torture at Abu Ghraib prison – is forcibly stripped of his clothes and civil liberties and fellated by Miss Naomi, who afterward proclaims, in the manner of George W. Bush, "Mission accomplished," to the camera that films the scene (218). The eroticism that informs that "spectacle" (214), in turn, serves as foreplay to the "spectacle" of war in the Middle East that concludes the book (232), anticipation of which has been "tantalizing America" and filling its aroused citizens with "longing" (223). With the exhilaration of the novel's fantasized ending – in which swift victory, found WMDs, hanged Hussein, and captured bin Laden combine – displacing the exhilaration that informs its opening, 9/11 is likewise displaced to the sidelines. A celeb at social events for having once worked at the World Trade Center, Marshall devolves into a "curiosity" for having survived the event that is the "alpha point from which history moved forward" at his decimated firm (176, 154), and finally into an embarrassment: a man who "seemed to have brought with him more than his share of the world's anxieties" (176), most of all his nation's after its temporary moment of vulnerability. "You're in the way!" shouts his daughter as Marshall stands in front of the television, pointlessly asserting the "basic human rights" he feels he has surrendered in the divorce settlement (226). And so he is.

Speaking for/about/with/to Others

John Updike has never shied away from what Linda Alcoff has termed "speaking for others" (6), having over the course of his career assumed the voice of an African American revolutionary (*Rabbit Redux* [1971]), an African dictator (*The Coup* [1978]), a Jewish American novelist (*Bech* [1970], *Bech Is Back* [1982], *Bech at Bay* [1998]), assorted women (*The Witches of Eastwick* [1984], *S.* [1988], *Seek My Face* [2002], *The Widows of Eastwick* [2008]), even Mohamed Atta, one of the four focalizers through whom September 11 is experienced in "Varieties of Religious Experience" (2002). That being said, the eponymous *Terrorist* of Updike's 2006 novel is not entirely Other, as eighteen-year-old Ahmad Ashmawy Mulloy makes a point of reiterating. A native-born American, the son of an Irish American mother and an Egyptian exchange student father, Ahmad has never been abroad, avoids the so-called Arab sections of his New Jersey hometown, and, in his limited travels around the state delivering furniture, "takes interest less in its pockets of a diluted Middle East than in the American reality all around" (177). The reality of the economically depressed city in which he lives, ironically named New Prospect, offers him daily proof of America's "failed experiment," however (177). To the extent that its citizens worship anything, they worship the unfettered capitalism of a bygone era, as typified by the old Wanamaker's department store that adults recall as a "paradise" (132). The few exceptions to that creed express themselves in ways that confirm what a Barbadian immigrant deems the "American hatred of decent order" (113), an antipathy evidenced most for Ahmad in female sexuality. His neglectful mother, Teresa, views religion as a matter of "saying *yes* to life," and her casual liaisons prove that she indeed "has a lot of *yes* in her" (91, 93). His African American classmate, Joryleen Grant – another "Yeaahuyess"-sayer (66) – tempts him with attire "both lower and higher than it should be" (8).

Islam offers Ahmad a Straight Path through this mess and confusion. Its strictness informs everything from his observance of daily prayers to the pressed white shirt and narrow black jeans that serve as his cleric's uniform, the somber shades of which contrast with both the vibrant colors of his high school's various gangs and the homeboy attire of those "co-religionists" for whom "Islam is less a faith, a filigreed doorway into the supernatural, than a habit" (244). Yet the Islam that Ahmad embraces as a faith "chosen rather than merely inherited" is a religion that he has selected at age eleven for personal rather than spiritual reasons (177): "He thought he might find in this religion a trace of the handsome father who had receded at the moment his memories were beginning" (99). Abandoned by his father at the age of three, Ahmad adopts his imam, Shaikh Rashid, as "his surrogate father" (13). Fascinated by the idea of brotherhood because he is an only child, he appeals to his immediate boss at Excellency Home Furnishings, Charlie Chehab, as a sibling. Surrounded by devils that seek to "*take away*" his God (3), he accompanies the God he views as "ever with him" and locates, in accordance with the Qur'an (50:16), "as close as the vein in my neck" (39, 233) – a custodianship as blasphemous as it is presumptuous, reflecting as it does not Allah's need for companionship but Ahmad's own.

The problem is that the proper relationship with the Muslim God from which Ahmad departs recalls all too well the distanced one that the Protestant Updike, following his reading of Karl Barth, early proposed for a Christian God conceived as "*totaliter aliter*" or "Wholly Other" (*Assorted* 273). Likewise, Ahmad's fear that his own death will be "as small and final" as that of insects recalls the existential angst that initially drove Updike to Barth and Kierkegaard in the first place (*Terrorist* 5). In fact, by the time that Ahmad agrees to drive a truck loaded with explosives to be detonated in the Lincoln Tunnel to mark the anniversary of 9/11, his motivations have very little to do with a religion that seems, like the Judaism and Christianity portrayed in the novel, "ground down to a lackluster sameness" (25). Derided as a "faggot" by his black classmates because of his limp handshake and girlish legs (98), Ahmad yearns to assert his manhood. Destined to a "life of barely belonging," he relishes the idea of being on the "verge of a radiant centrality" (234), to the extent of imagining the media coverage of his martyrdom and the gathering of his paraphernalia as part of the historical record. He thus continues with his mission despite his growing awareness that he is, as Joryleen correctly notes, being "fatten[ed] up" (227) – by the unfatherly imam who looks at him in the manner that Ahmad looks as bugs and has specifically targeted him as a patsy, by the unbrotherly Charlie who turns out to be a CIA operative and has been using Ahmad to flush out conspirators. He also continues despite his recognition that the Muslims to whom he has delivered an ottoman filled with cash are no different from Westerners in their "reverence" for American currency (194), that the newly shaven shaikh making his escape in a Western suit "as if dressed for a business trip among the infidels" looks "disconcertingly ordinary" (266, 271), that even the "Prophet himself was a merchant" (152).

Indeed, for all the transliterated Arabic and passages from the Qur'an that mark Ahmad's pilgrimage, it is by way of the observed details of American life – the menial details that inform Updike's particular brand of layered realism – that Ahmad inhabits Islam. A loading platform resembles "a place God has breathed upon" (153); a stained truck seat provides a means of ascent like that experienced when "the Prophet entrusted his body to the fearsome horse Buraq" (155). Similarly, it is by way of the details of the American Revolution that the jihadist revolution – in fact, any Third World revolution – takes shape. Thus George Washington, his "truly white horse" like the "winged white horse Buraq" (179, 5), and his "plucky band of threadbare freedom fighters" show the world "what can be done against the odds, against a superpower" (179, 181). It is not surprising, then, that Ahmad in the book's final pages chooses not to press the button that will detonate the explosives. Having earlier been struck by a lower Manhattan, even with a Statue of Liberty in "rather diminished side view" (186), that reveals an American "*beauty*" that "*must mean something*" (188), he is confirmed in his impression by a skyline that remains "one of the world's wonders" as he approaches the tunnel's entrance (293–94). Nor is it surprising that it is the sight of two African American children mischievously smiling at Ahmad from the Volvo in front of him that acts as his immediate deterrent. No longer an Other himself, Ahmad recognizes the ethical imperative of accepting the humanity of the Other, whether the *zanj* before him or the Jewish guidance counselor who has leapt into the truck to sit beside him. Because the injunction not to take life and thereby "desecrate His creation by willing death" is not unique to the God of Islam (306), Ahmad does surrender all hopes of the paradise he has envisioned after his own death when he returns to the Garden State from which he has been expelled. But as the route he takes to get back to his home reveals, there is no Straight Path through life, only a journey that involves driving through Columbus Circle.

Set in the final days preceding 9/11, in contrast, Andre Dubus III's *The Garden of Last Days* (2008) locates one of its eight narrative points of view in a fictionalized composite of the actual hijackers. The collision between Middle East and West portrayed in this novel, which follows the clash between a retired Iranian colonel and a rootless American woman in Dubus's earlier *House of Sand and Fog* (1999), takes place largely in a Florida strip club meant to approximate the kind frequented by the 2001 terrorists prior to relinquishing their own flesh. It is this club that joins together the book's three main characters: April Connors, a single mother who dances there under the name of Spring; Bassam al-Jizani, a young Saudi who hires April to perform for him; and Alan James (AJ) Carey, a heavy machinery operator who snatches April's three-year-old daughter when he sees her wandering around unattended the one night April is forced to take the child to her place of employment.

Hardly unusual in a state filled with "all those who weren't nailed down" after "God picked up the country and shook it" (208), Bassam has little difficulty fitting in with the *kufar* castoffs with whom he is instructed to mingle as part of his cover. One of eighteen children and the only son not to attend university, Bassam only begins attending prayers in order to escape work as a stock boy in a housewares shop; even when he finally commits himself to jihad, he mistakes the "lower meaning" of dying for Allah for the "struggle to live as Allah wishes," as the successful father who views Bassam as "the dull boy, the slow one," informs him (255, 256). Being selected by "the Egyptian" (Atta) provides the unfavored child who "had never done anything special" with a way to redeem himself in the eyes of his family (61, 477). As a bonus, the "chosen *shahid*" revealed with his martyrdom will become known to the "entire world" (377), transformed from the "nothing he was as Bassam" into "Mansoor, the Victorious" (58, 258).

This need to destroy the West, however, is largely rooted in Bassam's desire for the West. The "lush gardens watered by running streams" that he imagines awaiting him after death find their counterpart in the garden of April's land-lady that just keeps getting "more lush and breathtaking" as the book con-tinues (432, 239), and into which the "venomous snake" of sexuality slithers (527). When Bassam engages April to dance privately for him in the Puma Club's Champagne Room, it is as a twenty-six-year-old virgin who fears his resolve to "kill bodies he has never lain with" weakened by the bodies of Floridian women in scanty dress and casual contacts with helpful gym trainers and smiling waitresses that he admits to liking (230). He therefore does everything he can to humiliate the woman who, as a representative of all those women he deems whores, testifies to his own weakness – offering her $300 to tell him her real name, $600 to touch her C-section scar. And because April is a woman who takes pride in her fiscal responsibility and only sells herself in strip joints to save up for a down payment on a house – the emblem of American success that leads to catastrophe for the Iranian émigré of Dubus's second novel who plans on flipping the house he buys at public auction and reinvesting the profits in more real estate – Bassam's desire for her extends beyond sexual desire. A "good citizen" who always "needed more" (458, 499), April imagines the purchase of a house for herself followed by the purchase of three or four more to rent. As such, she is one with those American military officers the young Bassam has seen shopping in the *souq* years earlier, men "[t]all and strong and afraid of nothing" that impress the teen whose hunger derives from more than the fast of Ramadan: "there was something about these men [he] wanted to become" (91).

As the portrayal of AJ indicates, it is not only the "little foreigner" Bassam who is unable to live up to that model of American manhood (79). A "plain man who worked hard and wasn't good-looking or rich and never would be" but nonetheless "want[s] to be seen" (122, 181), AJ knows he is a disappointment to the wife he views as not "just a woman but home itself" (274). He also knows that he is in no position to keep her and their son – much less the homeland – safe from the unexpected in what he repeatedly refers to as the "hurricaneproof house" that it is his duty to defend with loaded rifle (288, 411, 514). Certainly not while living at his mother's after his wife throws him out of their home for beating her. So when he comes upon April's daughter abandoned at the strip club and crying, it is in the service of "doing something good for a stranger" (228), rescuing a "child only he could save" (197), that he drives away with her in his truck to "someplace safe" (242), even though he has no idea where such a spot might be. Yet "do[ing] something good" is exactly the way Bassam conceives of himself on board another large vehicle filled with passengers who think they are traveling to someplace safe (477). And just as the misogyny behind AJ's act is quickly exposed once he stops admiring little Franny's "spunk" and remembers how "[s]punk turns to sassy turns to bitch turns to whore" (274), the misogyny behind Bassam's mission reveals itself when he anticipates the sight of *kufar* women who "take from you your power" kneeling before the Judge and the Ruler – not God, but Bassam – and "beg[ging] for their souls" (462, 463). Only Dubus grants AJ a degree of conscience and misgivings that he denies Bassam. Imagining April combing her daughter's hair, AJ suspects "he'd done something wrong" (326), realizes "[y]ou can't just drive off with somebody's child" (384), and eventually accepts his prison sentence after being apprehended. Bassam, who suffers one last indignity when the "Already?" uttered by a hired prostitute confirms his inadequacies both as a man and a consumer (454), boards American Airlines 11 sure in his belief that "*good works are accomplished*" (511).

Such confidence is noticeably lacking in works written by authors of Middle Eastern or South Asian descent for whom 9/11 serves as a reminder of the provisional nature of their characters' American belonging. The Karachi-born hipster of H. M. Naqvi's *Home Boy* (2009), who has prided himself on being "self-invented" and attuned to the "great global dialectic" as a Manhattan "Metrostani" (1, 14), opens his account with a blunt assertion of his post-9/11 status: "We'd become Japs, Jews, Niggers" (1). These are characters suspect not just because of those visible markers (hijab, prayer caps, beards) that denote difference and trigger the kind of hatred portrayed by Shaila Abdullah's *Saffron Dreams* (2009) when a Pakistani widow's veil is ripped away by swastika-tattooed hoodlums who accuse her of belonging to a "race of murderers" the day she picks up the death certificate of the husband who has worked in Windows on the World (61). Rather, these are characters that are suspect for the simple fact, as Carol Fadda-Conrey argues, of no longer being "over there" but "over here in the US" (535), regardless of how ordinary, nonobservant, or assimilated they appear to be. The Lebanese American children in Alia Yunis's comedic *The Night Counter* (2009), for instance, model themselves on those "blenders" in Detroit who "just mixed into the rest of the country" before fanning out all over the country themselves as adults (93). One disguises pork as veal and serves it to a Dearborn mosque's elders, another alters her nose and name in lieu of joining the Daughters of the American Revolution (a stretch even she recognizes) in Houston, a third becomes an itinerant psychic who gives birth to a son conceived via sperm donor, who in turn grows up to become a gay actor whose Arabic links consist mainly of those bit parts as terrorists that after September 11 become increasingly available. When in the aftermath of 9/11, however, neighbors of the daughter living in New Castle, Pennsylvania, arrive with cakes to prove that "Arab Americans and Muslim Americans were Americans period," their support reminds the Vietnam War widow and her son that "they were no longer just Americans" in a way that the bungling FBI agents that wiretap the family's eighty-five-year-old matriarch because of her grandson's audition outfits do not (252).

Salwa and Jassim Haddad, the Jordanian couple of Laila Halaby's *Once in a Promised Land* (2007), are not entirely ordinary, surrounded as they are by those luxury items – towels as large as bedcovers, glittering Mercedes, "nestled-in-the-hills" Arizona home (22) – to which his job as a hydrologist and hers as a banker/part-time realtor grant them access. "But of course they have nothing to do with what happened to the World Trade Center," writes Halaby in the book's prologue (viii). Yet when a sixteen-year-old skateboarder sporting his own "Terrorist Hunting License" deliberately (and fatally) propels himself into Jassim's car and a pushy co-worker manipulates himself into Salwa's affections, the Haddads are forced off the American "autobahn" they think they have been traveling and "onto an American frontage road" (117). This unexpected detour not only exposes them to the America of Denny's and Wal-Marts to which they have been blind. It also exposes this wholly secular couple to the disparity between the true and the false desert promised land, between the American "once upon a time" fairy tale that "promises a happy ending for everyone if you just believe it hard enough" (119) and the Arabic *"[t]hey say there was or there wasn't in olden times"* folktale in which humans walk a frayed tightrope over the "impossible pit of [their] greatest fears" (vii, 331).

A Palestinian raised in Jordan but born in the US, Salwa grows up doubly "cursed" by that fairy tale (46). Citizenship instills in her a view of happiness as a constitutional right; silk pajamas evoke the worship of capitalist consumption through which the desires of the future economics major who "studies money" will be satisfied (70). Unaware that this America, a *ghula* (female sorceress/monster) in Halaby's formulation that has stitched itself under her skin and tugs at her with invisible threads, is the "exported America of Disneyland and hamburgers, Hollywood and the Marlboro man," and hence a simulacrum that does not exist (49), Salwa attends a lecture given by a hydrologist from America and accepts his marriage proposal upon their third meeting. Jassim, conversely, whose "threads" to land and home are "severed" with his renunciation of God but who does his Ph.D. in the US thinking he will return to Jordan to apply what he has learned (46), recognizes that marriage to Salwa will enable him to remain in the US forever: "America, once tasted, is hard to spit out" (64).

Far easier to expel are the geopolitics of water that have made Jassim study rainwater harvesting in the first place. Jassim initially learns these politics at the foot of an uncle who frames the Arab-Israeli conflict as a fight over water and not land, and later illustrates by way of the 1967 fight for the Golan Heights originating in a desire to control the Banyas River. He even expands on his uncle's tutelage when locating the first human settlements near sources of water, the one thing to which the Qur'an states all humans have a right and no one human an exclusive right, and tracing the conquest of America to European settlers who "diverted rivers and tried to harness them, with little regard for the people they might be affecting" (244). But in marrying a woman who habitually wastes water, whose profligate use of water and concomitant taste for luxury make her a First World "colonizer," as her father jokes (70), Jassim relinquishes all consciousness of the complicated politics of water. He separates books devoted to "*problems*" from those concerned with "*solutions*" (178), dismissing the role played by governments and corporations in order to focus scientifically on the promotion of "self-sufficiency" (65), an approach most impressive for its naïveté. As his uncle states, "we cannot be self-sufficient if the supplies are ho[a]rded from the beginning" (178).

As it turns out, both Haddads are no less naïve with respect to the presumed benefits that derive from a decade of good citizenship and their own hoarding. Jassim – who thinks the 9/11 terrorists did not intend to destroy the twin towers – truly believes what he says to the FBI agents that investigate him because of his professional access to the Tucson water supply: "I'm a normal citizen who happens to be an Arab" (232). This, however, is the same man who responds to defecation in the swimming pool he frequents with pity for the culprit's loss of control rather than recognize the act as a display of that unfettered American freedom allowed when "no one said anything, no one intruded in other people's business" (181). Such behavior contrasts markedly with what is allowed in Arabic lands filled with nosy neighbors and aunties whose warnings of "*You'd better not, or else*" provide needed restraint (181). Salwa, far less patient with the post–9/11 xenophobia she encounters, recognizes the emptiness with which drawers of expensive lingerie have left her as the product of an "American freedom [that] had given her exactly that: American freedom" (202). Yet rather than fill that emptiness in the manner of her friend Randa, who views happiness as a "luxury" and enriches her life by infusing a bland America that caters to basic necessities with the "smaller details" of her Lebanese heritage that add "flavor" (283), Salwa uses that freedom to retreat further into her Disneyland dream. She casts herself as a princess needing the kiss of a co-worker prince to awaken her, completely oblivious to the fact that the prince in question is also a crystal meth dealer "turned on" by her exotic "foreignness" (171) – bellydancer in the guise of banker – the racism of which is horribly exposed when Salwa goes to his apartment to bid him farewell and he reacts by smashing a picture frame into her face and cursing her as an "Arab bitch" (322).

Salwa misses the point, however, when looking at her rescue by an immigrant gardener who in coming to America has probably "risked his life so that he could prune trees and fix sprinkler heads" as an apt comment on her own years there (323). For the man who saves her is a Guatemalan she has earlier mistaken for a Mexican and suspected of vandalizing her car based on his class and color. The physical disfigurement that Salwa suffers at the hands of her lover, in other words, only makes visible a disfigurement of the soul that comes from being "twice displaced from lands holier than this" and learning the lessons of this land all too well (210). So when, in Halaby's final invocation of the Arabic folktale that frames the novel, the girl about to be eaten by the *ghula* to whom she is bound by invisible threads – America personified – is returned to her home across the ocean by a nightingale the sorceress has kept trapped in a golden cage of his own, it is with no guarantees that she will recover from her wounds even with the care of the bird-transformed-into-an-ordinary-man. Suspended between lands, neither knows what or where home is.

By contrast, Mohsin Hamid's *The Reluctant Fundamentalist* (2007), a novel inspired by Camus's *La Chute* (*The Fall* [1956]) that takes the form of a monologue addressed to an unnamed listener, is set in the birthplace of its twenty-five-year-old Pakistani narrator, the place to which he has retreated after a four-and-a-half-year stay in America. This is not to say that Lahore serves as home to Changez, a man who for most of his life has assiduously avoided the more obvious markers of home – nation, religion, and ethnicity – when defining the collective by which he determines his identity, his present-day pride in "we, the people of the Indus River basin," and despair over the poverty of "our cities" notwithstanding (34). He leaves Pakistan for Princeton to attend college, drinks alcohol in defiance of Muslim dictates, and plays the foreigner only when it suits his social advantage. When he jokingly tells his Princeton classmates that his goal in life is to be a dictator of an Islamic republic with nuclear capability, nobody bats an eye, so clearly is Changez not a religious fundamentalist.

Economic fundamentalism is another story, however, once Changez begins working at Underwood Samson & Company – Hamid's less than subtle formulation for the US – a valuation firm he worships for its "exalted brand name" (5), whose skyscraper offices he approaches with "wonder" (33), and whose guiding principle of "focus on the fundamentals" he quickly adopts as "our creed" (98, 116). As the book's allusions to *The Great Gatsby* attest, it is not money per se that drives Changez to replace the true God of Islam's Five Pillars with the false god of American capitalism: for all his $80K annual salary, he still lives in an East Village studio and eats at local delis. Rather, it is money as a means to satisfy his "poor boy's sense of *longing*" to recoup what his family of declining fortunes "had had and lost," desire for which has hooked Changez even more than it has those relatives whose nostalgia he compares to crack cocaine because his is a yearning for an imagined past that he has never personally experienced (71). It also is money as a means for Changez – whose shifting (and sometimes contradictory) self-fashionings all involve imperial longings (beginning with an Urdu name that recalls Genghis Khan) – to satisfy his own urge for power. Having grown up during a period when "finance was a primary means by which the American empire exercised its power" (156), yet living in a time when, as his boss reminds him, "soldiers don't really fight for their flags" but for "[t]heir team" (153), Changez and his fellow trainees of diverse backgrounds join Underwood Samson during the happy moment when the two coincide. Confident that the new century to be led by "my team [that] was shaping the future" will be no different from the American Century just past (66), he arrives in July 2001 for his first assignment in the Philippines – the emblem of US global preeminence after the 1898 Spanish-American War, now a nation of skyscrapers and superhighways that expose Pakistan even more as belonging to the Third World – and begins to speak "more like an *American*" (65).

It is during that same trip that a hostile gaze from a Filipino jeepney driver in whose eyes Changez sees himself reflected reminds Changez of how *not* American he is as compared with his fair-haired colleagues, a fact Changez again learns when he looks at himself in a mirror during a visit to Pakistan and reacts with the same self-hatred and concomitant need for exorcism that the glance from the Filipino has evoked. More than anger at being devoid of a "stable *core*" or "lacking in substance" (148, 125), which would make him a cypher, Changez's rage comes from being both self and Other, which makes him schizophrenic. This, of course, is the quality that has defined for quite some time his courtship of Erica, Hamid's version of the Fitzgerald golden girl and another weak embodiment of America, whose devotion to her dead boyfriend has left her unresponsive to Changez's sexual advances. When Changez finally overcomes that resistance by pretending he is the dead Chris and taking what he wants, satisfying what he admits is a desire for blood, he hides behind a veil of contrition: "I did not seem to be myself" (105). When he hears of the 9/11 attacks on an America gendered as female, however, Changez feels only joy at a supplication that combines the martial and the sexual, pleased that "someone had so visibly brought America to her knees" (73).

According to Changez, it is 9/11 – along with the US response in Iraq and Afghanistan that awakens him to the long history of American militarism – that forces him to leave America for good. Also according to Changez, it is a later business trip to Chile – whose legally elected government of Salvador Allende was overthrown by a US-backed coup on a September 11 twenty-eight years earlier – that forces him to recognize himself as a modern-day janissary, no different from those Christian boys captured by the Ottomans and trained to fight for their adopted empire. Yet Changez, who prefers "*gist*" to "accuracy" in relating the history that has occurred "more or less" as he describes it (118), is hardly a reliable narrator. No more is he a hapless victim of post–9/11 Islamophobia. Unlike the return to Pakistan of Naqvi's *Home Boy*, whose imprisonment in the Metropolitan Detention Center as a potential terrorist is the result of racial profiling combined with his own stupidity in breaking into a friend's Connecticut home days before his visa is to expire, Changez's return after deliberately getting fired from his job is entirely of his own making. It is this same propensity for self-destruction that prompts him to tease the American stranger he approaches in an Old Anarkali tea café, who may or may not be an assassin sent to kill him for promoting anti-American violence among the students he now teaches – with hints of poisoned foods and threats of lengthening shadows – in effect to spook the spook into doing that for which he has been dispatched. "I must meet my fate when it confronts me," Changez declares in the book's final paragraphs (183), his presumed martyrdom of a part with those televised political appearances he views as having issued a "firefly's glow bright enough to transcend the boundaries of continents and civilizations" (182). It is a firefly "bumping repeatedly against [a] window," however, that earlier has served as an emblem of barriers that cannot be breached (63), its meager glow over-whelmed by the luminance of New York City. When Changez therefore sees a metallic object being removed from his listener's jacket pocket in the book's last lines, it is with a spurned lover's hope that it is not a business card holder for which the man is reaching.

Mixed Media

In contrast to the many artist-protagonists in 9/11 fiction for whom the crisis of 9/11 also is experienced as a crisis of aesthetic representation, the thirty-four-year-old linguist at the center of Lynne Sharon Schwartz's *The Writing on the Wall* (2005) does not create art. Renata is nonetheless attuned to the representative potential of languages of all sorts, from the babbling of infants and private language of siblings to those (invented) world languages in danger of extinction on which she works at the New York Public Library and against which English appears decidedly lacking in nuance. But after 9/11 fulfills the book title's intimations of Old Testament doom, adding to the calligraphy panels hung on her apartment walls and information cards mounted on museum walls those posters of the missing that make every surface onto which they are taped a Wailing Wall, Renata is forced to reevaluate her trust in language and belief that the books of paper into which language is transcribed "inspired saintliness" (38). The "hurricane of paper" that blankets the city and that would have been a "treasure trove" for Renata on any other day is the same paper that, as the epigraph from William Langewiesche's *American Ground* (2002) makes clear, directly contributes to the collapse of the World Trade Center (46). More to the point, the historic trauma of the twin towers that results in thousands presumed lost or dis-appeared evokes the two traumatic events of Renata's own history in which the breach of borders by another outside intruder – an uncle whose affair with her twin sister ends in pregnancy – resulted in the loss of the twin who drowns at sixteen and the disappearance of the niece who vanishes from a carousel in a moment of Renata's inattention.

Unlike the crisis of representation that prompts John Hersey in *Hiroshima* (1946) to characterize the "first moment of the atomic age" as one in which "a human being was crushed by books" after a factory clerk is crippled by falling bookcases (21), the crisis on which Schwartz focuses does not concern the inability of language or previous literary genres to convey catastrophe. Schwartz, in fact, appropriates words from the natural world – the same world that perversely regenerates in Hersey's account as an explosion of "panic grass and feverfew" (89) – to depict the flames of 9/11 as a "huge marigold bursting open in the sky, across the river, flinging petals into the blue" (*Writing* 45). Rather, the crisis the novel delineates concerns the manipulation of language for political ends. Exemplified by the snippets of George W. Bush's televised talk about "struggle[s] of good versus evil" and "war[s] against civilization" that punctuate the text (64, 67, 74, 86, 101, 110), such a mutilation of language by what Laplanders term "*prashmensti,*" or "wrong words" (7), eventuates in the kind of language that, in the words of Socrates posted on a library worker's door, "infects the soul with evil" (26, 51, 87).

Renata knows, of course, that the acquisition of language is a prerequisite, if not for civilization, then certainly for survival: the cave-dwelling Neanderthals with whom she has been infatuated as a girl, she later learns, were "an evolutionary dead end" (74). Yet Renata also knows that the variety of words in Bliondan that signify to Laplanders the wide range of "wrong words" available – white lies, euphemisms, deliberate untruths – all derive from the same root word, "*mentasi,*" for speech (7), making the government's corruption of language for purposes of revenge almost inevitable. Assuming from her study of an extinct Mongolian dialect that the only alternative to such falsehoods is direct eyewitness – something Renata cannot claim for either 9/11 or the two losses that have traumatized her years before – Renata opts more and more for silence in her dealings with others, withholding any information about her past from her lover. Aware that these omissions of truth that constitute silence, "*emenast*" in Bliondan, constitute another form of lying, she rationalizes them as being at least "clean" in a way that "wrong words" are not (169).

These assumptions are put to the test when a call from her uncle's ex-wife trying to locate someone missing from downtown Manhattan also alerts Renata to her relative's whereabouts, and Renata is given the opportunity to exact her own vengeance on the man who has terrorized her family years earlier. Implored by the man dying of lymphoma in a Houston hospital to be the "righteous" person she has always enjoyed being and suffocate him, Renata realizes that helping to "rid the world of evil" in this manner will only "add to the past" in which she already is implicated (201). As the elderly people in her mother's nursing home state when 9/11 is explained as part of a history of the West "shitting on people" who not surprisingly "start shitting back" in response, "Everyone has history" (248). Instead, the linguist who has lived her life believing that "what we haven't named we cannot see or take into account" is forced to recognize that her own failure to act on knowledge of her uncle's crime has stemmed from a deliberate refusal to "frame the words that would make it real" (29–30, 158). This recognition, in turn, leads to another concerning the mute teenage girl wandering around the streets that Renata has taken in after 9/11, thinking she may indeed be the niece who vanished over a decade earlier. The act she justifies as combining Etinoian "*ahmintu*" (yielding to chance) and Hawaiian "*hanai*" (providing shelter to children) is without paperwork (178, 182), no different from the adoption of the child her uncle has tried to broker years ago and dependent on the same implanting of false memories in children, an evil "outrage" for which not even "*prashmen-sti*" has a suitable variant (146). Having thus recognized silence as a form of complicity, Renata ends by reembracing language in the final pages of the novel, albeit in a qualified manner. She communicates with her lover in the Arabic that the State Department has asked her to learn after 9/11, a language he does not understand but in which her request for love he can come close to imagining.

Less hopeful about language is Paul Auster's *Man in the Dark* (2008), which compares words and images in order to assess their respective powers of representation. Set over the course of a single night in 2007, the book opens with August Brill telling himself a story as he has done each night the retired book critic lies sleepless in the Vermont "house of grieving" he shares with his daughter and granddaughter, "making up stories about other worlds" to prevent him, as he admits, "from thinking about the things I would prefer to forget" (71, 2). In this particular story, the World Trade Center still stands, and the Iraq War is nonexistent. But because the America of this parallel world still has "strong historical links" to the America of the real world (50), the US is instead engaged in a second Civil War, spawned by the writings that emerge from the head of a guilt-ridden man named August Brill, whom the story's soldier-protagonist, Owen Brick, is charged with eliminating. Because, as Brill understands, letting one's guard down while telling a single war story allows many others to "come rushing in" (119), the Civil War story he imagines segues into stories he recalls of individuals saved by books during the Second World War and Cold War, and stories about himself and his dead wife, "[t]wo veterans who'd fought in the same war" (159), that form part of the memoir he is meant to be composing.

Yet the man in the dark who tells himself these stories is also a man who has been sitting in the dark for a few months watching movies with his film student granddaughter who needs their images for her own purposes of "distraction" (166), a practice that inevitably leads to discussions about the relative merits of words and images. Brill contends that books "force you to give something back to them, to exercise your intelligence and imagination" (15); Katya counters with those "[i]nanimate objects" that comprise the "language of film" (16) – a bundle of sheets in *The Bicycle Thief* (1948), a watch in *Tokyo Story* (1953), a hairpin in *The World of Apu* (1959) – that make words unnecessary in expressing human emotion or conveying societies on the brink of collapse. When Auster finally discloses that the inanimate object that has inspired Brill's story of American society on the verge of collapse is the head of Katya's former boyfriend shown in close-up on the Internet after being severed by the men who have taken him hostage in Iraq, there can be little doubt about the relative powers of words and images or the curative prospects of Brill and Katya collaborating to turn the tales he tells himself during sleepless nights into films. The son of two painters who appeals to Brill because he reads books, Titus only goes to Iraq as a civilian contractor to experience "the big rotten world" in order to be a better writer (173). Having known in advance that his "words would have no effect" in dissuading a young man of uncertain talent from pursuing a course as foolishly romantic as it is unwarranted (171), Brill is left with a final image of the young man who runs off "to redeem himself in his own eyes" getting his eyes stabbed out on camera (174).

Graphic narratives, predicated on a nonsynchronous presentation of verbal and visual (Chute, "Comics" 452), address this disparity in ways especially well-suited to an event whose images were repeatedly compared to those of a Hollywood disaster film, if not perpetrated with the production of such images in mind (Baudrillard 27–30; Žižek 15–17). When Jay Cantor and James Romberger thus trace the origins of terrorism in *Aaron and Ahmed: A Love Story* (2011) with respect to those bits of cultural programming that evolutionary biologist Richard Dawkins terms "memes," they portray the West's "magic words" ("war on terror," "clash of civilizations") and the East's "holy power words" (too holy to be quoted) that work on minds the way the "special words" of DNA work on cells as requiring images to be triggered (42, 100). In the case of the psychiatrist who journeys to Pakistan in the company of a Guantánamo Bay prisoner to investigate what makes suicide bombers willing to kill themselves only to become a suicide bomber himself, the image is as small as that contained on a gum wrapper. Distinguished by various ways of rendering temporal movement spatially – panels separated by gutters that rupture time, superimposed panels that juxtapose different times – graphic narratives also prove well-suited to depicting an event alternately perceived as halting time or too muddled to reconstruct in time but still requiring temporal contextualization. To that end, the time lines that display the "simultaneous histories" of the four hijacked planes in Sid Jacobson and Ernie Colón's *The 9/11 Report: A Graphic Adaptation* (2006), which show flight attendants reporting the first hijacking at 8:19 but American Airlines 77 not taking off until 8:20 and United 93 not taking off until 8:42 due to delays, offer a clear and trenchant critique of the FAA, NORAD, and airlines involved, whose failed communications resulted in deaths that might have been prevented (6–25). Perhaps most important, unlike photographs that presuppose accuracy by virtue of a presumed transparency, graphic narratives drawn by hand expose the limits of their own representation.

No text employs these qualities to better effect than *In the Shadow of No Towers* (2004), in which Art Spiegelman works from his belief that "[c]omics pages are architectural structures" formed by narrative panels that act like "stories of a building" ("Comic Supplement") to portray the "pivotal image" of the specific building that has haunted him since 9/11: the "looming north tower's glowing bones just before it vaporized" ("Sky"). So traumatized is Spiegelman by this image he still sees years later that he rejects the sequential narrative of comic books for a collage of ten oversized single plates of vibrant colors and garish styles to convey the fractured thoughts of his "unhinged" mind ("Sky"). Yet so resistant to his own painterly abilities is that image that he must resort to computer-generated pixels to represent a leitmotif of disintegration that first appears as a tower vertically framing both sides of the opening plate but broken into separate panels that depict its collapse from differently skewed angles (Versluys, *Out* 69). This traumatic unhinging that leaves Spiegelman feeling that "Time stands still" and fearing "the sky is falling" (2) – the perpetual nature of which is grammatically reinforced by a tower portrayed as "glowing" (2, 4), a world "ending" (2, 9), even Spiegelman himself "falling" through holes in a head whose brain is "missing" (6, 2) – is not just a function of his living close to the World Trade Center or bearing direct witness to its attack. The text, in fact, goes to great lengths to show what Spiegelman does not see (the first plane hitting the north tower, the south tower collapsing, people jumping to their deaths), in addition to what is obscured from his sight and what he only sees as mediated by television. It is instead the way the noxious air of Lower Manhattan recalls what his Holocaust-survivor father has described as the "indescribable" odor of Auschwitz that prompts Spiegelman to reappropriate the image of Jews as mice previously employed in *Maus* (1986, 1991) to suggest a victimization first instilled by parents who admonished him "to always keep [his] bags packed" in response to their familial wound (3, "Sky").

As Spiegelman also makes clear, this renewed victimization is perpetrated by the US government as well as Al Qaeda. For the president whose own wound is "reopened" by surgeons, as stated in the September 11, 1901, headline from the *New York World* reproduced on the book's flyleaf, is the same president, William McKinley, who mounted the Spanish-American War (fomented, ironically, by the two newspapers that introduced comic strips as weapons in their own circulation war) that led to "America's first colonialist adventure" ("Comic Supplement"). That three-month-long war Spiegelman directly connects – in an inversion of Wilson's defense of the First World War – to the Iraq "war to begin all wars" mounted by George W. Bush's "unelected government" (7). Having thus condensed a century's history of war into one ongoing war, Spiegelman marks the three-year anniversary of the event that sparked the "war on terror" with two new twin towers featured on his final plate (10), buildings that dwarf the pixelated images of the actual towers shown fading to black in the lower right-hand corner and reduce to naught the tiny plane hovering in the sky-blue background. In this resurrection, the idiomatic shoe waiting to be dropped, shown earlier as a single shoe suspended above fleeing crowds in an ad for "Jihad Brand Footware" (1), is replaced by a hailstorm of cowboy boots raining on fleeing mice as the transformation of New York City into a stage set for the Republican National Convention completes the translation of 9/11 from "Tragedy" to "Travesty."

To the extent that Amy Waldman's *The Submission* (2011) depicts the outcry that erupts when the design selected for a 9/11 memorial turns out to have been submitted by a Muslim American architect, the book continues this sense of travesty. ("It's Maya Lin all over again. But worse" [17]). Yet it also complicates the question of representing 9/11 by focusing on a medium distinguished by practical use as well as aesthetic contemplation and an artifact in which public space and private imagination necessarily combine. Or not. The conflicts surrounding the relatively quick move to build a memorial at Ground Zero – sacred ground in that the place for commemoration was also the place of devastation, urban ground requiring enhanced commercial viability for its renewal – only led to more territorial disputes after the Lower Manhattan Development Corporation split the site's rebuilding into two parts and gave priority to Daniel Libeskind's "Memory Foundations" master plan into which any design for a memorial was later to be fit (a fact omitted from both the "guiding principles" and "project elements" listed in the memorial competition's mission statement).

None of this concerns Mohammad Khan, whose design for the Garden – an element initially missing from the "Reflecting Absence" design that won the actual competition – is chosen by the jury in the book's opening pages, its emphasis on rejuvenation enabling it to beat out the darker-themed Void despite protests that gardens are not part of the American architectural vernacular. To him, the walled rectangular garden with raised pavilion, its order of straight lines and right angles a response to the disorder inflicted on 9/11, is modeled on the grid that is the "quintessential modernist form" and a discipline, geometry, that "doesn't belong to a single culture" (269). In much the same way, the aesthete who belongs only to the American Institute of Architects views himself as belonging to no single culture. The son of secular Indian parents who immigrated to America and "made modernity their religion" (28), he refuses to "traffic in labels" (64). When pressed, he identifies as "American" but defines his community as limited to "people like me," people "who are rational" (261, 194) – even though the commission he seeks is for an edifice experienced as "not a fully rational thing," as Paul Goldenberger writes when describing the final paradox of designing a "solid to make us feel the void" (209).

Not surprisingly, such naïve identity politics ends in that community shrinking to one after the public gets wind of Mo's name and a circus of self-serving agendas (a governor with presidential aspirations, a Muslim American organization looking for its own Rosa Parks), ambitions (a rabid talk-show host intent on ratings, a hack journalist looking for bylines), and needs (a dead fireman's brother without home or job, a jury chairperson retired early by his bank, a 9/11 suburban widow with a Harvard Law degree collecting dust) results in Mo withdrawing his design and making the familiar retreat back to the South Asian "more promising land" that has never been his homeland (293). Far more interesting is Waldman's portrayal of Mo's aesthetics as not just equally naïve in a time when it is counterterrorism experts rather than men like Gropius and Breuer who consult on overseas fortresses of "Standard Embassy Design" but completely wrongheaded in being a narcissism unconnected to time or place (46). Unburdened by any anxiety of influence because he acknowledges no influence stronger than his own imagination (good architects at most "quote" and never "plagiarize" [267]), Mo stubbornly refuses to compromise or comment on those elements of the Garden that architecture critics cite as having appeared in gardens across the Islamic world for centuries. He continues to do so when his Garden is likened to an Islamic martyrs' paradise after experts note the way those ancient gardens conceived for agricultural ends became so verdant as to represent the Qur'an's paradisiacal "gardens beneath which rivers flow" (116). He even does so after a scholar defends him at a public hearing by reminding attendees that the twin towers so deeply mourned displayed elements of Islamic design, evidence of a long-standing cross-fertilization between East and West.

It is not until the final pages of the novel that Waldman reveals the chance event that both inspires Mo's Garden and offers a more nuanced meaning to her own title: an inadvertent detour into the slums of Kabul while on a business trip that leaves Mo staring at a patch of green from an outhouse window and then venturing into the sixteenth-century Bagh-e-Babur, or

Babur's garden, where he joins a man in prayer whose "truest submission" comes from having "forgotten himself" (281). His own relinquishment doesn't last very long, however. An epilogue set in 2023 features Mo, now a "global citizen" of Mumbai and the subject of a retrospective on (ironically) his own influence on others (286), being filmed for a documentary amidst those objets d'art that "express his faith more than any ritual or text" (293). As that epilogue also suggests, the most eloquent memorial to 9/11 is provided not by the Garden of Flags that finally is erected in Lower Manhattan or the Middle Eastern pleasure garden in which Mo's original Garden eventuates in modified form. That honor belongs to the cairn of pebbles left in a corner of that private garden by the son of a man killed on 9/11, his anonymous tribute recalling the anonymous selection process that sets the book's plot in motion. For the America portrayed by Waldman does not have a climate hospitable to cultivating gardens of any sort. "I think a garden is right," asserts a Bangladeshi widow at the public hearing to debate Mo's design, "because that is what America is," a place where people come to take root and mingle their various traditions (231). But, as Waldman understands, getting a patch of earth to bloom depends less on the "creating of a garden" than on the "sustaining" of a garden (297). And in this inability to nurture the life that seeks sustenance from its soil, America fails miserably. "Don't feel bad," Mo's mother tells him when he phones to say he is withdrawing from the memorial competition (293). "Eden, paradise – all the best gardens are imaginary."

Chapter 5

Smooth Worlds

"They're part of the mirror-world," Cayce says.... "That's why you noticed that vent. They invented that here, probably, and made it here. This was an industrial nation. Buy a pair of scissors, you got British scissors.... Same thing in Japan. All their bits and pieces were different, from the ground up."

"I see what you mean, but I don't think it's going to be that way much longer. Not if the world's Bigends keep at it: no borders, pretty soon there's no mirror to be on the other side of."

– William Gibson, *Pattern Recognition* (2003)

For William Gibson, a writer whose fiction typically is set in the near future, "pretty soon" is the operative phrase in this passage taken from his first book to take place in the post–9/11 present and distinguished by the addition of post-1989 Russia to its locales. In Japan's "empire of signs," to recall Roland Barthes's 1970 characterization, visitors deplaning at Narita are greeted by Coca-Cola ads pulsing on huge screens, and confused tourists in Tokyo can locate their bearings by way of Gap billboards. Moscow sports a city center crowned by McDonald's golden arches. London is launching a Soviet yogurt drink purchased by Suntory and hawked by a British pop star whose face appears in promos for all three countries. Starbucks, of course, is everywhere.

Within this expansion of *Neuromancer* (1984) Sprawl from Boston-Atlanta to the entire globe, provenance no longer has much relevance. The "simulacra of simulacra of simulacra" that is Tommy Hilfiger is a "diluted tincture of Ralph Lauren," itself a diluted version of Brooks Brothers, itself a dilution of Jermyn Street and Savile Row (17). Nor is there any trace of the particular histories to which such commodities refer or suggestion of one-of-a-kind uniqueness. A damaged Buzz Rickson's flying jacket – a Japanese imitation "more real" than the American MA-1 garment it emulates (11) – is replaced by ordering a new one: "History erased via the substitution of an identical object" (194). If, in fact, objects are the main object in an economy in which far more energy goes into marketing products than making products. As Hubertus Bigend, the "nominal Belgian" who founds the "post-geographic" agency of Blue Ant and a subsidiary named Trans devoted to product mention (6), recognizes, "[i]t's about transferring information, but at the same time about a certain lack of specificity" (63), the model of which is viral and the goal the reduction of all experience "to price-point variations on the same thing" (341).

It is no wonder that Cayce Pollard, the freelance "coolhunter" that Bigend hires as, in effect, a one-woman R&D department (2) – identifying styles that later get "-ized" in all the appropriate ways ("productized," "monetized," "rationalized") and consulted on the logos into which those styles get crystallized – feels "complicit" in whatever it is "that dissolves the membranes between mirror-worlds" (194). The daughter of a Cold Warrior security expert who goes missing that day in September on which the perimeters that were his *raison d'être* were so easily breached, Cayce grows up aware of the specifics of bipolar politics and distinct nation-states. Even if she intellectually does not understand the reason for her allergy to certain logos – as opposed, significantly, to her neutrality toward national icons – the bodily revulsion induced by Michelin's Bibendum, the elephantine man employed by a corporation that marketed World War I battlefields even before the war had ended (Link 217), suggests otherwise. The one exception to Cayce's imperviousness to patriotic emblems, Nazi Germany's swastika, appalls precisely because the "scary excess of design talent" it displays is directly connected to the "historical evil" it perpetuates (263). When Cayce, in the book's last paragraphs, travels to the Stalingrad dig site beneath which bones of German and Russian soldiers have melded, her furious attempts to excavate a past smoothed over by mafiosi and magnates joined in dubious ventures are a form of atonement, even if she does not know if the tears she sheds for "her century" are for "the one past or the one present" (356).

Such uncertainty, no doubt, reflects the fact that the processes of globalization that Gibson depicts seem singularly lacking in direction or control, resulting in what Anthony Giddens has called a "runaway world" (20), governed by recklessness and risk. It also reflects the fact that, for whatever agreement exists on the elements that contribute to those processes (multinational corporations, footloose capital, new communications technology, information networks), globalization itself – a term first used in the 1960s–1970s to denote a phenomenon whose origins can be traced back to 1000 CE (Modelski 42) – remains rather amorphous in its meaning. Ursula K. Heise provides a helpful overview of the dominant positions taken (4): globalization as a function of modernization (Anthony Giddens, Ulrich

Beck); globalization as neoliberal economic culmination (Immanuel Wallerstein, David Harvey); globalization as uneven economic, political, and cultural realization (James Clifford, Néstor García Canclini). From such variations has emerged a host of related terms: "deterritorialization" (Arjun Appadurai), "mondialisation" (Jacques Derrida), "glocalization" (Roland Robertson), "cosmodernism" (Christian Moraru), "oneworldedness" (Emily Apter), "planetarity" (Gayatri Chakravorty Spivak), to name but a few. As with 9/11, beyond dispute as an event but bitterly debated as a limit event, how much the evidence on display signals new processes or an intensification of existing ones depends on how much differences in degree signal differences in kind. Does an increase in international trade evince a more pronounced version of the *belle époque* (1890–1914) market or a new world market? Have the rise of multinationals, outsourcing of production, and emergence of a postindustrial economy merely eroded or eliminated the sovereignty of nation-states? Does technology's compression of time and space lead to a renewed importance of place as a source of low-wage labor for economic operations or place as a locale with traditions that counter homogenization? Has America "sort of ended at check-in," as a Gibson character writing from Charles de Gaulle quips (*Pattern* 310), or has America, as the ubiquity of Coke suggests, transcended all borders?

Viewed in light of such vexed issues, Gibson's prognosis may be less dire than initially assumed. However much Poland looks like Kansas from the air, it is Pepsi and not Coke that residents of the former Soviet Union drink, evidence of the "but-really-it's-like thing" ("but really it's like Vienna, except it isn't, and really it's like Stockholm, but it's not") that Cayce experiences when confronted with "serious cultural novelty" (276). A US Army parka spotted in London is "recontextualized" by virtue of the RAF roundel embroidered on its back, the British military symbol itself "re-purposed" via "cross-cultural echo" (142). Doc Martens are "de-recontextualized" from fashion footwear back to the inexpensive shoes of their original design (235). Perhaps most important, a Claymore mine produced in an American armory that eventually finds its way into the brain of a young Russian years after the Cold War – the global intruding into the local in a most intimate way – leaves behind a T-shaped fragment from which damage springs the film footage that turns those who pursue its frames on the Web like a Holy Grail into a worldwide community. In so devoting themselves to the castoffs of global destruction, surveillance video remade as art by way of lodged ordnance, this community of Waste Not distinguishes itself from the lost souls of W.A.S.T.E. in Pynchon's *Lot 49*, exchanging paranoia for purpose.

The novels discussed in the sections that follow are indeed "fictions of globalization," as James Annesley claims (74), works that often query the very phenomenon they represent – in this case, novels whose interrogations of what Hardt and Negri term a "smooth world" steadily proceed in the direction of increasing striation (xii, 332–36). The first group, by Don DeLillo and Dave Eggers, concern those information flows that bypass geography and make touchable money a thing of the past, but question the role that the US has played in its own decentering, in turning Tom Wolfe's 1987 "Master of the Universe" into an endangered, if not extinct, species (*Bonfire* 12). The second, by Joseph O'Neill, Colum McCann, and Teju Cole, focus on migrants joined by the very specific geography of New York City into a community of the "unhomely" (Bhabha 141), as portrayed by authors who have immigrated to that part of the US themselves and made it their postnational home. The third, by Gary Shteyngart, Yelena Akhtiorskaya, and Anya Ulinich, reflect the sensibility of the immigrant writers perhaps most shaped by the collapse of the First and Second World binary so pivotal to globalization, those Russian-born writers who convey the tension between a US no different from the Soviet Union and a US that, for all its flaws, is celebrated as vastly superior to the Soviet Union. The last, by Barbara Kingsolver and Karen Tei Yamashita, typify the large group of novelists whose environmental concerns make a planet-centered as opposed to a nation-centered perspective seem "open and shut," as Lawrence Buell asserts (227), but whose advocacy attaches itself to the local more than the global, based on their recognition, as Buell concedes, that "there's simply no possibility that the nation form, however much nation-centrism be deplored or deconstructed, will go away any time soon" (228).

Smooth Operators

Arguably the smoothest operator in the American fiction of globalization is Eric Michael Packer, the billionaire assets manager of Don DeLillo's *Cosmopolis* (2003), who negotiates fluctuations of the yen on a single day in April 2000 as his limo negotiates traffic in crosstown Manhattan. A self-styled "world citizen with a New York pair of balls" by virtue of trading in any and all currencies (26), the twenty-eight-year-old Packer is as divorced from national geography as he is from physical materiality: "three-dimensional" dollars signify "everything he'd left behind or never encountered" (64); the words "office" and "computer" sound "outdated" and "dumb" (15, 104). So devoted is he to a market to which there appears to be "no outside" (90), in which "[m]oney is talking to itself" via sacred flows of information (77), that he has no response to his wife's query about where the money of hers that he has confessed to stealing and losing on the market has actually gone. All he desires, much like the console cowboys in Gibson's early fiction who yearn to exchange the corporeal meat of their bodies for the transcendence afforded by cyberspace, is to be one with those information flows himself: "It would be the master thrust of cyber-capital, to extend the human experience toward infinity as a medium for corporate growth and investment, for the accumulation of profits and vigorous reinvestment" (207).

That Packer suffers excruciating pain after shooting a bullet into his own hand in an attempt to outman a disgruntled employee turned would-be assassin dispels any such notions near the end of the novel. That Packer is outmaneuvered throughout the book by the yen that keeps rising despite his having bet against it to speculate in high-yield stocks shows his limited mastery over the market itself, whose asymmetrical tics and quirks when graphed resemble, ironically, the shape of his own prostate. However much his losses contribute to the failure of those institutions with which his wealth is linked, resulting in a "whole system [that] was in danger" (116), it is in fact a "system that's out of control" itself that is responsible for the "[h]ysteria at high speeds" – nanoseconds, zeptoseconds, yoctoseconds – that distinguishes the opening of the twenty-first century (85). But unlike the "hysteria" that led Henry Adams to dub the onset of the twentieth century a "Nunc Age," encapsulated in a frantic New York City in which "[p]ower seemed to have outgrown its servitude and to have asserted its freedom" (499), the result of continuity having "snapped" in the year 1900 (457), this new century's frenzy is the product of a spiraling that comes from too much having been connected.

Just how lacking in control that system is becomes even more apparent when this work published three years into that new century is compared with the DeLillo novel published three years before the end of the previous one. A sprawling, encyclopedic text that spans the early 1950s to the early 1990s, and mixes actual figures (J. Edgar Hoover, Lenny Bruce, Jackie Gleason) with invented ones (Jesuits in Minnesota and nuns in the South Bronx, bombardiers in Vietnam and bombheads in New Mexico, hipsters in Manhattan and highway killers in Texas) to provide an under- or counterhistory to the official accounts of the second half of the twentieth century, *Underworld* (1997) introduces the United States as a nation "that's in a hurry to make the future," its "burgeoning economy" based on a three-word mandate (39): "Consume or die" (287). Yet *Underworld* portrays consumption as a function of specific brand names, the "venerated emblems" that are "easier to identify than the names of battlefields or dead presidents" (39). If those seemingly innocuous items produced also are portrayed as connected – as is "everything" according to the book's refrain – to the decidedly more destructive implements of war, the Cold War that joins them is defined by a balance of binaries.

It is that balance that offsets the terror of nuclear annihilation that pervades the novel, beginning with the stunning set-piece that opens it, in which the October 3, 1951, battle between the New York Giants and Brooklyn Dodgers for the National League pennant is juxtaposed against the US-USSR arms race, and the Shot Heard Round the World joins Bobby Thomson's winning home run and the Soviet Union's testing of an atomic bomb. From this prologue emerges a series of pairings that counter waste with weapons, rubber kitchen gloves and plutonium protection gloves, orange juice and Agent Orange, Watts Towers and Twin Towers. Evidence, on the one hand, of "some horrific system of connections in which you can't tell the difference between one thing and another ... because they are made by the same people in the same way and ultimately refer to the same thing" (446), such twinnings also provide reassurance, on the other hand, that the system whose connections may operate "at levels outside your comprehension" is still one whose dynamics are unvarying (465). "Power meant something thirty, forty years ago," recalls the artist who incorporates abandoned B-52 bombers into a landscape painting that uses the landscape itself as canvas. "It was stable, it was focused, it was a tangible thing. . . . And it held us together, the Soviets and us" (76). And because it may not be as all-encompassing in that Cold War period as the book's refrain suggests – the New York City blackout of 1965 can signal a "whole linked system down" or "not linked sufficiently perhaps" (634) – there remains room for acts of cultural critique. Graffiti artists in 1974 can "vandalize" the same eyeballs control of which the advertising Mad Men of 1961 use to "run the world" (435, 530). A pennant-defining baseball of 1951 can be deemed "not for sale" by the young African American boy who claims it (55).

No such possibility exists in the early 1990s of the book's epilogue, "Das Kapital." When Nick Shay, the waste management operator who serves as the book's primary protagonist, journeys to Kazakhstan to broker a deal with a company that trades in nuclear explosions for cash and has an army to protect its assets, he learns just how much the undoing of the "balance of power" and "balance of terror" that was the Cold War has ushered in an era in which "[t]hings have no limits," as the landscape artist who once was his lover asserts near the novel's beginning (76). It is in Kazakhstan that Nick is forced to recognize that the territorial expansion by which he used to conceive of vast empires has been supplanted by the miniaturization of computer chips, the same technology responsible for the Internet in which "[e]verything is connected" and where, in DeLillo's rendering, J. Edgar Hoover achieves his apotheosis as his twin, Sister Edgar, experiences the "grip of systems" in a "world without end" (825). At the same time, it is in Kazakhstan's Medical Institute and Museum of Misshapens that Nick is confronted with the human proof that disposing of hazardous waste by putting it into the ground and vaporizing it does not destroy nuclear waste but increases it, the superfluity upsetting any earlier balance between waste and weapons. By the end of the book, then, it hardly matters that Nick dutifully separates his household trash according to official guidelines so that it can be "sorted, compressed and baled, [and] transformed in the end to square-edged units, products again, wire-bound and smartly stacked and ready to be marketed" (809). The man who once made his living arranging global transports for a company named Waste Containment now lives in a time in which the invention of ways to make synthetic feces precludes any assumptions about containment. No longer a global "[p]oint of reference" (170), the nation in which he makes his home loses its center to become, in the words of *Falling Man*, the "center of its own shit," distinguished most by its own "irrelevance" (191).

Perhaps nowhere is that irrelevance better embodied than in the figure of Alan Clay, the "virtually broke" American waiting in Dave Eggers's *A Hologram for the King* (2012) to pitch a virtual product to a Middle Eastern monarch who has not been seen in the mirage that is King Abdullah Economic City (KAEC) for eighteen months (4). Such geographical displacement from home, of course, is hardly unusual in Eggers's writing, which progressively incorporates more and more of the globe into its purview. The memoir introduced as *A Heartbreaking Work of Staggering Genius* (2000) follows the move of Eggers and his younger brother from their home in Illinois to California after the deaths of their parents. The updated road trip of *You Shall Know Our Velocity!* (2002) traces the week-long journey of two friends intent on dispensing $32,000 while making their way around the world. The autobiography that asks *What Is the What* (2006) depicts the flight of Valentino Achak Deng from Sudan to Ethiopia to Kenya and finally to Atlanta, a forced escape from a twenty-two-year civil war (1983–2005) that Eggers presents as not only an internal conflict between north and south, Khartoum and SPLA, Arabs and Dinka, but the product of a "web of money and power and oil" that involves a host of nations (notably, Britain, Egypt, US, and China) and an extended colonialist history (438).

The situation that leaves Alan Clay at fifty-four sweating in a tent by the Red Sea in 2010, however, differs from those in Eggers's earlier works in two important ways. First, it reverses the roles of donor and supplicant. If the story of *You Shall Know Our Velocity!* that serves as a "neat and tidy allegory" for any kind of intervention meant to redress economic inequities focuses on two Americans whose altruism is premised on recipients not asking for money but docilely accepting money in acknowledgment of the giver's power (274), it still ends by portraying the act of giving – however compromised or self-serving – as a "sacrament," an "outward symbolic act of an inward grace," that it is incumbent upon those with more to perform on behalf of those with less, and leaves no doubt as to which citizens of which country have the greatest obligation (287). So bankrupt is the America of Alan Clay, by contrast, that his Transcendentalist neighbor freezes to death after deliberately walking into a lake because budget cuts have prevented any of the responders called from learning the rescue techniques needed to save him. (So much for Walden Pond.) Second, it portrays the supplicant – in this case the American suppli-cant – as complicit in his own predicament. Alan is overseas pitching a teleconference system for an IT supplier that gets its lenses from Korea because the man who helped move Schwinn from Illinois to Mississippi to Hungary to Taiwan to China in an attempt at more "efficient" bicycle produc-tion that bypassed American unions ended up with a junk product and a process that was more efficient without himself involved (*Hologram* 188–89). Glass for the new World Trade Center is being made in China because the Pittsburgh company that invented the blast-resistant product licensed the patent to firms overseas that could make it for less. No wonder the Statue of Liberty is rumored to be moving back to France, as a drunk next to Alan on a plane quips. When the whole world is heeding the call of CEO Jack Welch to think of manufacturing as a barge circling the globe for the cheapest possible conditions, even Lady Liberty is looking for a better deal.

What Alan, who cut his teeth selling Fuller Brushes door-to-door at a time when an exchange of names was presumed enough to form a bond with consumers, is looking for in Saudi Arabia is more than a commission that will help pay his daughter's college fees, though. He seeks evidence that beyond that Economic City built solely to attract foreign investment (to the extent that three buildings constitute a city), the "triumph of systems designed to thwart all human contact, human reason, personal discretion and decision making" is not yet complete (139). What Alan fails to realize is that these values were already obsolete when attributed in 1949 to Willy Loman, who made "well liked" a measure of self-worth and modeled a salesman's death on the number of people that attended the funeral of one who expired in a Pullman car (A. Miller 97). The first prospective client on whose door a younger Alan knocks marvels that Fuller Brush salesmen are "still out there" (*Hologram* 72).

Such ignorance of this economic past merely embarrasses Alan while in the Middle East: he thrills to hear that his driver's father sells sandals in Jeddah's Old City only to discover that the man whose "clean" and "honest" work recalls his own father's work at Stride Rite has never made a shoe in his life but only marked up shoes made in Yemen that he buys wholesale (222). His obliviousness to the political realities of the area's present, however, jeopardizes lives. A jokester who "had never felt in danger anywhere" his assignments have taken him (9), Alan thinks nothing of telling a Saudi who sees him photographing the countryside that he is doing freelance work for the CIA, the humor of which escapes the driver whose family makes its home in that remote outpost. Even worse, Alan thinks nothing of using those surroundings as a tableau on which to address his male inadequacies. Too young for the "good war" of his father and spared the Vietnam War because he drops out of college after the 1973 end of conscription (256), Alan yearns to test his manhood on the Sarawat range frontier on which he pictures himself perched with a rifle in his hands. When he finally takes the shot during the wolf hunt that serves as an analogue for the US presence in the region, compelled by a "waiting" that – like his time in KAEC – "must end" (260), the bumbling Leatherstocking almost kills a shepherd.

It is only when Alan stops trying to heal himself and submits to the ministrations of others that he can begin to reverse the path – his own and, by extension, his nation's – that has led to such acts of careless overcompensation. That submission begins with his decision upon his return from the mountains to have the lump on his neck that protrudes from his spine (which he attacks with various implements throughout the book to excise what he suspects is the cause of his spinelessness) surgically removed. This procedure literally exposes a vulnerable Alan, lying naked on his stomach beneath a sheet, to a medical team composed of doctors from China, Germany, Italy, and Russia, and led by a woman whose mixed Saudi, Lebanese, Swiss, Greek, and Dutch ancestry makes Alan, with his amorphous origins, feel "like a less necessary species" (287). It continues with Alan recognizing that, however much the "dreaming's being done elsewhere for now," as an American architect who cannot remember the last time he worked in the US states (143), the opportunities for dreaming still exist. The man-made canal that runs through the dusty city of KAEC that "might never be" offers proof of a "bewildering beauty [brought] into a place in which it did not belong" (283, 284). It ends with Alan, the company he represents having been outbid by the Chinese, submitting his own skills to the Saudi in charge of KAEC's operations, aware that the offer "to help" the American that is extended by the young man with the posh British accent depends upon the man's amnesia as much as his goodwill (312).

(New) New York, New York

Among the authors who have zigzagged around the globe prior to settling in New York City, few can rival Joseph O'Neill. Born in Ireland but raised in the Netherlands after migrating with his family through South Africa, Mozambique, Syria, Turkey, and Iran, O'Neill is a self-described "mongrel," as he writes in *Blood-Dark Track* (2001), an "outsider" belonging to no one nation or culture (244, 65). As the grandson of two men incarcerated by the British during World War II, however – one for being an IRA member, the other for being an alleged German spy – he is acutely aware of the importance of citizenship and the duties attendant upon it. Those duties, as his investigation into his grandfathers' lives and the parallels between his Irish and Turkish relations make clear, are only partly a function of birthplace. They approximate much more the ancient concept of *xenia* or "guest-friendship," portrayed in *The Dog* (2014) as the obligation of "exercising for the guest's benefit the power of shelter" and extending the family home's "relief from the outside" to the nation as home (150). Looked at from this perspective, the expat "abracadabrapolis" of Dubai fails miserably in providing mere denizenship to the thousands of stateless bidoons whose residency depends on their continued employment (*Dog* 11); when the narrator's assistant is fired, the man has no choice but to accept the "unrefusable offer of citizenship" granted by the Union of the Comoros, where he can live on $1.25 a day while extracting the oil used in Chanel No. 5 perfume (236). Yet no less blameless are the men in O'Neill's family memoir who inure themselves to the contingent nature of citizenship, to the fact that what separates majority from minority is often context and time. Blind to the fact that the Protestant admiral marked for death by the IRA in 1936 is descended from a family that came to Ireland in 1692 to escape persecution by Catholics in Scotland, O'Neill's great-uncle shoots, clear of conscience because "morally self-sparing compartmentalization" prevents him from seeing his act as a sectarian killing (*Blood-Dark* 329). Bound by the "politics of good citizenship" to a Turkish nation-state that demands compliance from its ethnic and religious minorities (312), O'Neill's Syrian Christian grandfather silently colludes in the persecution of Armenians; opting for neutrality in order to play the grand hotelier, he succumbs to the "misconception about the responsibilities of neutrality" and ends up arrested while traveling to Palestine to buy lemons (318).

In awakening the phlegmatic Hans van den Broek to the obligations of postnational citizenship in *Netherland* (2008), New York City plays a pivotal role. An equities analyst born in The Hague, Hans arrives in New York in 1998 thinking that making millions is "essentially a question of walking down the street" and entranced by the two "exhilaratory skyward figures" that form the island's "most beautiful sight" (91, 92). All of that changes when the collapse of those towers on 9/11 and imminent war with Iraq cause Hans's British wife to return to London with their son, so appalled is she at the prospect of living in an "ideologically diseased" nation while married to a "political-ethical idiot" of a husband (95, 100). And O'Neill does not disagree. The DMV employee that forces Hans to get a new green card because of a minor spelling discrepancy illustrates in miniature the "unjust, indifferent powers" that are about to be unleashed in the Middle East by a US that later is likened to a McDonald's float that runs amuck during a Thanksgiving Day parade (68) – a nation all the more dangerous for appearing to have "mislaid its power" (193), as confirmed by the 2003 black-out, yet prone to such propensities from its inception. As O'Neill informs readers in one of the many historical details that punctuate the text, the bald eagle adopted by Congress as the great seal of the nation was opposed by Benjamin Franklin, who preferred the turkey to a bird he considered a scavenger.

But O'Neill also provides an alternative to such bullying in the community of other immigrants that Hans encounters once he starts playing cricket after his wife's departure and discovers in New York's outer boroughs the "new City of Friends" imagined by Whitman in the book's epigraph. Chief among these is Chuck Ramkissoon. A "rare bird" from Trinidad (251), Chuck guides Hans through that urban "miscellany" of kosher sushi and curried goat, and awakens him to those relics of the city's Dutch past that link Yankee and Netherlander (146). Yet Chuck also reveals the contradictions of having unquestioningly adopted the city, and the country it emblematizes, as his own. A businessman for whom "complication represents an opportunity" (57), Chuck opportunistically gets Chinese and Jamaicans to play the weh-weh game he runs as banker, hires Bangladeshis to do the labor that leaves him as contractor-boss white-faced from plaster debris, even terrorizes employees with a baseball bat when the occasion warrants. A sportsman also devoted to a game that inculcates civility and civic responsibility, Chuck promotes cricket, a sport played in New York since the 1770s, as the "first modern team sport in America" and pitches a New York Cricket Club international arena as offering the "crash course in democracy" that will enable America to fulfill its destiny (101, 211).

What that destiny is in the twenty-first century remains to be seen, how-ever. Cricket's link to Britain's past empire exposes the flaws in Chuck's political reasoning: the first thing he does to turn the nature preserve he leases, and through which hundreds of migrant birds travel on the Atlantic flyway, into a cricket field is "kill everything with Roundup" (83). And the economic reasoning that assumes a New York arena will propel a faltering US into the future is sunk by Internet markets and media coverage that make the specific locations in which cricket is played wholly irrelevant, as the Indian backer Chuck has sought out recognizes. Unable to adapt to the times, Chuck – Gatsby to Hans's Nick in O'Neill's updating of Fitzgerald's classic – ends up like his prototype dead in the water, the Gowanus Canal in his case. Hans, whose drifting back to his dead mother and lost childhood attests to the past's strong hold over him, realizes that he does not want to join the New York dead when shown the graves behind Brooklyn's Reformed Protestant Dutch church. Unlike his fictional antecedent, then, whose return to the Midwest to seek moral sanctuary betrays a nostalgic longing for that which never was, Hans's return to England and reconciliation with his family signals moral growth. "New York's a very hard place to leave," a colleague warns him on the book's first page (3), and so it is. Hans's final memory of himself and his mother on the Staten Island Ferry as the boat passes Ellis Island to approach the "extraordinary promise" of "two amazingly high towers" conveys beautifully – and movingly – the "wistfulness" he earlier allows as a "respectable, serious condition" (255–56, 179). Yet the scene that precedes this memory, in which Hans approaches the "tattered lawn" of Jubilee Gardens and then looks down upon the "crushed, squashed" once-imperial capital while at the summit of the London Eye (253, 254), displays an understanding that there can be no drifting away from a descent that is inevitable.

Another "international mongrel," by his own admission, Colum McCann cites "elsewhere" when describing where someone like himself who belongs to many different places feels most at home despite having made his home in New York City ("Conversation with Strout" 314). It is that desire for "else-where" that inspires the numerous geographical crossings to and from his native Ireland that the historical and invented figures in *TransAtlantic* (2013) make (177, 289). These crossings, as McCann's title suggests, do not typically involve land, portrayed as unstable and politically contested, but sea and sky, and the journeys that take place through the latter medium are governed by the dual meaning of flight as escape and flight as airborne elevation. In this sense, the 1919 flight of John Alcock and Arthur Brown from Newfoundland to Ireland that opens the book provides less a "unification of the continents," as its promoters claim, and more an alternative way of connecting continents already unified by the carnage of World War I (19), as the modified Vickers Vimy being used proves. Navigated by an Englishman born in Scotland to American parents, someone who already thinks of himself as "a man of the mid-Atlantic" and who would "happily live in constant flight" (14), it also introduces the first of many figures in whom migration and mixed heritage combine. George Mitchell, who flies almost two hundred times during the three years he works on the 1998 Good Friday Accords, is the son of a Lebanese immigrant mother and ethnic Irish father. Tomas, the young maths student shot twenty years before that treaty takes effect, is a child of Newfoundland, Holland, Norway, Belfast, London, St. Louis, and Dublin – his family tree formed from "twigs taken from everywhere, bits and pieces, leaves and branches, crossing and crisscrossing" (261).

This happiness that comes from having multiple homes is to be distinguished, however, from the precariousness of having no one home, as McCann's earlier portrayal of Rudolf Nureyev – another man "in flight" by virtue of ballet jumps that keep him aloft (193) – in *Dancer* (2003) attests: the constant travel that leaves the aesthete reveling in being "stateless" is what makes him vulnerable to the totalitarian Soviet state that tries him in absentia as a traitor after his defection (159). That being said, negotiating the "middle space," as Alcock and Brown do, comes with its own set of risks: notably the prospect of "flying blind" (*TransAtlantic* 29), of "go[ing] up in a plane knowing, sometimes, that not all of you is going to come down" (215) – or where. When Alcock and Brown land in Ireland in 1919, the first thing they see is British soldiers with rifles. When Frederick Douglass arrives in 1845, the fugitive slave looking to buy his own freedom finds wage slavery akin to plantation slavery and religious oppression akin to racial oppression. Conversely, when the fictional Lily Duggan decides to "try New York" after walking from Dublin to Cork that same year (89), the fugitive maid fleeing a family to which she "as good as belong[ed]" – as in "[o]wned" (188) – awakens on her first day in New York to the scream of a horse being beaten with a truncheon.

The characters in McCann's 9/11 novel, *Let the Great World Spin* (2009), awaken in New York to a very different kind of spectacle on August 7, 1974: the sight of Philippe Petit suspended in the sky as he walks a tightrope between the towers of the World Trade Center. Yet rather than focusing on the airborne performance to offset 9/11 with the triumph and transcendence to which the city's verticality traditionally testifies, McCann focuses in this opening scene on Petit's audience, in keeping with his stated concern with "life on the ground" ("Conversation with Englander" 366), with those threshold spaces in which collapsed spatial distinctions produce collapsed social divisions. As a result, the diverse set of characters – a radical priest from Ireland, a nurse from Guatemala, a painter from Michigan, a whore from Ohio – later brought together by the accident on the FDR Drive around which the plot pivots are prefigured by the cross-section of races, ethnicities, and occupations – "Doctors. Cleaners. Prep chefs. Diamond merchants. Fish sellers" (4) – joined by Petit's artistry and transformed from "[p]erfect strangers" into a "family" by virtue of shared spectatorship (5, 6).

And not, significantly, just shared spectatorship but shared language, as a comparison with McCann's first novel illustrates. In *This Side of Brightness* (1998), which chronicles New York between 1916 and 1991 through the sandhog's life below ground and the skyscraper construction worker's life above ground, it is an environment in which "[d]ifferent languages blend" that produces the "democracy beneath the river" in which "every man's blood runs the same color" (17, 9). But because no one language is commonly understood by the largely immigrant and African American workforce that builds the tunnels, the warning that forms an Italian worker's first English sentence gets garbled as it is passed along, resulting in a catastrophic blowout. In *Let the Great World Spin*, by contrast, the characters from different nations and states already know the English language that, in Whitman's view, served as "a sort of universal absorber" ("Slang" 68), consolidating immigrants into citizens. The question that pertains to them concerns the acquisition of the particular kind of English that makes them New Yorkers, specifically those swearwords and slang the visiting Frenchman on the wire can neither hear ("Do it, asshole!" [*Let* 6]) nor fully appreciate ("get off the motherfucking wire right motherfucking now" [241]) but that unite his witnesses as much as physical proximity. It is this language that, expanded from subgroup to society, can be the "prelude to real social change" (Allen 7), the kind McCann terms "*justful*" rather than "just" (287).

Not everyone in this book filled with figures remarkably attuned to the myriad ways in which language works is receptive to the slang that Whitman deemed a "lawless germinal element" ("Slang" 68). The Upper East Side matron Claire, who chooses to "*slide*" out of her depression rather than conventionally "*snap*" out of it (*Let* 90), opts for a word her dead son has liked, the same cosseted child whose urgings not to "*freak out*" because he is "*cool*" display a "new language creeping in[to]" his phone calls from Vietnam (101). Her Manhattan judge husband, who is "not fond of bad language" (249), combines linguistic and legal absolutism and extends the sentence of a prostitute who uses bad words during her allocution, which eventuates in the woman's suicide. As a consequence of that ruling, however, an African American woman who has lost three sons in Vietnam performs the highly illegal act on the ground that puts into perspective all those performances enacted above the ground – the mean-spirited one from a courtroom bench as much as the truly magnificent one atop the twin towers. Like Petit, who finds all questions of "why" irrelevant (243), Gloria understands that she does not "need a reason" to lie about her relationship to two orphaned girls about to be consigned to social services after a car crash kills their mother and blind justice leaves their grandmother hanging from a pipe in prison (322). Unlike Petit, whose spectacular act above the ground can end up, if he falls, killing dozens of people on the ground, Gloria's act of *communitas* on the ground – accompanied by no fanfare or acclaim – saves two little girls and harms no one. Even more, it recalls a quality built into the fabric of New York City, quite literally, between the late nineteenth and early twentieth centuries, when Beaux Arts tenets prevailed and depictions of the skyline took the form of a mountain range ensemble rather than a set of differently towering peaks in competition with each other (Bender and Taylor 195, 212–13). In thus locating its climax in a South Bronx moment that collapses time, McCann also brings the book full circle to collapse space, affirming its early rejection of the "honey-soaked heaven" of Christian geography as a "dressing room for hell" and embrace of the "real world" as the place where one might find "some sort of triumph that went beyond theological proof, a cause for optimism against all the evidence" (*Let* 20).

The young Nigerian who wanders aimlessly around New York City in Teju Cole's *Open City* (2011) spends most of his time in that real world between 2006 and 2007, much as the nameless narrator of *Every Day Is for the Thief* (2007; rpt. 2014) does when he returns to Lagos after a fifteen-year absence. Not quite *tokunbo* (Yoruba for "from over the seas") and not entirely black (his estranged mother is German), Julius is born in Nigeria, educated in the US, and making his home in Manhattan while completing a psychiatry fellowship at Columbia Presbyterian as the book opens. The New York where he engages with strangers of all sorts during the perambulations that form this nearly plotless work – a Haitian bootblack, a Barbudan museum guard, a Berliner refugee – is indeed an open city where bird migrations confirm the "miracle of natural immigration" and the sparrows that God looks after as "homeless travelers" offer proof that "we, too, were under heaven's protection" (4, 181). In extending this welcome, New York is much like Brussels, another city distinguished by the number of residents that seem to have "just arrived from a sun-suffused elsewhere" with whom Julius converses during a winter visit (97–98). Yet much like Brussels, a historical crossroads for "Europe's fatal tussles" that only escaped the devastation of World War II by declaring itself an "open city" (97), and Lagos, a city being pillaged in the new century by foreigners drawn to its "open economy" (*Every* 145), New York is also a city perceived as under siege – from illegals, from bedbugs, from AIDS. All are emblematized by the "invasive [plant] species" brought over from China in the 1700s that became a "pest" after those trees of heaven grew so freely as to "displac[e] native species" (*Open* 179, 180). When residents respond by xenophobically trying to contain (or, in the case of undocumented arrivals, detain) the threats to the "sanctity of the home" posed by enemies as "vague" as they are "constantly shifting" (176, 173), they end up the first humans "completely unprepared for [global] disaster" for failing to recognize the transnational nature of the phenomena they fear (200).

Such obliviousness is quite antithetical to Cole, an avid Internet communicator who began his first book as a thirty-day experimental blog, and a writer whose movements between the US and Nigeria recall the borderless biographies of cohorts like Chigozie Obioma (*The Fishermen* [2015]), Okey Ndibe (*Foreign Gods, Inc.* [2014]), Chimamanda Ngozi Adichie (*Americanah* [2013]), Sefi Atta (*A Bit of Difference* [2012]), and Chinelo Okparanta (*Happiness, Like Water* [2013]). Such willful obtuseness is, however, portrayed by Cole as fundamental to the palimpsest that is New York City, a naturally "riverine city" covered by concrete and stone (54), a layered city that for all its monuments and plaques to the past prefers to bury the past when it proves inconvenient. When Julius looks at the empty space that has become a metonym for 9/11, he sees in his mind's eye a site redolent of erasure. The small businesses obliterated in the 1960s to make way for the World Trade Center evoke the Levantines of the 1800s pushed out to Atlantic Avenue, and the Lenape before them, and finally all the communities that once occupied what is now Lower Manhattan whose presences there have been forgotten. But not, significantly, foreclosed in a book that argues for the past's continuation into the present. When Julius looks at the old Customs House behind which Bartholdi's green figure suggestively peaks from Ellis Island, he is reminded of the role played by New York in outfitting the slave ships that transported those Africans "who weren't immigrants in any case" (54), the profits of which helped to found all those companies – City Bank of New York, AT&T, Con Edition – that emerged from an area in which the circuit from Customs House to Wall Street to South Street Seaport was less than a mile. Similarly reminded, by the imposing buildings named after donors that he sees uptown, of the link between memorials and money, Julius needs no explanation for what the African burial ground with unmanned security post that he stumbles upon in a downtown side street signifies. Shrunk to a patch of grass from an original six acres, its unguarded holy ground mocked by the zealously patrolled Ground Zero, this home to mostly enslaved blacks lies mostly beneath office buildings that evince "the endless hum of quotidian commerce and government" (220).

The triangulated cities in his work show that Cole has no illusions that such burial of the past is unique to New York. The plaque to Belgium's kings near the Brussels Musées Royaux d'Art et d'Histoire that offers an inscribed HOMMAGE A LA DYNASTIE LA BELGIQUE ET LE CONGO, RECONNAISSANTS gives no evidence of the colonialist past accorded that gratitude (100). The plaques to military dictators on the walls of Lagos's National Museum mention the human trafficking in which the port city partook as just an "obnoxious practice" (*Every* 78). With the detail from Julius's past that Cole unearths near the end of *Open City* – the rape at fourteen of a friend's sister at a party in Ikoyi – he indicates, however, the degree to which the Nigerian immigrant has naturalized himself to his new homeland. Indeed, for all the claims of having "hewed close to the good" all his life and hints of Barthes and Borges, Augustine and Appiah, that make erudition a sign of civilization (*Open* 243), the doctor who deems himself among the few psychiatrists concerned with patients' souls reveals himself with this narrative twist as having lost his own soul, and in a way for which no intellectual name-dropping can compensate: when he runs into his victim in Union Square eighteen years later, he does not recognize her much less acknowledge his earlier violation. It is no wonder, then, that Julius presents his decision to remain in New York after his fellowship ends as "the only choice that makes emotional sense" (248). Much like those birds in the novel's closing image, lured to Manhattan by the Statue of Liberty during the days it served as the nation's biggest lighthouse, clever enough to dodge the city's skyscrapers but fatally disoriented by the monument's single flame, he loses his bearings. And just like those secondhand *tokunbo* planes bought from the West that make Africa host to more than a quarter of the world's aviation accidents, all he can do is crash.

From Russia with Lyubov'yu

Gary Shteyngart is one of the many Russian-born novelists – Olga Grushin (*The Dream Life of Sukhanov* [2005], *The Line* [2010]), Ellen Litman (*The Last Chicken in America* [2007]), Keith Gessen (*All the Sad Young Literary Men* [2008]), Irina Reyn (*What Happened to Anna K.* [2008]), Boris Fishman (*A Replacement Life* [2014]) – living in the US and writing about the collapsed binary of First and Second World. Having arrived in 1979 as one of the Grain Jews allowed to emigrate as part of an exchange brokered by Jimmy Carter, though, he is arguably the writer most shaped by a Cold War heritage that has made him – quite literally – a marked man according to his memoir. In fact, the giant keloid that testifies in *Little Failure* (2014) to a "Soviet inoculation gone terribly wrong" (171) is just the visible manifestation of a victimization inflicted by a series of patriarchs whose commingling of cruelty and love ("*Tot kto ne byot, tot ne lyubit*" ["He who doesn't hit, doesn't love"]) leaves a lasting imprint (125): "Here is Father, above me, and here is Lenin above him, and this is my family and this is my country" (49). That scarring does not fade with the Shteyngart family's move from East to West, *The Six Million Dollar Man*'s tele-promise that in America "you can swap out the parts of yourself that don't work" and "rebuild yourself piece by piece" notwithstanding (158). The family swaps his birth name of Igor for the Americanized Gary, and his classmates still beat the boy they taunt as a "Red Gerbil" (119), as does his father who alternately calls him "*zhidovskaya morda*" ("Yid-face") and "*mudak*" ("dickhead") (171, 319). The capitalist-enclave garden apartment is also part of a Queens cooperative surveilled by cameras and patrols. Perhaps most telling, the Publishers Clearing House that informs the gullible newcomers they have already won ten million dollars lies as shamelessly as the Politburo that lies about everything from wheat harvests to crickets singing the "Internationale" in honor of Brezhnev (133). Aware that in New York's multicultural landscape his refugee family is admittedly privileged for being "something that we never really had the chance to appreciate back home," namely white (109), the young Gary still remains skeptical: having once tasted the "forbidden fruit" of the fake sweepstakes, "We won't bite again" (143).

The unlikely heroes of Shteyngart's first two novels, by contrast, are eager to take a bite out of the Big Apple and take advantage of any means to do so. In *The Russian Debutante's Handbook* (2002), Vladimir Girshkin does not know if being "fifty percent functional American, and fifty percent cultured Eastern European" grants him "the best of both worlds" or "the remorse of fitting finally into neither" (409, 306). But having prioritized acceptance and love over his parents' pursuit of wealth as a mark of assimilation, he invokes his Russian half to play the "rootless cosmopolitan" to the Fifth Avenue princess who thinks he looks like Trotsky and Count Vronsky to the "downtown nobility" that forms her coterie (60, 104). It is only when plans to pay the high costs of hipsterdom by posing as a young Catalan for a college interview end in threats to his life that Vladimir is forced to abscond to Prava, Republika Stolovaya, where he implements a Ponzi scheme to defraud the hapless American expats who flock to this "Paris of the 90s" (67). It is in this former Soviet-bloc country, complete with K-Marts and American Express machines, that he sees what the Soviet Union has been reduced to in 1993: a giant Foot guarded by *babushkas* wielding portraits of Stalin, which is all that remains of the Great One after his statue is steadily dismembered with each regime change. Yet it is also in Prava that Vladimir learns how much the gendered legacy of that "precious gray planet of our fathers and forefathers" has "marked for life" anyone who grew up on it (402), how little is left for the people he recognizes as "my people" now that history has "totally outflanked" them (407).

In *Absurdistan* (2006), in which Mikhail Borisovich Vainberg makes a similar journey to a former Soviet republic (the "Norway of the Caspian") from the opposite direction in an attempt to buy the Belgian passport that will allow him to return to New York after a two-year absence, those paternal markers are both more pronounced and more pathetic (111). On the one hand, Misha's trip is occasioned by the US State Department repeatedly denying his visa application after his father kills an Oklahoma businessman, an act meant to keep Misha by his side but prompting the question, "Are we best off with abusive parents or no parents at all?" (300). On the other hand, the assassination of that patriarch in the book's opening pages leaves no doubt as to the Russian's standing in the world at large. "Let us be certain: the Cold War was won by one side and lost by another," this son of Russia's 1,238th richest man categorically states (57). Absurdsvaní's Svaní City thus welcomes visitors with Benetton billboards and Microsoft flags, as befits a nation run by a Halliburton subsidiary and a population so "completely in tune with globalization" as to revile the G8 summit protester whose death draws attention away from the staged civil war starting to gain international media traction (224). Unfortunately, this same embrace leaves Absurdistan without any of the distinguishing features – geographical, racial, genocidal – needed to attract that American sponsor it courts after losing its Soviet patron ("We don't want the United Nations," "We want the big time"), not even the kind of name that can be used as a child's first name as is required "to get anywhere" (225, 309).

As Soviet Jews, however, Shteyngart's surrogates *are* distinguished by a heritage that even after 1989 serves as nationality, ethnicity, and race, depending on the whim of the persecutor. Vladimir, for all his alpha-immigrant mother's attempts to get him not to "walk like a Jew" (*Russian* 45), finds proof of the continued precariousness of being a Jew when he returns to Europe. Stolovan skinheads attack him with cries of "*Auslander raus!*" ("Foreigner out!" [355]), as do Stolovan skinheads who surround him with an "ethnic-cleansing *cordon sanitaire*" (440). Germans that photograph him at Auschwitz II–Birkenau recall his grandmother's injunction – "Run, before the *goyim* get you" – at the precise moment that he is poised to toss aside the century about to end and all thoughts of his family as the "clearing-house for global confusion and uncertainty" for having survived both Hitler and Stalin (427, 428). Misha, for all his attempts at separating "good Jews" from "bad Jews" (*Absurdistan* 108), "*secular* Jews" from "second-rate Jews" (251), learns that he is "the biggest Jew" of all (as evidenced by his own botched *bris*) and not "a new kind of man" (304). Likewise, for all his plans to pitch Absurdistan as "the most Jew-tolerant place on earth outside of Brookline, Massachusetts," while Minister of Multicultural Affairs by appealing to the "New Tribalism" arisen in "angry response to global homogenization" (269, 270), he learns that the Absurdis that profess undying love of his Jewish nationality are the same KGB agents that once chanted "Suitcase! Train station! Israel!" to get Jews to leave their country (69), that the Sevo minority claiming a willingness to assist Jews should the Germans have reached their borders are the same people who tried to get Absurdistan's Mountain Jews sent to the gulags in order to take over their ancestral villages.

All of which makes the crazed Russian intent on getting US citizenship in *The Russian Debutante's Handbook* all the more lucid when stressing the dangers of being "a man without a country" in a world in which "[e]verywhere is Russia" (176, 10): the first step on the road to extinction for European Jews were those 1935 Nuremberg Laws that deprived them of citizenship and made them stateless. Therefore, despite the Statue of Liberty's "Soviet-cafeteria green" that does "not inspire confidence" or, more pointedly, America's "sorting mechanism" by which beta immigrants are "discovered, branded . . . , and eventually rounded up" (119, 179), it is the US passport that does not have "Jew" listed as nationality that guarantees Vladimir will not be extinguished by morons as he makes yet another airport run at book's end, this time to escape Russians relocated to Prava who are looking to kill him after the exposure of another scam. If the Cleveland of the 1998 epilogue in which he works as an accountant lacks the maniacal ecstasy of his youth, it nevertheless provides shelter and insulation for the married man whose son will be born "[a]n American in America" (476). This is exactly what the Mountain Jews of Absurdistan's frontier offer Misha after his own escape from a capital about to be bombed by Putin looking to profit from a sham conflict that has produced all-too-real casualties – a place where any Jew "will always find a home" (*Absurdistan* 324), much like Israel, a place one is not required to love so long as it exists. Only in this 2006 work, the *schlemiel* cannot claim that security. When Misha in the epilogue opts to make his home on the corner of 173rd Street and Vyse where his Bronx Latina girlfriend awaits him, to "take to the air" but keep his "feet on the ground" as his psychiatrist advises (viii), he takes flight the second week in September 2001 and so travels to a nation in which the sanctuary of home is as uncertain as the defense of the homeland.

The fiction of writers who emigrated to the US after 1989, by contrast, relies far less on the Russian state as patriarchal oppressor, as evidenced by the various renderings of former Soviet heads of state: Lenin a twenty-foot-high portrait that resembles the head of a gigantic caterpillar (Vapnyar 64), Stalin a decapitated head on a medal in deplorable condition (Akhtiorskaya 188–89). In the case of Russian women writers in particular, that patriarchal decline is corroborated further by the number of absent fathers that appear in their work. Lara Vapnyar's *There Are Jews in My House* (2003) portrays fathers in the Soviet Union as at the front during wartime or abroad on business when in fact dead, abandoning their families for other women or becoming emasculated upon arrival in the United States. Yelena Akhtiorskaya's *Panic in a Suitcase* (2014) depicts the Nasmertov men as either "sickly from the outset" or "shr[u]nk" by America (3, 40), weaknesses exacerbated by having been born Jewish, "which in Russia qualified as a separate nationality if not species," and not even born in "Russia proper" but Ukraine (290). As such, they prove no match for the matriarchal Esther, who, with "top-of-the-line primal-mother tool kit" (21), has saved the family from "scavenging garbage dumps" as she has "all the children [that] were under her care" as a pediatrician, which is to say the "future of Odessa" (56), and by extension the "motherland" itself in Akhtiorskaya's gendered delineation (127).

Strong-willed but not strong-arming, this "motherland" is one from which the characters who uproot themselves in Akhtiorskaya's post-Soviet novel are unwilling to sever their ties completely. When they arrive in the US and replant themselves in Brighton Beach, a "tidy replication of the messy, imperfect original they'd gone through so many hurdles to escape" (17), they display the ambivalence of the émigré-immigrant. The Nasmertovs, after two years, still count the days since their arrival, much like prisoners marking off days of their sentences. Conversely, thinking they have a son still living in their prized apartment "in the epicenter of Odessa" and watching over their treasured dacha enables them to feel that they have not "exchanged or betrayed but simply enlarged in scope," have not relinquished the center in coming to America even if re-creating it in an outer borough attests to Odessa's never having been much of a center to begin with (127, 128). But when the book makes its fifteen-year jump from the 1993 of its first half to the 2008 of its second, and the journey of the Nasmertovs to the US is juxtaposed with the reverse-trip made by their twenty-five-year-old granddaughter back to Ukraine, Akhtiorskaya exposes the extent of the disinheritance that

Esther's death at the end of Part One has only implied. For while Frida has prepared herself to "feel nothing" upon returning to a place she barely remembers, and is preempted from having to feel anything about the Potemkin Square flat her feckless uncle is revealed as having been forced to vacate years ago, she is not prepared that "there would actually *be* nothing" when she finally arrives at the site of the dacha reduced to a mound of rubble (274). Left with only the facsimile of a home that no longer exists, the Nasmertovs end up "[h]omeless," albeit not in the way that Frida's mother means when earlier expressing a desire to exchange the claustrophobia that is Brighton Beach for the freedom that comes from lying under the stars and listening to the ocean (178). Having attempted to straddle two worlds, they get neither First nor Second World. Instead they remain afloat, much as the grandfather imagines in his recurrent dream: in a canoe with no oars, searching for something to paddle with and only finding a suitcase that crumbles to dust the moment it is touched.

Even more dramatically displaced are the protagonists of Anya Ulinich's fiction. "*Homo Sovieticus* is pretty well extinct, but at least he's documented," Sasha Goldberg states near the end of *Petropolis* (2007). "But what am I? *Homo Post-Sovieticus? Homo Nowhere?*" (311), as indeed she is, having already been abandoned by her father at ten and raised by a mother pining for Mandelstam's prerevolutionary world of the intelligentsia. Born in a former gulag administrative center located in Siberia and hence even farther from the Soviet center than Odessa, Sasha grows up in a town named after a toxic substance, "where everything had already fallen apart" by the 1990s and without anything to take its place (79). Once the mines that have produced its primary source of income become depleted and Asbestos 2 begins to disappear without a trace (save for what has worked its way into the lungs of its poisoned inhabitants), Sasha is as homeless as the "barrel people" living in concrete pipes whose bulldozed residences she earlier has seen "*sail through the air like a giant egghell*" (288). The eponymous heroine of *Lena Finkle's Magic Barrel* (2014) thus unequivocally declares herself "an immigrant, *not* an expatriate" at the start of Ulinich's autobiographical graphic novel (8). As she goes on to state when challenged about missing her gendered homeland, "I don't have a motherland . . . ! It's all just . . . land" (180).

Like Shteyngart's *schlemiels*, these heroines find a lot that resembles Russia after they actually land in the US and, much like Ulinich herself (who emigrated with her family in 1991), make their way from west to east with each successive escape. Sasha arrives in Phoenix as a sixteen-year-old mail-order bride and finds Russians crammed four to a bedroom. Chicago greets her with abandoned factories and concrete apartment blocks. New York is filled with plumbers that never call back and buses that peel away as passengers run to board them. Unlike Shteyngart's *schlemiels*, they do not run to escape Jewish persecution. "Being a Jew wasn't all that bad" – indeed, better than being a Chukchi – to Sasha, who does not know what matzo is and only has a Jewish surname because her mixed-race father (an illegitimate result of Moscow's 1957 International Youth Festival) was adopted by Jewish engineers (*Petropolis* 30). In fact, their greatest escapes involve slipping the bonds of other Jews who force their heritage upon them. The Oak Grove Tarakans take Sasha in after she flees the husband that keeps her passport under lock and key only to enslave her to the Torah during the two hours each day they are not using her as unpaid labor in their "house of collections" (162) – aka tchotchkes – or trotting her out at benefits to raise money for Soviet Jewry. The Hasidic landlords teach Lena, whose family is seeking asylum to pursue "freedom of worship" even though they do not know the first thing about worship, "how to be a proper Jew" while she scrubs their floors on her hands and knees (*Lena* 73).

The chains of cultural bondage, however, prove less easy to shed because they are matrilineal in origin. Sasha, after she gets her green card, returns for two weeks every summer to the "Mother Russia" she knows will pour "all of its thirdworldness" on visitors "like a bottomless bucket of shit" because it is there that her own mother, a woman as tenacious in love (her first name is Lubov) as loyalty (she keeps her apartment clean for the future when things will get better), is raising as her own the daughter that Sasha has left behind when she departed Asbestos 2 for Moscow (*Petropolis* 268). It is only after the former librarian is found frozen over a copy of Mandelstam's *Tristia* (1922) and Sasha takes the child back to Brooklyn that she can begin to see herself as "living in the *world*, not in a town" (310). In much the same way, Lena continues to play what she knows is a "game of passive-aggressive one-upsmanship" with the mother she urges to "arrive" in America instead of harping on the "coming to America" of twenty years past (*Lena* 150). It is only after reviewing her own disastrous history with men – some of whom see her as a waif in need of rescue, others a combination cook-caregiver – that Lena realizes that she is not that different from her mother, that her desire to "move through life . . . like an ancient traveler, ignorant of borders" (241), has only left her "an interesting third world country" that a succession of men has "toured" prior to abandoning (294).

Such aspirations to complete independence – that life, liberty, and pursuit of happiness that Lena identifies as "not inheritance" and "not 'mommy'" (62) – are ones to which she feels so entitled as a new American that she buys a copy of Jefferson's Declaration when she takes her daughters to Monticello. They also are ones that the various interlocutors and nagging conscience that Ulinich has following Lena around in this second work continually upset. "What makes you think you should be happy all the time?" a friend inquires of the immigrant who has acquired "a sense of self the size of the Empire State Building" (333). And so when Lena in the book's end notes finally meets up with the father who has been MIA since allegedly leaving for Pinsk to settle a family inheritance, she does not harangue him with having arrived in America. Having come to recognize that "no one ever truly arrives," that we all "just nudge each other along muddy ruts of suffering, occasionally peeking over the edges" (361), she accepts herself as in the middle of a journey accompanied not just by her conscience but by her "caricature of a Russian soul" (361).

Glocal Geographies

The characters in Barbara Kingsolver's historical novels travel the globe: to the Congo in *The Poisonwood Bible* (1998), between the US and Mexico in *The Lacuna* (2009). Those in the works set in the present gravitate to the two places – Appalachia and Tucson – that frame the heroine's journey in *The Bean Trees* (1988), her first novel. Such settings have little to do with satisfying any autobiographical impulse of an author who was raised in rural Kentucky and resided in Arizona for two decades. Rather, they afford the environmentally conscious Kingsolver a canvas on which to depict the local implicated in the global. In this endeavor, she is hardly alone. Linda Hogan, for example, portrays the drilling for oil in Oklahoma (*Mean Spirit* [1990]), the building of a hydroelectric power plant between Minnesota and Canada (*Solar Storms* [1995]), the endangering of the Florida panther (*Power* [1998]), and the killing of whales in the Pacific Northwest (*People of the Whale* [2008]) as part of a history of colonialism as devastating to the earth as it is to those tribal communities dispossessed of their place on it. Kingsolver, a trained evolutionary biologist, focuses instead on places that "belong entirely to themselves" by virtue of a distinct ecosystem in order to explore what happens when their biodiversity is reduced by the "human passion to carry all things everywhere, so that every place is home," a "homogenizing [of] our planet" that results in the extinguishing of indigenous species from the planet (*High Tide* 204).

In the southern Appalachia of *Prodigal Summer* (2000), the farmers of Zebulon County grow up thinking it is their "destiny" to occupy the same plot of land for "eternity" (33), safe in the knowledge that everybody within sixteen miles is a relation by blood or marriage. Their belief is seemingly confirmed by the loose connections among the three focalizers whose intertwined narratives comprise the novel: a wildlife biologist ("Predators"), a widowed entomologist ("Moth Love"), and an elderly farmer ("Old Chestnuts"). Yet these preservers of all things local have depended for generations on crops that can be shipped around the world for profit. Tobacco can be "lit and smoked on a different day of the year, in a different country of the world" (108). Ginseng can be "packed off to China" and sold for "good money" (193). Conversely, these yeomen rooted to the land are steadily being forced by species foreign to the land to mortgage, subdivide, even leave their land and seek work in Knoxville's Toyota plant. This, however, is a battle they have been waging ever since another Japanese invader, a "fungal blight [that] stepped off a ship in some harbor" a century earlier, "grinned at America, and took down every chestnut tree from New York to Alabama" (100), thereby anticipating those other non-native species – honeysuckle, kudzu, Japanese knotweed – that have produced a "new world entire" that indigenous species like the bobwhite chick are unable to negotiate (138). Such upsetting of the region's ecosystem by botanical "introduction[s] from someplace else" (360), moreover, is only exacerbated by humans armed with shotguns and spray cans intent on removing from that system the natural predators upon which its pyramidal structure, defined mathematically by Vito Volterra and Alfred J. Lotka, rests. To the biologist Deanna Wolfe, who has relocated to a cabin to await the return of the coyote, the consequences to Appalachia are all too clear: "North America's richest biological home was losing its richness to one extinction after another, of plants and birds, fish, mammals, moths and stoneflies, and especially the river creatures" (63).

No wide-eyed romantic, Kingsolver is aware that accepting a system in which "[l]iving takes life" is easier said than done (323): Deanna defends a snake that devours mice as just "doing its job" but is distraught when it later kills the nest of baby phoebes she has appropriated as her own (329). Kingsolver also knows that the entire web of "fine, invisible threads" by which "[e]verything alive is connected" is impossible for humans to apprehend (216). That being said, she portrays the urge to own what can only be occupied as gendered, part of the territorial need of man to "mark" his land (25), just as the ruination of the landscape itself is depicted as a propensity of the American man. The men who organize the Mountain Empire Bounty Hunt during the season that female coyotes give birth and nurse have as their goal "willful extermination" (29). Yet no less does Garnett Walker III, who views himself as enacting God's plan while spraying his property with broad-spectrum insecticides so that the "landscape of his father's manhood would be restored" (130). The only difference is that Garnett – who has refused surgery for his cataracts and left unexamined the vertigo caused by (crystal) rocks in his head – has willfully blinded himself to the consequences of his acts. Myopic about the impact that spraying toxic chemicals can have on the organic orchards of his neighbor, he is amnesiac with respect to the impact they already have had on his wife who died of cancer.

In *Animal Dreams* (1990), which details the attempts of a group of women to fight the polluting and diverting of their Arizona town's river by selling as folk art those "nice things" that the "ladies here do" (as their leader admits, "we don't know how to use dynamite" [266–67]), that habit of proceeding "as if there were no other day but today" is portrayed as having produced a whole "nation of amnesiacs" (240–41). Codi Noline thus characterizes what the Black Mountain Mining Company is doing to the Jemez Mountains as "such an American story" (240), identical to what her sister Hallie sees in Central America, where a "whole land-based culture is being relocated out of its land" after having been turned by the First World into a "toilet bowl" for chemical dumping (88, 223). Yet Hallie, a woman who is – as the Nicaraguan minister of agriculture carefully puts it after her abduction by contras – an "exceptional person" but "not an exceptional case" (270), also understands that "[w]ars and elections are both too big and too small to matter in the long run," and so devotes herself to the local, laboring in the cotton fields to do the "daily work" that "goes on" and "adds up" (299).

The characters in *Prodigal Summer* approach ecological threats by similarly focusing on what they can feasibly hope to do in their area, combating the unnatural interventions that have spoiled the land with, surprisingly, the unnatural intervention of humans to restore the land – some by artificially breeding, others by artificially culling. Garnett crosses and backcrosses American and Chinese chestnuts in the hopes of producing blight-resistant seedlings that can "go forth and multiply" (130). His neighbor, Nannie Rawley, crosses Transparents and Stayman's winesaps to produce the apples known as "Nannie's Finest." Perhaps most paradoxically, the Polish Jewish-Palestinian American Lusa Maluf Landowski – a crossbreed transplanted from Lexington herself – saves the farm she inherits from her husband by getting Spanish and brush goats to kid out of season, aware that the offspring of her reproductive efforts will end up on the plates of New Yorkers celebrating Id-al-Adha in April. In choosing to base her business on the same animals that have left the county with a "goat plague" after a 4-H project "kind of overgrew" itself (208, 209), however, the city girl who once saw all killing as an affront to God's creation comes to learn why intervening in that creation is needed when nature, as her husband has tried to teach her, is "on [a] bender" and must be persuaded to take "two steps back every day or it will move in and take you over" (45). In a world in which solitude is characterized as a "human presumption," as the paragraphs that frame the novel assert (1, 444), part of the human prerogative is to act when faced with those "passionate excesses" that can "wear out everything in [their] path" (51), but to do so thoughtfully, mindful that "[e]very choice is a world made new for the chosen" (444).

The Japanese who carve out the colony of Esperança from the Brazilian forests in Karen Tei Yamashita's *Brazil-Maru* (1992) are quite mindful of this point, viewing their 1925 creation of a "new world" on "new land" as a "special and sacred gift given only to a chosen few" (22). As such, the "story" that Yamashita – a Californian who spent nearly a decade living in Brazil – introduces as "belong[ing] to all of us who travel distances to find something that is, after all, home" (n. pag.) is indeed "part of something larger," as one of the last original founders concludes in 1992, although not necessarily as he means (248). For having been established in Brazil because of exclusionary legislation passed by the US in 1908, Esperança is born of the triangulated relationship between one nation founded upon exceptionalist principles (Puritan election) and two others in the process of uncovering or recovering the principles of essentialized identity (*nihonjinron, brasilidade*), making the book's saga of oceanic migration a cautionary tale of the perils of artificial isolation. Intent on producing "a new breed of youth" modeled on Rousseau's *Emile* (1762), excerpts of which preface the novel's four main parts, the Japanese settlers resist the historical connections between aboriginal Ainu of Japan and Brazilian Indians, whose remains their tractors unearth. But unschooled in the Portuguese of their adopted country, severed by wartime politics from their ancestral home, and, in the case of those who move to the New World Ranch compound, divorced from their own families, their off-spring grow up as depleted as the "pure form" of chickens the settlers have also attempted to breed (177). The result, as Yamashita notes near the end, is a colony "preserved, [and] picked in miso" (202).

The Brazilian interior in Yamashita's *Through the Arc of the Rain Forest* (1990), by contrast, is portrayed as a global nexus, especially after the nation introduced as "the sort of place that might absorb someone who was different" (starting with a Japanese man with a whirling ball a few inches from his forehead) is overrun by citizens of all nations (an American businessman with three arms, a French ornithologist with three breasts) after the smooth surface known as the Matacão is revealed, in "a breakthrough tantamount to Teflon," to be a five-foot-deep block of plastic both indestructible and magnetic (9–10, 97). Formed from the compression of nonbiodegradable materials from around the Earth, the liquid deposits of which have squeezed through underground veins to virgin areas, the Matacão literalizes Kingsolver's claim that "throw[ing] away" means "out of sight somewhere" for "someone else to run into further down the road" (*Prodigal* 206). Yet the magic realist tale predicated on this geological phenomenon is not the expected one of desecration, and subsequent pillage, of the local by the global, the number of businesses that spring up in the wake of the region's development – relaxation feathers (pitched as a healthy alternative to coffee and tobacco), karaoke bars (franchised in every South American town), carrier pigeon networks (sold door-to-door like Tupperware) – and vertically integrated businesses (plastic food and plastic surgery paid for by magnetized plastic credit cards) notwithstanding. For, in Yamashita's sly delineation, the Amazon Forest that has become synonymous with the human despoliation of the planet (and a photogenic site used by environmental groups seeking cash for calendars) has long ago surrendered its primeval attributes. No "virgin soil," as the one character born in the region states, its "tubes had been tied long ago" (*Through* 17). And once the most artificial substance of plastic becomes, in effect, a natural resource to be mined like any other profit-generating mineral and the feathers of actual birds are forced by the laws of supply and demand to be marketed along with plastic reproductions, the entire distinction between natural and artificial collapses (Song 559–60). So, too, does the ability to determine an identity based on local roots, since the primary place that might provide for such definition, the Matacão, is mainly a destination, an area to which characters cannot easily return because it is not "naturally" their home (Heise 107).

Yet the local in Yamashita's work, in contrast to Kingsolver's, pushes back against human incursions all by itself. In an ecological return of the repressed, the birds threatened with extinction because of the comfort their feathers offer humans turn out to carry in their feathers the lice on which travel rickettsia, whose migrations lead to a typhus epidemic that does not confine itself to those "poor people in the Third World who cavorted with communism and the like" (*Through* 184). Bodies start falling down from the sky as hallucinating cultists, clutching the feathers they worship, are abandoned to the sky by the birds they mistakenly assume will keep them aloft. Eventually, the Matacão itself disappears, invaded by devouring bacteria that reduce even this most nonbiodegradable area – along with everything built on its foundation – to a giant pit. That being said, the magic realism that informs the novel does not extend to Yamashita's portraying this push-back as leading to a happy ending: it comes only after enhanced DDT meant to eradicate the rickettsia indiscriminately kills every small animal, insect, and occasional child in the region, including, ironically, those carrier pigeons freed by their owner to escape the poison bombs only to return within hours to die in "the home they had been trained to return to" (201).

It is in a place seventy-two kilometers outside the Matacão, however, that Yamashita offers an alternative to a battle waged between humans and nature. In this setting filled with abandoned vehicles dating back to the early Cold War, the paving of paradise to put up a parking lot (to recall Joni Mitchell's lyrics) has eventuated not in a conflation of natural and artificial but an accommodation of natural and artificial. Butterflies nest in corroding Fords and Chevys, mice burrow in exhaust pipes. Miracles of adaption, with exquisite reds and glorious greens that come from feeding on ferric oxide and paint chips, and suction cups and prehensile tails that come from nesting in cars sinking beneath fields of napalm, they pale beside the phenomenon of entirely new species coexisting with known varieties of flora and fauna. None survives the toxic bombing any more than the species native to the Matacão do, of course. But in a junkyard littered by the detritus of war, these offspring of an "ecological experiment unparalleled in the known world of nature" – unassisted by humans in any way – testify to a place in which all, and against all odds, were able for a brief moment to "somehow found a home," a "way of life" (101).

Chapter 6

Borderlands and Border Identities

About twenty years after the turn of the century, the border became stabilized and eventually abolished. Although the border area had a few Lower Life Existence concentrations like Chula Vista, now all people lived a Middle Life Existence. . . . I recalled Grandfather's descriptions of how the Border Patrol tried to stop Mexican immigration into the United States and how the Immigration and Naturalization Service swept through Mexican neighborhoods arresting brown faced "illegal aliens." . . . What irony that today the Mexican population dominated north of what once was the international border and that Euroamericans fled to the Mexican States of North Baja California and South Baja California.

– Alejandro Morales, The Rag Doll Plagues (1992)

And what irony that the plagues that decimate populations in the three places in which Alejandro Morales's novel is set – Mexico City between 1788 and 1792, Orange County during the mid-1970s, a hemispheric coastal corridor in the late twenty-first century – bypass not just geographic lines but class, race, ethnic, and gender lines. As the mention of "Lower Life Existence" in the book's final section attests, an absence of national borders does not mean an absence of other divides. Circumscribed areas where the dregs of society reside still exist, the Philippine Islands still serve as a waste dump, and Mexicans still evoke fear in Canadians and United Statesians. More than simply a "just disease," as a priest in New Spain remarks, each plague is also a justice-dealing disease, its threat of an "Empire exterminated" payback for those "many European plagues" brought to the New World and the centuries of colonialism that followed (21). Don Gregorio Revueltas, the physician dispatched during the period of American and French independence to replace *curandero* with modern treatment, thus views his charge initially as being as much political as medicinal: "I was here to quell the fires of revolutionary fervor by extinguishing the illnesses in the fevered populace" (16). His descendant Gregory, a Los Angeles–Mexico City Health Corridor geneticist, by contrast, celebrates the "amazingly primitive" cure he uncovers (187) – transfusing infected patients with antidotal Mexican blood – as restorative: a reclaiming of all the blood shed, from the Indian blood sacrificed to the sun god to the Mexican blood that serviced the gods of industry, and a regaining of land lost almost 250 years earlier as infusions of Mexican blood produce a new *mestizo/a* bloodline.

Except that the restorative bloodline that Gregory envisions also results in a multimillion-dollar blood business and a new caste of MCMs (Mexico City Mexicans) contracted by "blood enslavement" to pharmaceutical companies that develop breeder communities and Euroanglos that demand 24/7 access to their (quite literal) liquid assets (195). The "hope for the new millennium" that he embodies in the child to be born to a Mexican Chinese couple at the book's end must therefore be set against a future to this future that may simply recapitulate the past (200). Likewise, his assertion of being "no longer me" that signals a reinvention of the self must be set against a "transfigur[ing] into all those that have gone before me" that suggests a relinquishing of all chances to determine his self (200).

In portraying *mestizaje* in this manner, Morales typifies a large number of contemporary writers for whom the geography of the US-Mexico border serves as a means to explore questions of identity – familial (Arturo Islas's *The Rain God* [1984] and *Migrant Souls* [1990]), generational (Roberta Fernández's *Intaglio* [1990], Denise Chávez's *Face of an Angel* [1994]), sexual (Emma Pérez's *Gulf Dreams* [1996], John Rechy's *The Coming of the Night* [1999]), aesthetic (Gloria Anzaldúa's *Borderlands/La Frontera* [1987], Guillermo Gómez-Peña's *The New World Border* [1996]), to name but a few – and with varying degrees of success for their characters. For a straddled border – its compensations notwithstanding – is, as Anzaldúa admits, "not a comfortable territory to live in" (n. pag.). Rudolfo Anaya's *Alburquerque* (1992) is filled with characters of mixed bloodlines (Indian Mexican, Anglo Mexican), purchased bloodlines (an offspring of Marrano Jews made Catholic with the right papers, a New York Italian given conquistador ancestry with a Spanish duke's cloak), and renounced bloodlines (a banker who names himself after the tobacco smoked by hobos on his train west from Chicago). Yet it is the character who heeds the injunction of "[t]ú eres tú" ("you are you") while searching for his birth father that becomes the "new mestizo" at book's end, as Abrán "create[s] his own image" by "drawing the two worlds together" without "letting them tear him apart" (23, 215). The critic introduced in Walter Abish's *Eclipse Fever* (1993) as possessed of pre-Columbian Toltec face and post-Cortés gentleman's disposition, by contrast, only resolves his ambivalence on the last page when, with the acceptance of his wife's "blanco" family as "his new family," Alejandro "give[s] up [his] own self" as his mother has long ago predicted (335, 134).

Moving beyond the myth of Aztlán in the formation of an essentialized identity, these authors adopt a borderlands paradigm to signal the fluidity of identity, what José David Saldívar, borrowing from Mary Louise Pratt, calls the *"[t]ransfrontera* contact zone," that "Janus-faced border line in which peoples geopolitically forced to separate themselves now negotiate with one another and manufacture new relations, hybrid cultures, and multiple-voiced aesthetics" (13–14). Depicting the 2,000-mile-long US-Mexico border as one such zone reflects, of course, the specifics of the contemporary period: the post-1989 shift in interest from East-West relations to North-South relations and the increasingly vital role in the global economy, especially after the ratification of NAFTA (North American Free Trade Agreement), that those relations have come to play. Karen Tei Yamashita's *Tropic of Orange* (1997), which juxtaposes Visa cards and visa crossings, concludes with a championship wrestling match ("El Contrato Con América") between SUPERNAFTA and El Gran Mojado (The BigWetback), the latter of whom has just dragged the Tropic of Cancer over the border into "the second largest city of México, also known as Los Angeles" (211). Yet as the signing of that free-trade pact the year that marked the quincentenary of European conquest suggests, such fictional depictions also reflect the particular demographics of that border region's history: racial heterogeneity due to intermarriage and the success Spaniards had in Christianizing the indigenous populations; an ethnic minority created not through immigration or even migration but by the incorporation of their own homelands, as occurred when Mexico surrendered its claim to Texas and the Southwest territories with the 1848 Treaty of Guadalupe Hidalgo (R. Saldívar, *Chicano* 13–14).

The novels that explore borderlands and border identities in the pages that follow are not limited to works concerned with that 2,000-mile region. For one thing, as Claudia Sadowski-Smith points out, the formal acquisition of land geographically contiguous to the US paved the way for incursions onto land not contiguous (4), as evidenced by the invocation of the Monroe Doctrine (1823) to justify intervention in Santo Domingo (1904), Nicaragua (1911), and Haiti (1915), and the creation of semiprotectorates and colonies beginning with Hawaii, Cuba, and the Philippines. The result is an expansion of Latino/a fiction from writers of Mexican American and Cuban American descent to fiction distinguished by a much wider spectrum of Latinidad and greater engagement with global concerns (Delgadillo 602). For another, as the history of immigration traced by Lisa Lowe makes clear, the contemporary debates aimed at stemming the flow of *indocumentados* from Latin America recall the late nineteenth- and early twentieth-century laws barring Asian immigration and naturalization (19–20). If it takes no time for the "liberal humanist" protagonist of T. Coraghessan Boyle's *The Tortilla Curtain* (1995) to blame "the Mexican" he hits with his car for all the subsequent miseries that befall him (3) – the snatching of his designer dogs by coyotes, the stealing of his Acura left unattended, the spoiling of the canyon to which this faux Thoreau has retreated from LA – it takes only slightly longer for him to start seeing in the man's specter "all those dark disordered faces" that the word "borders" brings to mind (101), of which China and Bangladesh have replaced Mexico as chief supplier by the book's end.

The chapter opens by discussing two authors – Cormac McCarthy and Leslie Marmon Silko – who situate the borderlands they portray within an extended geographical and chronological purview, 300,000 and 500 years respectively. It then looks at a sampling of novels composed by second-generation writers (Sandra Cisneros, Julia Alvarez, Gish Jen) and writers of what Rubén G. Rumbaut has termed the 1.5 generation (1162) for being born abroad but raised in the US (Jhumpa Lahiri, Chang-rae Lee) in whose works, often *bildungsromane*, questions of Americanization and hyphenization are portrayed with respect to articulation and naming: names inherited, names attributed, names selected. From questions of imposed or chosen identities, the chapter turns to novels by Oscar Hijuelos and Frank Chin that query the role played by popular culture in the formation of identity, with the aim of complicating the depiction of popular texts as not just tools of cultural imperialism but also sites of conflict that lend themselves to polysemy, as scholars such as John Fiske, Stuart Hall, and Douglas Kellner contend. It ends with works by Jessica Hagedorn that bring the chapter full circle by casting the Philippines as both ongoing and original contact zone.

Home(less) on the Range

Cormac McCarthy's Border Trilogy opens with a 1949 border crossing portrayed as a forced leaving of home, a response to disinheritance, dispossession, even emasculation: John Grady Cole takes off from western Texas with a friend in *All the Pretty Horses* (1992) after his grandfather dies and his mother sells the house that had been in the family for generations. Billy Parham follows suit a decade earlier in *The Crossing* (1994) and repeats that journey with his brother after their parents are killed and their New Mexico property ransacked. By the time the two are joined in *Cities of the Plain* (1998), working on a ranch from which they soon are to be evicted by the US Army in the early 1950s, the home lost has come to signify the West lost, what with cattle ropers reduced to dog ropers and Colt 45s collecting dust in pawnshops while atom bombs drop from planes in the sky. These changes that Billy traces to the Second World War – a war without a cavalry, as he discovers during his three failed attempts to enlist – are signaled in the trilogy's opening pages, however, as John Grady on horseback travels the old war trail of an Indian "lost nation," a "man come to the end of something" even though only sixteen himself (*All* 5, 6).

Such forced evictions, on the one hand, attest to a US imperial project come back to exact vengeance on its perpetrators. McCarthy thus hints at the Hearsts' inability to retain control of their Chihuahua estate for much longer. More important, he depicts his two protagonists not just bilingual Anglos but *mestizos* – one raised by a Mexican servant he calls "abuela," the other possessed of a Mexican maternal grandmother – each of whom is transformed into a "mojado-reverso" (reverse wetback) with his journey to Mexico (*All* 128; Limón 201). On the other hand, in focusing on protagonists that conceive of Mexico as an unspoiled "paradise" or "new country" (61, 50), a tabula rasa in accordance with maps that represent everything south of the Rio Grande as undifferentiated white space, McCarthy presents the two as engaging in the extension of that project. Crossing the border – without passport or papers of any kind – to them means "just passin through," not trespassing (*Crossing* 122, 145), much as it does to all those Americans driven by what Renato Rosaldo has termed "imperialist nostalgia" (69–70). "Dont you think if there's anything left of this life it's down there?" (*Cities* 220), asks John Grady, who still speaks of outlaws and desperados despite having earlier worked the hacienda of a family with a 170-year-old pedigree, to which the older Billy responds by locating the imaginary of "down there" in the younger man's head. No longer a land of peasants sharing victuals with lone riders in acts of generosity, Mexico is by this point a market economy – as exemplified by the border town of Juárez, where visitors are met by vendors hustling cheap goods and whores are appraised on a value per pound on the dollar basis – different from a US of agribusiness and oil fields only in its vulgarity being more blatant.

Nowhere does McCarthy more graphically expose that nostalgia for the lie it is than in *Blood Meridian, or, The Evening Redness in the West* (1985), in which another teen – known only as "the kid" (based on Samuel Chamberlain's self-portrait in *My Confession*) – experiences how the West was won by allying himself with, first, a group of army irregulars that foray into Mexico in 1849 and, then, a band of scalphunters hired by the governor of Sonora to kill Apaches at the rate of $100 a head. At the same time, nowhere in this book of bloodletting that quickly becomes blood sport does McCarthy depict the "taste for mindless violence" introduced in the first paragraphs (3) as unique to the American character (Comanches attack wearing the garb of dragoons and conquistadors) or particular even to the West (an epigraph cites a 300,000-year-old skull found in Ethiopia that shows evidence of having been scalped). Character, as the theatrical venues like carnivals, tent shows, revival meetings, and dances that punctuate the text imply, is a matter of performance (Parkes 107–14). The scalphunters led by John Joel Glanton are designated as "refugees," "barbarians," "partisans," "victors," "mercenaries," even "pilgrims" depending on context. The name John Jackson, conversely, identifies both a white man and a black man. "Blood's blood," John Grady will later state after his pal, Lacey Rawlins, expresses fear of being "part Mexican" because of a blood transfusion he receives while in a Saltillo prison. "It dont know where it come from" (*All* 216–17). Billy Parham will taste the blood of a wolf and find it to be no different than his own.

All of which makes any act based on presumed natural supremacy – whether racial, ethnic, even anthropocentric in its divide – profoundly unnatural, however justified as God-given or cloaked in the rhetoric of errands into the wilderness, Manifest Destiny, or white man's burden. The incursion into Mexico that is explained to the kid as a "liberation" of a "mongrel race" incapable of self-governing is a land grab pure and simple (*Blood* 34), one that as a bonus offers the filibusters a chance to assert their manhood while the "mollycoddles" in Washington draw up boundary lines (35) – an act equally unnatural as McCarthy's depiction of the landscape illustrates. The wolf that crosses from Mexico to the US nearly a century later in *The Crossing* recognizes no such boundaries. The maps that try to formalize them are mere "fantasma[s]" (*Crossing* 189), ascribing names and coordinates to phenomena lacking both to satisfy the human need to find a way already lost, the futility of which is exposed by the father's efforts in *The Road* (2006) to locate his bearings in a postapocalyptic landscape by piecing together the pages of a tattered road map.

The mistake made by the American border crossers in McCarthy's trilogy is to assume that their acts are devoid of agency. Given how badly the rescue missions they attempt turn out, this is not an unreasonable conclusion. Billy Parham makes three trips to Mexico in *The Crossing*: to return a wolf to its natural habitat, to recover stolen horses, to reclaim his lost brother. Only once does he come back with what he goes for – the bones of his dead sibling – which, as he admits, "sure as hell wasnt what I wanted" (*Crossing* 427), but which teaches him the difference between "quittin and knowin when you're beat" (*Cities* 220). John Grady fares much worse. A believer in fate, he sees his pursuit of the wealthy Alejandra in *All the Pretty Horses* as something over which he has no control, "quit[ting]" being as antithetical to his sense of self as "stick[ing]" is inimical to it (160). As illustrated by the number of characters in McCarthy's fiction who (in a nod to Ahab and the doubloon) take the coin toss as their guide, however, such abdication of agency leads more often to the blood spilt by the psychopath than the blood oath of the knight errant. The murderous Judge Holden in *Blood Meridian* blends Gnosticism, Platonism, and Nietzschean materialism to argue the pointlessness of man having any thoughts about war since it is war that predates man in a universe that "no man's mind can compass" (245). The hit man Anton Chigurh in *No Country for Old Men* (2005) forces the innocent to call a coin toss before killing them so as to maintain the illusion that he has had no say in what he deems accountings already tabulated. The imperious Dueña Alfonsa, who foils John Grady's plans to run off with her grandniece, thus has "no sympathy with people to whom things happen" (*All* 246), as she tells him in no uncertain terms. Having witnessed the "deaths of great men in violence and madness" during the Mexican Revolution (1910–1917), she knows full well what can come of conceiving of the world as a puppet show of strings that extend ad infinitum (236).

John Grady, though, refuses to listen to what she says, just as he refuses to listen to what any of the Mexicans who better understand the workings of the world tell him. For all his fluency in Spanish, the American does not "speak the language," as the inmate who runs the Saltillo prison correctly observes (193), hobbled as he is by a "picture of the world [that] is incomplete" (197), blind to the existence of evil, and tempering the fatalist's lack of agency with the exceptionalist's faith in being "release[d] from [his] confinement in some abnormal way" (196). The Adamic teen thus continues on the same path in *Cities of the Plain*, casting his desire for the young prostitute Magdalena as something he "cant help" (120), and this time the naïveté that is stupidity destroys him. Because he still thinks of himself as not having a price, John Grady is pathetically equipped to succeed in an economy in which women are as much commodities as horses. And unable to see that what to him is chivalry is to his lover's pimp the "coveting of another man's property" (241), he is completely outmatched by the Mexican who bargains with him at knifepoint – for an eye, for an ear – prior to passing a blade through his body and proclaiming his own nation's devouring of "[y]ou and all your pale empire" in some not-too-distant future (254).

The Indian troops about to make that future a reality at the end of Leslie Marmon Silko's *Almanac of the Dead* (1991) are far more ambitious in their goal: the return of all tribal lands stolen from them, which will result in the return of justice and then peace. To that end, they dismiss all borders as "[i]maginary lines" imposed by whites to restrict the movement of indigenous peoples that had traveled freely for thousands of years (216), and view "control" of the US-Mexico border (even though "no such thing existed to control except in the white man's mind") as inspired by gringo dread of "a great Indian army moving up from the South" in "spontaneous mass migration" (592). In fact, the troops that comprise that army see themselves as engaged in an ongoing hemispheric war that "never ended in the Americas," as the "Five Hundred Year Map" that serves as the book's frontispiece attests (n. pag.), a pillaging of land followed by the desecration of land, as mining for silver in the sixteenth century eventuates in the "ripping open [of] Mother Earth" for uranium in the twentieth (34).

Silko, however, goes further than the ancient Maya texts her title tropes, which predicted both the arrival of Cortés and the final disappearance of all things European, by attributing global dimensions to that hemispheric conflict. In a world in which "[n]o outsider knows where Africa ends or America begins" (421), and "[n]othing could be black only or brown only or white only anymore" (747), the war chronicled in her almanac will end with a global erasing of borders imposed by colonialists whose desires respect no borders. Consistent with that expanded perspective, Silko refuses to locate that war's onset in New World contact. The separation of tribes from their ancestral lands – in the Americas as well as Africa – is portrayed by her encyclopedic text as the "kind of thing [that] had been happening to human beings since the beginning of time" (88), initiated by a worldwide network of Destroyers, sorcerer-sacrificers called Gunadeeyahs who ask sorcerer-cannibals from Europe to join them, an invitation that Spaniards fresh from an Inquisition that has whetted their taste for blood cannot refuse. Likewise, the enslavement that satisfies that lust is portrayed as part of an extended pattern in which "[e]veryone was or had been a slave to some other person or to something that was controlled by another" (412), with the hungers aroused by ownership in the Americas unchecked by any restraints that proximity to the colonizers' own people or culture might have had. No wonder, in Silko's depiction of the spirit realms that connect Africa and the Americas, Ogoun the "gentleman-warrior" is transformed into a "guerrilla warrior," the Middle Passage crossing having "changed everything" (417).

Tucson, a Southwest "Saigon in the days of the Vietnam War" and the book's primary setting (*Yellow* 139), displays these ongoing processes through a large cast of juxtaposed characters: Indians smuggling guns, dope, and political refugees, and Anglos smuggling porn, coke, and CIA agents; *mestizos* of mixed blood intent on restoring the earth and aristos obsessed with *sangre pura* preparing Alternative Earth modules to flee a tainted earth; cyberterrorists devising computer viruses and racists contemplating biological viruses; psychics locating lost bodies and psychotics harvesting (not always volunteered) body parts. To the *mestiza* Zeta, who goes from smuggling tires and parrots to stockpiling guns and gold in abandoned mine shafts, every shipment of contraband is a victory against the US government since politics "always went where the gold was" (*Almanac* 179). So confirms the history of Tucson. A city where all that separates pimps from politicians is a single generation, Tucson is not just a frontier city *in* America. Tucson, which "had always depended on some sort of war to keep cash flowing" (598) – from Indian Wars that paid for its founding fathers' mansions to Mexican civil wars that fund a Mafia wife's plan to build a dream city with canals in the desert – is the embodiment *of* America. A financially impoverished city that also depends on rich Mexicans coming across the border to shop in its malls, Tucson is not only a city whose "fate was closely tied to the fate of Mexico" or a city "close to Mexico" (598, 759). Tucson, as the porous nature of free world trade illustrates, "*was* Mexico, only no one in the United States had realized it yet" (759). The one item exempt from an economy ruled by "no sentimentality" is dark cadaver skin (565), and that is only because the developer who traffics in biomaterials cannot find a market for it.

It is precisely because of such exemption, however, that the various groups converging on both sides of the border at the book's end – eco-warriors and keyboard warriors, Vietnam vets and Green Berets, Army of the Homeless and Army of Justice – subordinate class-based revolution to racially based restitution, whatever their own differences. The woman leading the pan-Indian Army of Justice and Redistribution thus rejects both Marx and Marxism. The former is a tribal Jew inspired by the *gens* of Native American society, alert to the power of sacred stories and respectful of the fact that the earth belongs to no one, but blind to the spirit beings and the "earth [as] mother to all beings" (749). The latter is an ideology that, as enacted by Stalin and Mao, runs entirely counter to the sensibility of indigenous peoples for whom "no crime was worse than to allow some human beings to starve while others ate" (316). The Indians approaching from Mexico adhere instead to one simple precept – "land first, talk and ideology later" (524) – as they foment the "civil strife, civil crisis, civil war" envisioned by the Maya almanacs (756). And because, as Silko earlier indicates in the opening to *Ceremony* (1977), the naming of things by Thought-Woman sitting in her room causes those things to appear, the retelling of the old almanacs' stories makes her own *Almanac* a participating agent in the realization of their prophecies. When Sterling, the Laguna Pueblo exiled for allowing the great stone snake that has reappeared by the uranium mine to be photographed, returns from Tucson to his community in the book's last pages, the "homing" that is a trademark of Native American fiction signals more than an individual reintegration (Bevis 580). When Sterling looks at the sandstone serpent, he finally understands why the sacred reptile is looking south, in the direction from which all "the people would come" home (763).

The Name Game

The daughter of a Mexican father and a Mexican American mother, Celaya responds with "[f]ront and back" when asked in Sandra Cisneros's *Caramelo* (2002) if she is Mexican on "both sides" (352). Yet given the book's destabilizing of those sides while tracing four generations of the Reyes family from Mexican Revolution through sexual revolution – the way that "over here" and "over there," "*este lado*" and "*otro lado*," shift according to speaker – Celaya's proud identification of herself actually reveals more about the splintering that is her self. The "girl born on the other side who speaks Spanish with an accent" to Mexico City relations (266) is also a "*gabacha*" to Chicana classmates (354), and just a "Mexican" to Anglos who make no distinction between "Mexicans from this side" and "Mexicans from that side" against whom they discriminate equally (235). Positioned in the interstices of two politically opposed cultures, each of which promotes a single national language (González 4), Lala occupies a linguistic middle complicated further by variations of dialect, from formal Castilian to Mexican-Aztec to Tex-Mex Spanglish, and the class-based differences attendant upon them. Familiar enough with two languages as to be aware of the nuances of language ("*¡Me mato!*" a more dramatic way of expressing a threat to kill oneself [11]) and the problems of translation ("*tristeza de hilo blanco*" a "goofy" line of poetry when rendered as "sadness of white string" [316]), she is not quite skilled enough to detect the clunkiness of those idioms that she transposes into English literally ("he who is destined to be a *tamal* will find corn shucks falling from the sky" [210]). As a child who still confuses words based on how they sound, she sometimes finds herself completely lacking in words, as occurs when the dining room ceiling of her grandparents' house collapses and she has neither the English nor the Spanish to convey what has happened. It therefore is not surprising that, having grown up a girl in-between, Lala becomes prone to what she terms the "funkadelics" by the time she becomes a teen (316), stranded in a house "made up of this and that" after her family moves from Chicago to San Antonio (306), "a town halfway between here and there, in the middle of nowhere" (380). Nor is it surprising that the "nostalgia for home when home is gone" that is exacerbated by a geographical border just three hours away is never placated (380): the country for which Lala is homesick, as she realizes in the book's last lines, "doesn't exist anymore," and "never existed" except in her imagination (434).

What this young Chicana does have, however, is a name, the importance of which Cisneros makes clear in *The House on Mango Street* (1984) when Esperanza describes having inherited her great-grandmother's name but not her "place by the window," where that "wild horse of a woman" retreated after being tamed by marriage (11). To be sure, such domestication might itself seem tame when set against the violation portrayed by other Chicana writers – the beatings and near-rapes of women whose "greatest transgression" in Ana Castillo's *The Mixquiahuala Letters* (1986) is to have "traveled alone" (59); the stalking and mutilation of women in *So Far from God* (1993) by "dudes" whose centuries-old misogyny "held the weight of a continent" (128, 77). Cisneros, by contrast, approximates such acts in *Caramelo* by way of fleeting reference: a father mentioning Asian women abused by soldiers during World War II; a grandfather (incorrectly) turning the volcanic origins of Popocatépetl and Iztaccíhuatl into a tale of a prince killing the princess he loved too much. Her focus instead is on the fairy tale figure rescued from one form of enslavement (Cinderella and her stepmother) only to suffer a later imprisonment (Rapunzel in the tower), and the deserving party that can be dispatched with wonderfully sly wit (a grandfather who never lifted a broom dying under a mountain of brooms after his car crashes into a truck packed with them). When Celaya's mother thus names her only daughter after the battle at which "Pancho Villa met his Waterloo" (231), and not Leticia as per her husband's instructions, she initiates what becomes a lifelong revolt, one that Lala imagines as a tossing of her "glass shoe flying flying flying across the broken-glass sky" and depicts as waged through words (66). Rejecting the cultural admonition that women speak "just enough but not too much" (151), Zoila "hurls words like weapons" at her husband in two languages (84). She uses the familiar "*tú*" when addressing the mother-in-law who derides her for not speaking a "proper Spanish" and looking "as dark as a slave" (342, 85), her own humble roots and "*dark as* cajeta" complexion notwithstanding (116). She forces a man chained by bonds of (s)mother love to choose between wife and woman worshipped (as are all the book's matriarchs) as la Virgen de Guadalupe by adult sons infantilized with nicknames like "Fat-Face" and "Baby."

And when Lala of the "Big-Mouth" chooses to become a storyteller (351), one who – in Cisneros's deliberate phrasing – "like[s] weaving stories just to make trouble" (93), she follows suit. For in portraying the art of *cuentos* as kin to the art of *rebozos*, the Mexican shawls of the book's title that *"like all mestizos"* derive *"from everywhere"* (96), Cisneros not only links storytelling to an art born of matrilineal succession, "one thread interlocking and double-looping, each woman learning from the woman before, but adding a flourish that became her signature, then passing it on" (93). She links it to an artifact that, woven on indigenous looms during the colonial period by *mestizas* prohibited by law from dressing like Indians but too poor to clothe themselves like Spaniards, testifies to female rebellion. Lala embroiders her family saga in a similar manner, as befits the child of an upholsterer: "knot[ting] the words together for everyone who can't say them" (428), crisscrossing *historias* with "healthy lies" (188), and finishing her fabric(ation) with appliquéd footnotes and chronology trim. In so adhering to the writing of stories as Latina feminists urge (Gómez, Moraga, and Romo-Carmona vii), she avoids becoming part of the story her grandmother tells of Mexican women leaping from church bell towers in such large numbers as to prohibit visitor access. Having learned the difference between destiny and destination from her own romantic misfortunes, Celaya concedes the first but chooses the second.

Another "Big Mouth" who aspires to be a writer, Yolanda de la Torre is similarly splintered in Julia Alvarez's *How the García Girls Lost Their Accents* (1991), which traces, in reverse chronological order (1989–1956), an upper-class family's narrow escape from the Dominican Republic to the US and the bastardizing of the authorial surrogate's "pure, mouth-filling, full blooded" Spanish name into abbreviations (Yo, Yoyo, Yosita), English mispronunciations (Joe, Joey), and downright falsifications (Jolinda), with the result that "her real name no longer sounded like her own" (135, 81, 79). To Alvarez, who elsewhere describes her native Spanish words as "illegal immigrants trying to cross a border into another language" (*Something* 24), command of language is more than just a mark of assimilation, with the García girls' lost accents as much a source of pride as their fixed teeth to a father who speaks English with a heavy accent and mother whose English is a "mishmash of mixed-up idioms and sayings" (*García Girls* 135). Command of language is a means of survival, quite literally a matter of life or death to a family shaped by Trujillo's dictatorship. Its servant Chucha barely survives the 1937 massacre of Haitians identified by their inability to pronounce *"perejil"* (parsley) with the proper Spanish trill (an ethnic cleansing of thousands at the center of Edwidge Danticat's *The Farming of Bones* [1998]). Horrified as she is that her four young daughters are "picking up the national language of a police state" in which every word is "a possible mine field" (211), Yolanda's mother also recognizes the absolute need for such discretion. Yolanda as a child nearly gets her father killed after she tells a neighbor that he has a gun; when members of the secret police (SIM) come looking for him years later, he hopes from his closet hideout that "Yoyo will keep her mouth shut" (196). Conversely, when her father literally rips to shreds the speech in which the teenage Yolanda "finally sounded like herself in English" because he finds its Whitman-inspired celebration of the self-boastful rather than grateful (143), she responds to his quashing her American right to free speech by calling him "Chapita" (147), the worst word she can think of for being Trujillo's hated nickname.

Compounding the problem for sisters whose struggles with language coincide with their struggles with adult sexuality, as critics have noted (Hoffman 23–24; Gómez-Vega 90–92), is the fact that they come from a country in which the silencing of citizens and the violation of women also coincide. Fifi, the youngest sister, imagines that it was she who almost got their father killed for refusing to sit on the lap of one of the SIM men whose hands at their holsters remind her mother of a "man fondling his genitals" (211), a point that Alvarez later expands in *In the Time of the Butterflies* (1994) when relating the story of the Mirabal sisters whose execution by Trujillo (publicly slapped by one for his predatory advances) occurred just months after the Alvarez sisters' flight to safety. Therefore, when Carla, the oldest Gracía girl, is left speechless while trying to describe the man whose earlier exposing of himself has left her with "[n]ot one word, English or Spanish" (157), it is not only because she has left the Dominican Republic "before she had reached puberty in Spanish" and is being taught English in the US by nuns who had not "ever mentioned the words she was needing" (163). It is also because she is reporting the incident to American policemen whose "masculinity offended and threatened" (160). Likewise, when Yolanda, who has become skilled in the nuances of two languages, rejects her husband's sexual overtures, prompting her "proudly monolingual" Anglo mate to force his tongue between her lips and push "her words back in her throat" (72, 75), his physical silencing becomes part of an ongoing war waged through language: he compensates for his verbal inadequacy by humiliating his poet-wife with hated nicknames, and she responds by "taking on his language" to appease him (73). When this suppression of language finally erupts in the babbling that gets her hospitalized for a nervous breakdown, Yolanda discovers that the most offending of the words to which she has developed an allergy is the word for "love," which makes a rash erupt whether rendered in English or Spanish (85).

All of which makes Yolanda's 1989 return to a Dominican Republic still plagued by "incidents" (10), and an extended family that lives in a compound patrolled by private guards, such a misguided attempt to find a safe home after coming to the conclusion that "she has never felt at home in the States, never"

(12). Because this return occurs in the book's opening chapter, it informs the events of the fourteen chapters that follow, as does the life of the sister in whom the "wrong turns" of all the García girls' "turbulent lives" combine (11). Yolanda literally does not know the words for the *antojo* that consumes her, a longing that cannot be satiated no matter how many guavas (or *guayabas*) she eats. What she does know, however, is menace. Unlike the woman in a Palmolive ad, her mouth open in ecstatic cry, that she finds tacked to a cantina post while searching for the fruit in the remote countryside, Yolanda feels as if her tongue "has been stuffed in her mouth like a rag to keep her quiet" when approached by two *campesinos* with machetes who offer to help her with a flat tire (20). So when she recalls the poet she has earlier met at a party who asks her in what language she loves, the *dominicana americana* does not reply in a way that confirms or denies his theory about people reverting to their mother tongue when experiencing profound emotion. Alvarez withholds from the reader any reply that Yolanda makes to his query.

Gogol Ganguli, by contrast, responds not at all in Jhumpa Lahiri's *The Namesake* (2003) when presented with a plate holding soil, pen, and dollar bill at the *annaprasan*, or rice ceremony, that serves as the first formal ceremony for Bengali babies for whom there is no ritualistic naming or baptism. Forced at six months "to confront his destiny" – landowner, scholar, or businessman – he touches nothing, after which he beings to cry (40). Thus begins a lifetime of opting out for this son of Indian immigrants who later latches onto the term "ABCD" – "American-born confused *deshi*" – because it encapsulates so well the conflicted identity of a second-generation child who understands and speaks a mother tongue that he neither reads nor writes (118), and whose avoidance of other ABCDs is matched by his dalliances with women of no Indian heritage whatsoever. As the naming and name-changing that marks the first thirty-two years of his own life reveals, however, that prioritizing of consent over descent, to employ Werner Sollors's terms, testifies less to agency and more to accident, beginning with the accidental train wreck from which Gogol gains his name after his father is saved by holding up a page of Nikolai Gogol's short stories for rescuers to spot. That pet name (*daknam*) is recorded on his birth certificate as his good name (*bhalonam*) when the letter with the name chosen by his great-grandmother gets lost in the mail between Calcutta and Cambridge. It is formalized again when his grandfather's sudden death forces his parents to get an express passport for him before they can come up with a suitable good name for him. As a result, Gogol grows up with a "pet name turned good name" in a country where no such distinctions exist, not to mention a "last name turned first name" (78). Even worse, when he goes to India for family visits, he learns that he has a last name so common as to fill six pages of the Calcutta telephone directory. Far from testifying to that sacred inviolability of names that makes the naming of children after their parents unknown in Bengali culture, Gogol's entire name, as he discovers, testifies to cultural divestment: Ganguli an Anglicized abbreviation of Gangopadhyay; Gogol a simplification of Gogol-Yanovsky, the surname of a writer who once simplified his name to the point of signing his work "OOOO."

In fact, as designating a nineteenth-century Russian writer who starved himself to death, those four characters that equally signal four zeros testify to the cancellation of the self. They thus prove especially appropriate for the twentieth-century namesake whose serial alternation of names is character-ized less by the choosing of a name he wants as it is the discarding of a name he hates. Unwilling to start kindergarten as Nikhil, the good name on which his parents finally decide and to which they are certain he will "grow accustomed" (the paradigm for their own immigrant experience), he allows his teacher to keep the name Gogol for him (59). Unwilling to begin college as Gogol, he legally changes his name to Nikhil, offering "I hate the name Gogol" when ordered by the judge to supply a reason for his request (102). And because the serial alternation of names meant to resolve the conflicts of hybridity deprives him of the benefits of hybridity, Gogol remains not just without a "B-side to the self" (76); he remains without much of an A-side as well. When later surrounded by young marrieds discussing the "perfect name" for a child (244–45), the man whose rejected/accepted good name means "he who is entire, encompassing all," argues that humans should use pronouns for themselves until they turn eighteen (56). It is, then, not surprising that he twice fails the architect's licensing exam that is a prerequisite for him to design structures under his own name and that the contributions to those devoted to tourism on which he does work are "incidental, and never fully his own" (125). How can he build when his characteristic response is to banish?

It is not until the collapse of his marriage to the *deshi* daughter of family friends – the seemingly perfect mate who knows him as both Gogol and Nikhil but finally rejects him for reminding her of the life she "had struggled so mightily to leave behind" by immersing herself in all things French (250) – that Gogol begins to realize just how poorly his strategy has served him. Her "reinvent[ion]" by way of a new third culture, one embraced "without misgivings, without guilt," is something that Gogol, in "all likelihood, will never do" (233). For one thing, Gogol has never bothered to learn another language. For another, Gogol has never bothered to move more than four hours away from his parents, a fact made even more apparent by the distances the women who surround him are traveling by book's end. His sister, Sonia, moves to California and gets engaged to a man half-Jewish and half-Chinese; in so doing, she does become the "citizen of the world" that her Russian, European, and South American name bespeaks (62), a fully integrated person whose pet and good name are one and the same. His widowed mother, Ashima, gives up her home of twenty-seven years to live half the year in India and half in the US: "True to the meaning of her name, she will be without borders, ... a resident everywhere and nowhere" (276). These geographic departures prompt Gogol to recognize those more permanent generational ones that will eventuate in the disappearance of all those who knew him as Gogol Ganguli before he ever has had the chance to know Gogol Ganguli himself. Lahiri, though, ends the novel with a final accident that grants him a reprieve. Gogol, back in Massachusetts to celebrate a last Christmas in his family home, enters his old room and happens upon the unread volume of his namesake's stories that his father has inscribed on his fourteenth birthday, a book "salvaged" by "chance" from a pile awaiting donation that reminds him of the parent saved from a pile of debris years earlier (291). It is at that point that the boy who has never outgrown adolescent naysaying opens the book and decides to read.

The decision of sixteen-year-old Mona Chang to become Jewish occurs at the beginning of Gish Jen's *Mona in the Promised Land* (1996), "before you can say matzoh ball" in fact (32). That "switch" (14) – the word used throughout to designate the fluidity/performativity of identity – has little to do with self-cancellation, however. When "Mona-also-known-as-Ruth" steps out of her ritual mikvah with a new religion and new name, she emerges "a more or less genuine Catholic Chinese Jew" (44). Her conversion is an act of accumulation, her choice a celebration of her nationality: "American means being whatever you want," she tells her mother, "and I happened to pick being Jewish" (49).

To her immigrant parents who "adjust" rather than "switch" (4), and whose backstory forms the subject of *Typical American* (1991), such thinking is beyond their comprehension. In large part, this is because the initial Americanization of Ralph-born-Yifeng and Helen-born-Hailan is a matter over which they have had no choice, stranded as they are in the US when China falls in 1949 to the Communists. It is only when the unlikelihood of any Nationalist return forces them to embark upon the process of assimilation, assisted by those guidebooks they take as their bibles (*The Power of Positive Thinking* [1952] for engineer-turned-imagineer Ralph, *House Beautiful* for happy-homemaker Helen) and become "Chang-kees" themselves that they relinquish their contempt for "typical American[s]" (127, 67). Never do they look back. Ralph fails his driver's test three times because he will not heed his instructor's advice to check his rear-view mirror. Nor do they ever question the foundation on which they base their new sense of self. Indeed, the man who writes his dissertation on crack stress in airplanes remains oblivious to the literal and figurative cracks in his own domiciles, personal and professional, and with increasingly disastrous results as the Changs move from slum to suburb. A Harlem rental loses an entire bedroom corner. A purchased fried chicken joint resting on unstable land collapses into the ground. A doghouse improperly staked leaves Ralph's sister in a coma after being struck by a car while running from the vicious animal that has destroyed its home. Adjusting to events and "moving on" (120), as per the first-generation immigrant's creed, the family moves from Tarrytown to Scarshill and opens up a new establishment that caters to American tastes (pancakes). Accepting that the "language of *outside the house* had seeped well inside" (124), they decide that their children will learn English before Chinese so as not to speak with accents.

Except that Callie-born-Kailan, who starts studying Mandarin at Harvard, and Mona-born-Mengna, who starts peppering her speech with Yiddish in high school, have absolutely no interest in identifying themselves as "plain" Mayflower Americans (*Mona* 135). Nor do any of their suburban friends who grow up during the 1960s "blushing dawn of ethnic awareness" untroubled by cultural binarism (3). The Rapunzel-haired Eloise Ingle starts attending Temple Youth Group after she learns of her dead mother's background, only to stop a few weeks later after "having decided to go back to being Wasp," and another teen points at "the Changowitz" to ask "why can't a person be both?" (56). The "authentic inauthentic Jew" in-the-process-of-becoming an "inauthentic inauthentic Jew" Seth Mandel becomes convinced by his impersonation of a Japanese student that he has been, if not Japanese, at the very least "something else Eastern" in another life (112, 279). Fittingly, the one time that talk about plastic surgery – which typically involves Mona enlarging her nose to look more Jewish – ends in someone actually going under the knife, the procedure backfires: so mortified is Barbara Gugelstein by the new nose her mother has duped her into getting that she starts making plans to work on a kibbutz.

Jen, who freely cites the mash-up of literary antecedents that contribute *to* her work (*Tiger* 142–43), makes it clear *in* her work that this freedom to cherry-pick and mix-and-match is more complicated when it comes to personal identity. In the case of Mona and her friends, it is predicated not just on privilege – on Seth's "authentic canvas teepee" being furnished with reel-to-reel tape player and push-button Princess phone (*Mona* 113) – but on ignorance. For the actual Sherman Matsumoto, who knows that the atomic bomb was dropped on only one people (and by whom), becoming "American" as per Mona's suggestion is not as easy as it is for Mona, whose knowledge of Asian history has her thinking the Nanking Massacre is the Napkin Massacre, to become "Jewish." More to the point, it founders completely when confronted with the subject of race. Mona, who "has never thought of herself as colored before" and needs to get used to the idea of being "yellow" because "she is not exactly a textbook primary" (170), concedes that her classmates who are "studying to be Bobby Seale" are "finding the color row tough hoeing" (49, 118). She even, with her BFFs, devises a point system for their "comparative-tragedy project" and arrives at "the shining truth" that, the Chinese Revolution and the Holocaust notwithstanding, it is advantageous "to look more like Archie Bunker than Malcolm X" (140). Yet in trying to convince the African American cook at her parents' restaurant that being Jewish "too" will improve his prospects, citing Stokely Carmichael's desire to attend Brandeis as proof, they are blind to the fact that African Americans are, as Alfred informs them, *"black motherfuckers"* who are likely to end up doing time in a concrete hotel if they do not mind their manners (137). And this is exactly what happens after Alfred is evicted from his home and the three install him in the vacated Gugelstein home, but with so many restrictions to avoid nosy neighbors as to amount to incarceration, an arrangement that falls apart when a silver flask goes missing and photos of Alfred cavorting with Barbara's cousin surface.

The "*[g]emilut hassadim*" or acts of "loving-kindness" from which their clumsy efforts spring (141) – superior to *tzedakah* according to the Talmud in that the giving of the self is more virtuous than the giving of physical possessions – testifies, however, to a view of the self defined less by what one is than by what one does, what Jen elsewhere terms the "interdependent" or "relational" self (*Tiger* 3, 164). To that end, she introduces the failed experiment of Camp Gugelstein by recalling an earlier "nice experiment" predicated on "remain[ing] true" to oneself, only to dismiss Thoreau's experience in the woods as "*self-centered*" (*Mona* 121–22), a luxury in a country without enough room "for everyone to be authentic all day long" and in which people "need to have *consideration for others*" (122). This Mona has understood even before she becomes Jewish; arguably, it is the reason she becomes Jewish in the first place, drawn not by faith (her scrupulous hyphenation of the deity's name notwithstanding) or canonical law (which would require her to give up *treif*), or even diasporic precedent (how better to be a model minority than to learn from the best?), but by a need to ask rather than obey and a sense of duty to the circles that extend beyond the family circle. It thus hardly matters when, at the wedding to Seth that ends the book, Mona hedges when asked about legally changing her surname to Changowitz, something that at one point in her life "mattered more than anything" (303). The daughter to whom she already has given birth does not have to perform identity or change her name to suit her identity. A child "part Jewish, part Chinese" whose favorite cuisine is Italian (303), Io already *is* her identity. What remains to be seen is what her self will be.

The mixed-race child who embodies that possibility in Chang-rae Lee's *Native Speaker* (1995) is remembered as having spoken English "beautifully" by his Korean American father (222), who has wished "whiteness" and a "life univocal" for the boy accidentally smothered by friends on his seventh birthday (265, 249). That Henry Park values Mitt's proficiency in one language more than the child's skill negotiating two (his immigrant grandfather's mixture of Korean and English, his speech therapist mother's standardized English) reflects Henry's own discomfort with language. An American citizen only because born "on this end" of his mother's plane trip from Seoul (310), who still freezes when addressed by his Korean name, Henry speaks English without an accent, but still stumbles over the second language that remains a "scabrous mouthful" (217). This personal liability that makes Henry a "native speaker" in the double sense of Lee's title – "native" signifying birthplace as well as racial otherness – proves a professional asset, however, when Henry is recruited as a "[d]omestic traveler" by a firm specializing in "ethnic coverage" (15, 16). More than just a spy whose adoption of "serial identit[ies]" can end in the erasure of all identity (30), an updated version of the duplicitous Asian in a genre long linked to colonialist adventure (Chen 178), Henry is a spy whose success depends on using his invisibility to ingratiate as well as infiltrate. The latter, in fact, is predicated on the former. Henry can only "stay in the background" and be "unapparent and flat" as per his employer's instructions after having used the visible marker of race to gain the trust of those Asian subjects to whom he is assigned (40). When he is tasked with infiltrating the organization of a rising Korean councilman in an attempt by his boss to get him "back to [his] old self" (21) – the "good Henry, good Harry, Parky" that is his office self (158) – after the Filipino doctor of his last assignment turns up drowned, Henry is faced with a dilemma. The Korean American who has avidly cultivated a native American persona must, as Christian Moraru notes, "reconstitute a sort of 'pre-native,' pre-Americanized profile" in order to bond with John Kwang's own "native Korean self" ("Speakers" 71).

Just how much of that self remains is open to debate, of course, given the vexed relationship between politicians' performativity and authenticity. Kwang is "in the language," as a colleague of Henry's asserts (157), not only because the telegenic self-made man – an Asian Gatsby who renames himself John upon arriving in the US after his family is obliterated during the Korean War – speaks "a beautiful, almost formal English" (21). It is also because Kwang knows enough of all the languages spoken by the Queens constituents he courts by melding their ethnic and racial differences into the same historical paradigm: his own. It is this same command of languages that he uses to expand his business ventures beyond neighborhood dry-cleaning to car dealerships, from Korean to European suppliers, as befits someone whose ambitions extend beyond being "just another ethnic pol from the outer boroughs" (283). At the same time, Kwang is not above financing his campaigns by expanding the model of the Korean *ggeh* into a "giant money club" (261). Nor is he immune to lapsing into Korean and English in private or displaying in public a "mysterious dubbing" at odds with his stylized Anglo gestures (167) – slippages that Henry can recognize as clearly as he can the smells of those pickled Korean foods kept sealed and double-wrapped in Kwang's basement because they are so familiar. On the one hand, Kwang's defrauding of other Koreans reenacts, on a larger scale, the "exploit[ing] his own" in which Henry's greengrocer father has engaged (50), making the role of "obedient, soft-spoken son" that Henry assumes in his dealings with the councilman more than filial performance (188). On the other hand, Kwang's adopting a persona that is simply a more polished and confident version of Henry's turns Kwang into Henry's double. When the job that Henry begins intending "to give a good scratch to the surface" and "come away with some spice or flavor under my nails" leaves Kwang with just a final mask after his various faces have been stripped away (131), the person who also is revealed as lacking is Henry himself. As this lackey understands, "in every betrayal dwells a self-betrayal, which brings you that much closer to a reckoning" (292).

The bomb in Kwang's headquarters that forces that reckoning by exposing the councilman's complicity and, later, duplicity "speaks volumes" (248) – a reminder that in New York's "city of words" there is no one to speak for the Dominican volunteer and East German janitor killed by fumes (319), any more than there is someone "who can speak" for the cabbies being murdered across the boroughs because as a group "they're too different from one another, they're recently arrived Latvians and Jamaicans, Pakistanis, Hmong" (229). Lee thus proposes that "*[h]ave mercy*" be the city's first lesson, to be uttered in "forty signs and tongues" (229). To that end, he portrays New York as incarnating ancient Rome's "first true Babel," its people of the outer boroughs no different from the "outer peoples" earlier brought as "ambassadors, lovers, soldiers, slaves," carrying with them their "native spice and fabric, rites, contagion," and – most important – languages (220).

When Lee adds that entering Rome's "resplendent place" required those "new ones" to "learn the primary Latin" and "[q]uell the old tongue" (220), however, he hints at what distinguishes the two imperial centers. By the end of his novel, such new ones are not even allowed to enter, much less stay, in late twentieth-century New York. Hounded by the press, Kwang and his family depart for Korea. Rounded up by the INS, the undocumented who fund his mayoral bid are sent back to their native countries. Taken into police custody after a freighter smuggling Chinese men runs aground off Far Rockaway, the survivors await deportation. Yet the novel's final pages that show the spy introduced as a "*[f]alse speaker of language*" teaching a class of students with the wife introduced as the "standard-bearer" of language suggest a heteroglossic alternative (5, 11). What those students see is a "pale white woman horsing with the language to show them it's fine to mess it all up" and a man wearing the mask of the Speech Monster whom they can subdue by repeating the day's secret phrase (324). The men aboard the *Golden Venture*, the actual vessel that went aground in 1993, did not go "*[g]ently down the stream*" – as the book's secret phrase of the day would have it (323) – or any waterway during their 120 days at sea. But the children who sing the line exit their classroom hearing their names spoken in a "dozen lovely and native languages" and wearing badges that certify that each "has been a good citizen" (324).

The Late-Night Zeitgeist

Oscar Hijuelos's *The Mambo Kings Play Songs of Love* (1989) takes its title from the 33⅓ LP released by a Cuban dance band prior to its quick slide into the obscurity of New Jersey *quinceañeras* the following year. More than just alluding to that 1956 record, the book itself assumes the form of a record, with "Side A" and "Side B" sections framed by chapters that serve as overture and encore, which enables Hijuelos to partake of the dual temporal meaning of that structuring device. As the chronological account of two brothers who come to the US from Cuba in 1949 with the vague idea of "hook[ing] up with an orchestra" (34), much as they earlier have when leaving Oriente Province for Havana, the record traces a history of loss – of home, family, musical idiom – losses certainly exacerbated once Castro makes Cuba itself one of those "things [that] don't exist anymore" (353), but not specific to Castro for being the inevitable products of time's passing. Yet as a circular disk meant to be replayed again and again, the record also testifies to the longing for return. It is that yearning that plagues the surviving Castillo brother as he drunkenly relives memories of his sixty-two years to the tunes of his best-selling (though hardly platinum-record-selling) album over the course of the final night in a seedy hotel from which the text radiates.

Concerned more with cultural exchange than mere cultural imperialism, Hijuelos is careful to situate the brothers' 1949 move to New York within a larger historical context, as part of a wave of musicians departing Cuba since the 1920s, prompted, first, by the loss of orchestra jobs after talkies replace silent films and, later, by the influx of big American jazz bands that relegate "more authentic" Cuban music "to the alleys" (31). That being said, and for all the attempts of the Cuban immigrants who surround them to look like Hollywood movie stars, neither Cesar nor Nestor displays any assimilationist angst regarding the loss of their Cuban identity. The machismo and melancholy that define both (inversely) are too engrained personally; the mambos played by Latin bands "given balls by saxophones and horns" and sappy boleros in which the siblings specialize depend on the men's professionally retaining their island heritage (24). Any reinvention of themselves as Americans, after learning the English required for practical dealings, is limited to achieving monetary success (Nestor's underlined copy of *Forward America!*) or emblems of that success (Cesar's turbo-thrust 1956 DeSoto), aspirations validated by the Hollywood careers of Cubans like Cesar Romero and Gilbert Roland. As *musicians*, however, the brothers take their cue from performers like Machito and Pérez Prado, and, most of all, Desi Arnaz, the *compadre* who "parlayed his conga drum, singing voice, and quaint Cuban accent into fame" while always "present[ing] the proper image of a man" (33, 138).

That image, of course, had little to do with the actual facts of Arnaz's past – wealthy family, forced exile after Batista's 1933 military coup – or the fact that his Hollywood success was as much a function of his being a shrewd businessman as a skilled musician. As portrayed by Hijuelos, it depends upon Arnaz being a *gallego*, a "white Cuban" allowed to enter the living rooms of Americans watching television (in contrast to the "ebony-black" Cubans forced to use the back doors when the Mambo Kings tour America's heartland [165]), who is domesticated further as the beleaguered "Ricky," the Anglicized diminutive that precedes "Ricardo," a name that is seldom a Spanish surname (Firmat 67). Fittingly, it is his easy-listening recording of the brothers' "Beautiful María of My Soul" that eventuates in the Muzak versions piped into supermarkets and bus terminals. Yet when Cesar is questioned about Arnaz by a nostalgia-hour interviewer who criticizes the performer as not having been "very authentic or original," Cesar responds by describing what the untrained Arnaz did as very "difficult" and his music as "Cuban enough for me" (339). As Hijuelos suggests, it also is for those Cubans force-fed "jive Eastern European jazz like pompom waltz music" who seek out short-wave radios broadcasting from the US and Mexico after 1959 in order to "listen to the real stuff" (324). When Cesar, then, watches late-night reruns of *I Love Lucy*, in particular the episode in which he and Nestor playing Alfonso and Manny Reyes appear on the Ricardos' doorstep as per the show's formula, his being struck by a "world where everything happens because of the door" (268), a welcome of outsider into inside, is not proof of his having been hoodwinked by the worst kind of American self-congratulation. Within the confines of the world established by the novel, the sitcom's fiction is ratified. When the two Sánchez brothers, suitcases and instruments in hand, later appear on the doorstep of Cesar himself, their appearance jettisons all ideas of the "television personality" as celebrity simulacrum (124), with Ricky Ricardo a refracted version of Desi Arnaz, the name used for the bandleader in the original TV script (Shirley 78). More than "Cuban enough," Arnaz is the Cuban last seen welcoming Nestor's troubled son, Eugenio, into the home he continues to live in because California's climate evokes memories of the home he has had to leave.

It is, significantly, through the final dissolving of barriers that occurs in that home that Hijuelos grants this Castillo second-generation American male who narrates the book's framing chapters a moment of grace denied the first. Having opened the novel by recalling the strains of *I Love Lucy* that resurrect his deceased father in eternal rerun, Eugenio ends it by writing himself into that TV scene while sitting in Arnaz's living room. Embracing, through the magic of Desilu's satin heart and the miracle of Jesus Christ's "fiery heart" (195), the father who dies when a steering wheel crushes a vein near his heart, Eugenio is "pulled back into a world of pure affection, before torment, before loss, before awareness" (404). Yet identifying as a dream the final image of his uncle Cesar's heart swelling to the size of that satin heart and floating free from his chest, he qualifies the extent to which the desire for a lost home can ever be realized. As Cristina García concludes when describing her own *Dreaming in Cuban* (1992), "Cuba is a peculiar exile ... We can reach it by a thirty-minute charter flight from Miami, yet never reach it all" (219).

China, as portrayed in the work of Frank Chin, is eminently reachable, provided one is skilled in the art of "bullshit detection," the ability to distinguish between "the real and the fake" ("Come" 39), so crucial to the Confucian model of life as warfare within which "[a]ll art" – writing as much as swordsmanship – is "martial art" (35). Completely "real," which is to say authentic, are the heroic traditions encoded in fairy tales and Asian classics (*Romance of the Three Kingdoms, The Water Margin, Journey to the West*), as relevant to Asian American as to Asian experience. The eponymous *Donald Duk* (1991), for instance, educates himself about the history of the Chinese in America by grafting the Chinese god of war, Kwan Kung, and Soon Gong's 108 outlaws onto the building of the transcontinental railroad. Completely "fake" are the distortions of those tales by writers who falsify both Asian and Asian American history to suit their own agendas (promotion of Christianity in the autobiographies of Yung Wing and Jade Snow Wong; exposure of misogyny in the novels of Maxine Hong Kingston and Amy Tan), which contributes to the perception of Asians as sojourners rather than settlers and Asian men as alternately passive or perverse. Within that paradigm, Charlie Chan is not the antitype of the demonic Asian purveyed by writers such as Sax Rohmer, the desire of creator Earl Derr Biggers to subvert racial stereotypes with his hero's smarts notwithstanding (Rzepka 1472–76). Rather, the obse- quious male detective is its flip side, the "acceptable pervert" as opposed to Fu Manchu's "unacceptable pervert" ("Come" 17). His initial appearance in 1925 coincided with laws restricting Chinese women from entering the US and revoking the citizenship of women who married "alien[s] ineligible to citizen- ship" (Chan 123–24), and this quite literal erasing of Chinese men was later exacerbated by cinematic adaptations (1931–1949) in which the leading role was played, successively, by three white actors.

Chin, who has returned to the figure of Charlie Chan throughout his career (most recently, in Calvin McMillin's reassembling of the "lost" novel of the 1970s, *The Confessions of a Number One Son* [2015]), is fully aware of how indestructible that figure is. In "The Sons of Chan" (1988), the narrator relegated to playing Number Six Son (in movies that, in actuality, did not go past three) embarks upon a mission to kill his father on behalf of a secret society of sons engaged in "holy war" (*Chinaman* 141), but is unable to lift a finger against the man who shames him with his lowly filial status. In *Gunga Din Highway* (1994), which opens with plans to reboot the franchise and a Number Four Son desperate to be the first Chinese man to play the lead, the sleuth's films are studied (without protest) in universities. Indeed, far from dead and buried, Charlie Chan is portrayed as perennially alive on late-night TV, the "brilliant zeitgeist" of America's "local collective subconscious" (38), whatever the professional fortunes of his cinematic offspring – Keye Luke a blind Buddhist priest on *Kung Fu*, Victor Sen Yung a cook on *Bonanza* – might suggest. His claim to fame the fact that he is "The Chinaman Who Dies" – having followed his stint as Number Four Son by playing expendable Asian sidekick to just about every Hollywood A-list (and sometimes B-list) actor, as per the pattern set by RKO's Gunga Din (played not by an Indian but by a Jewish American) – Longman Kwan is perfectly positioned to advance from "symbol of helpless, struggling China" to emasculated star (7). No longer a cinematic representation of a fictional character based on an actual Honolulu detective named Chang Apana, the reel has completely eclipsed the real. In *Donald Duk*, such displacement results in no actor's dismay: when the tween who wants to be Fred Astaire imagines asking his idol if he ever dreamed of being anyone but himself, he is told by the Omaha-born Frederic Austerlitz that he has "always dreamed of being Fred Astaire" and cannot be certain of what his real name is anymore (124). In *Gunga Din Highway*, by contrast, the characters who imagine themselves starring in what is repeatedly termed "The Movie About Me" invariably find themselves in the "wrong movie."

Nothing exposes that disjunction more clearly than the 1960s Revolution Chin deems pure "showbiz" (*Gunga* 220), as Chinatown Black Tigers impersonate Black Panthers that swear by unread copies of Mao's *Little Red Book* while taking their cues from *Ozzie and Harriet*. But no one suffers that mash-up more than the Number Two Son (who later discovers he is the Number Three Son) of the father who played Chan's Number Four Son on screen. A self-described "camper" rather than "homer," Ulysses Kwan (like his Greek namesake) is a wanderer who "*play[s]* the part" rather than "*live[s]* the part" because he conceives of his life as a series of location shoots (178) – Mother Lode, Oakland, Berkeley, Seattle, New York. When he finally appears to have found a part he wants to live – creator of an Asian American theater – he discovers that actors refusing to be typecast in *Flower Drum Song* only want to star in productions of *Jesus Christ Superstar* and *Hair* with all Asian American casts.

It is not until he attends a Washington music festival and happens upon the father he has hated for his absence and reviled for promulgating stereotypes that have turned entire generations into "the sons of the sons of Charlie Chan" that Ulysses witnesses subversion by way of appropriation (311). "I want to laugh at the paranoid stupidity of what's real here," he remarks when seeing his own father and Longman's Belgian cinematic father in obviously fake toupees bemoaning the Chinese presence in film, given the chimpanzee's advance from *King Kong* to *Planet of the Apes* (200). He thus defends his later decision to star in the American Face Theater's production of *Fu Manchu Plays Flamenco* by citing what he has learned about genre: "Satire is where you make fun of how *they* think and what *they* say in order to make *them* look stupid" (257). And, inspired by "divine stupidity" after waking from a dream of playing the corpse of the last white man to play Charlie Chan (345), he proceeds to write *Night of the Living Hollywood Dead* and *Night of the Living Third World Dead*, staking his own claim to fame – his saving of face, as it were – on a genre predicated on zombies "slipping the face back on over the skull only to have it gradually slip off again and dangle" (382). The screenplays he writes under a pseudonym, the novelizations under his own name.

Under no illusion is Ulysses that he can completely control reception of work reviewed in terms of ethnicity rather than genre in a town that has just green-lighted a new Charlie Chan film scripted by a thinly disguised Kingston, directed by a thinly disguised Oliver Stone, and starring (of course) a white actor. Even at the funeral of Longman that ends the book, at which both "real and fake" fathers and sons converge for publicity hype, his father remains "second banana" (389). But in following that scene with Ulysses being given the reels of the 35mm film his father has kept as a paternal "ace in the hole" (45), Chin suggests the degree of control that parodic ironizing does make possible. "[H]ave you noticed the Americans really show what they think of you by who they let pilot planes in the movies?" Longman is asked early in the novel by one of his cinematic brethren (42). In the war movie shown only in China and named after the expert in dying on screen who countered Orientalism with camp, the sons of Charlie Chan who form the first Chinese American B-24 crew step into the *Anna May Wong* and take to the sky.

The multimedia performance artist Jessica Hagedorn is far less sanguine about the prospects of flight, given the state in which she leaves her Filipina surrogates. At "home only in airports," Rio Gonzaga ends her coming-of-age in *Dogeaters* (1990) dreaming of "fly[ing] around in circles" in "futile attempts to reach what surely must be heaven" (247). The journalist Paz Marlowe "wander[s] the planet" of *Dream Jungle* (2003) like "some cosmic detective without grounding or direction" (285). Exacerbated by US immigration, these expatriates' demons originate in the particular nature of the Philippines' colonization, notably the fact that the archipelago of over 7,100 islands, forty ethnic groups, and eighty languages and dialects was only unified under one name after its sixteenth-century conquest by Spain, and the fact that Spain's three-hundred-year rule was succeeded by nearly a half-century of US rule. Having been "baptized and colonized to death" by those two imperial powers, the *mestizos/as* descended from warring tribes emerge "united only by our hunger for glamour and our Hollywood dreams" (*Dogeaters* 101), a mixture of Catholicism and cinema that displaces animism and paganism with the worship of God as "Charlton Heston in robes, with flowing white hair and matching beard" (190).

As *Dogeaters* makes clear, however, that displacement does not signal an entire replacement of indigenous with imposed. A collage of historical figures (William McKinley, George Hamilton, Rainer Werner Fassbinder) and invented figures (a radicalized beauty queen, a young street hustler, a showbiz wannabe), actual documents (Associated Press bulletins, 1846 anthropological excerpts) and fabricated documents (*Metro Manila Daily* clippings, *Celebrity Pinoy* datelines), the book duplicates the "crazy-quilt atmosphere" and "hybrid ambiance" that is the Philippines itself to the self-described "hybrid" Hagedorn ("Interview" 97, 94). As such, its characters are as glued to radio dramas, Tagalog soap operas, and *bomba* movies as they are to imported Douglas Sirk melodramas. There is no question, though, of which artifacts are the most desirable in a country where cashiers acclaim "Made in de USA!" when ringing up customers' prized purchases (234). Nor is there any question of whether the image of the suffering woman conveyed by those artifacts lends itself more to dominant or oppositional readings. In a nation where even upper-middle-class *mestizos* like Rio's father feel like "guest[s]" in their own country (7), the specter of imperialism still hangs over the post-colonial Philippines. Only now it emanates from the "haunted palace on the edge of a swamp" from which a First Lady being photographed displays her "romance with Western culture" (223, 221), lamenting the film career that could have been hers had she and her husband not been "chosen by God to guide and to serve," and extolling the Filipinos' embrace of movies and ability to endure (224).

It is this "[q]ueen of beauty queens" (218), so much like that other self-sacrificing icon Eva Perón, who literally embodies the politics of popular culture hinted at by all the spectacles that punctuate the book (beauty pageants, TV game shows, shower dance clubs), the underlying brutality of which is exposed when the interrogation of an opposition leader's daughter is crosscut with dialogue from that week's episode of *Love Letters*, and the gang-rape that follows occurs while the general in charge watches. It is that same linkage of politics and popular culture that makes the two assignments that Paz pursues in *Dream Jungle* – the 1971 discovery of a lost rain forest tribe (based on Manuel Elizalde Jr.'s purported discovery of the Stone Age Tasaday tribe on Mindanao) and the 1977 filming of the psychedelic Vietnam War epic *Napalm Sunset* (based on *Apocalypse Now* [1979]) – variations on the same assignment. Choreographed by a master showman and documented by an independent filmmaker, each production is coordinated with a Marcos regime that supplies equipment (if not actual bodies, both live and dead) in return for information about leftist activities in remote areas. More to the point, in featuring one man revered as "Spirit Father" by scantily clad tribes-men and another served by natives who double as extras to show a white man worshipped by loincloth-clad tribesmen (11), each production reprises Magellan's original contact with villagers that grant him obedience along with food and tribute – at least according to the excerpted account of that 1521 expedition interwoven into the text. It therefore matters that Tony Pierce be referred to as a "great American director," contrary to Paz's doubts about the need for adjectival qualification (220), just as it matters that Zamora López de Legazpi Jr. be referred to as a "conquistador" even after the revelation of his hoax turns him into a social pariah (151). Together they trace not just the past colonization of the Philippines but a colonization that Hagedorn portrays as ongoing.

When the anthropologist who collected data on the Taobo finally admits to his role in that fraud and ponders the reasons for its perpetration, he sees the First Couple as driven by 40,000 acres of prime real estate and, as a bonus, the international cachet accorded protectors of the environment and indigenous peoples. The playboy born into a family empire of rum, guns, minerals, and logging he views as motivated by the simple fact that "he could" (308). His own twenty-six-year silence he ascribes to fear of retaliation, citing the "omnipresent specter of the president" whose "mummified corpse" in an air-conditioned Hawaii vault is "still capable of casting a long shadow over those of us who remember" (306). When Paz remembers watching the documentary of Zamora's expedition on PBS, she recalls being overcome in Los Angeles by longing, "[h]omesick for gaudy spectacles and contradictions" (304) – much like that most famous (and photogenic) Taobo boy that Zamora sent back to the jungle only to have Bodabil return to the conqueror's Hollywood Hills, Manila, home. As the Great *Mestizo* Father explains when introducing Paz to the teen scampering across his lawn, "he wanted to come back here, to me" (154). Witness to a willingness to which she herself falls prey, this Marlowe experiences a horror that Conrad could only imagine.

Chapter 7

Race Relations

The group, family and guests, was a menagerie, Tino thought. Human; nearly Human with a few visible sensory tentacles; half-Human, gray with strangely jointed limbs and some sensory tentacles; Oankali with Human features contrasting jarringly with their alienness; Oankali who might possibly be part Human; and Oankali like the ooloi who had spoken to him, who obviously had no Humanity at all.
                                – Octavia E. Butler, *Adulthood Rites* (1988)

It is not surprising that the community that presents itself to Augustino Leal upon his arrival at the Lo settlement is perceived as a menagerie. The genetic engineering that has produced the mixed population in this second volume of Octavia E. Butler's Xenogenesis trilogy is the result of ménage-à-trois couplings between males, females, and ooloi neither male nor female in whose bodies the combining of human and alien occurs. To the Oankali who have rescued the survivors of a nuclear holocaust as the first volume, *Dawn* (1987), opens, such exchanges go beyond mere "interbreeding" or "crossbreeding" (41, 42). As portrayed by Butler, they originate as attempts to modify the acquisitive tendencies of aliens and the hierarchical tendencies of humans, in particular the "natural fear of strangers and of difference" that has led to the situation in which the remaining humans find themselves and their sterilization by Oankali who seek to prevent its recurrence (202). They eventuate in *Imago* (1989) in the emergence of an entirely new species – ooloi constructs – whose "reproductive independence" can be conceived as a postrace "true independence" in signaling an evolution beyond the human race (217).

Viewed in this manner, Butler's speculative fiction anticipates by a decade the flurry of pronouncements about race's end that bracketed the millennium – "Race Is Over" (Stanley Crouch), "Race Over" (Orlando Patterson) – a period in which the computer-morphed mixed "New Face of America" that graced *Time* magazine's November 18, 1993, cover was seemingly realized by the November 4, 2008, election of a president who described being born to a black man from Kenya and a white woman from Kansas, and related to people "of every race and every hue," as a "story" that "in no other country on Earth [would be] even possible" (Obama, "More"). Its scientific elements predate those advances cited by Paul Gilroy – in cellular research, organ transplants, and genetic manipulation – that suggest epidermal differences to be no more than skin deep and have led to a "crisis of raciology" (14), the question of whether any place exists in today's new paradigm for those differences based specifically on "race," a word he surrounds with quotation marks. Or, as Walter Benn Michaels argues with respect to Butler's work ("Political" 650), given the difference in the trilogy between humans and walking mollusks, the difference between white and black skin pales (pun intended) by comparison.

It is not, however, eradicated. In *Adulthood Rites*, the construct abandoned on Earth by the Oankali to learn about humans because he still looks completely human is driven out of an English-speaking village because his skin is browner than that of the residents, proof, as Toni Morrison writes in her refutation of *Time*'s celebration, that "the move into mainstream America always means buying into the notion of American blacks as the real aliens" ("On the Backs" 57). Indeed, for all her portrayal of national differences – Indian, Chinese, Brazilian, French, Israeli, Filipino, American – collapsing in the face of interspecies differences, Butler goes to great lengths to show the resilience of familiar racialized thinking when characterizing the encounters between members of those species. On the one hand, the "true xenophobia" evoked in Lilith Iyapo (*Dawn* 22), the first human awakened after a 250-year suspended animation, by the sight of an Oankali derives entirely from what she perceives as his ugly appearance, even though the African American anthropology student admits it is not "that different" from what she earlier has seen on Earth (16) – the tentacles growing out of his head that serve as markers of that ugliness are in fact not "that different" from dreadlocks. Her mixed son, Akin, conversely, is prized by the men who kidnap him because, as a baby whose only suspect feature is a gray tongue, he still "*looks* okay" (*Adulthood* 92), which is to say he can "pass" as human and be sold to human resisters who accept infertility over miscegenation and are desperate for a child. On the other hand, the Oankali whose name means "traders" engage in coercive practices that recall all too clearly those of the slave trade: enforced captivity, impregnation without consent, and perhaps the longest Middle Passage ever imagined. More to the point, they specifically recall the antebellum practices portrayed by Butler in *Kindred* (1979), in which another African American woman who travels through time (backward) and thinks she can survive slavery through careful negotiation learns that as a commodity she has "no enforceable rights" (202), a lesson from the past that is imprinted on her body when she returns to the present with a scarred face and a severed arm. When Lilith, then, asserts to the survivors in the future that they are to "stay human," she refers not just to those abstract notions of "humanity" that concern Tino but to particular acts that resonate with her historically: "Nobody here is property. Nobody here has the right to the use of anybody else's body" (*Dawn* 188).

Possessed of a similar sense of the past's persistence, Michael Omi and Howard Winant propose a theory of "racial formation" when negotiating the degree to which race is determined or constructed, a matter of classification or contingency (53–76). Modern racial awareness having evolved in the Americas from the time of the conquest (a religiously justified advance of civilization) to the eighteenth century (of scientifically based natural hierarchy) to the twentieth century (with its politically determined social constructions), race remains a matter of "'common sense' – a way of comprehending, explaining, and acting in the world" (60). Yet as Ta-Nehisi Coates makes clear when acknowledging that being black has "no inherent meaning" (black blood being no more black in color than black skin [55]) and being white is a function of perception (what people who "believe themselves to be white," in his characteristic phrasing, need to think [6, 42, 97, 104, 105]), the racism from which those conceptions of race spring is a "visceral experience" that "dislodges brains, blocks airways, rips muscle, extracts organs, cracks bones, breaks teeth" (10). As such, the history he charts in the letter to his son that is *Between the World and Me* (2015) – the title taken from a 1935 Richard Wright poem whose speaker stumbles upon "the thing" that is a lynched body – of enslaved bodies requiring whips or tongs or "whatever might be handy" to "get a human being to commit their body against its own elemental interest" and children endangered by police endowed with the authority to destroy their bodies forms an American "*heritage*" (103–04), eventuating in a permanent sense of "[d]isembodiment" that "is a kind of terrorism" (114). Hence his repeated urgings that the teenager named Samori after the nineteenth-century West African who struggled against French colonizers "for the right to his own black body" must always "be responsible for your body" (68, 71), because as a black boy "the price of error is higher for you than it is for your countrymen" in a land where "the story of a black body's destruction must always begin with his or her error, real or imagined" (96).

Cultural critics who address the "postrace" phenomenon, even those who contribute to the plethora of adjectival "post"-ings that infuse the conversation – "postethnic" (David A. Hollinger), "post-black" (Thelma Golden, Holland Cotter, Touré), "post-soul" (Nelson George, Mark Anthony Neal, Bertram

D. Ashe) – thus do not confuse any end of race with an end of racism. Touré distinguishes between "post-Black" and "post-racial," the former signaling a limitless range of identity options, the latter a bankrupt colorblindness that "reflects a naïve understanding of race in America" (12). Gilroy counters the prospect that "the time of 'race' may be coming to a close" with a proliferation of emerging "racisms" (44), the virulence of which stems from these new hatreds no longer deriving, "as they did in the past, from supposedly reliable anthropological knowledge of the identity and difference of the Other but from the novel problem of not being able to locate the Other's difference in the common-sense lexicon of alterity" (105–06). I write just months after news of the self-serving identifications of Spokane NAACP president Rachel Dolezal was followed a week later by the massacre of nine at Emanuel A.M.E. Church in Charleston, South Carolina.

What distinguishes the "post"-tings provided by contemporary African American fiction writers is not only their frequent – and often humorous – dismissals: Danzy Senna approaching "The Mulatto Millennium" (the year the US Census allowed respondents to check more than one box for race) with a listing of coinages ("Jewlatto," "Blulatto," "Tomatto," "Fauxlatto") from which she selected "Postlatto" for herself (23–27); Colson Whitehead addressing the "branding problem" posed by "The Year of Living Postracially" by offering "PWBJHTPMMATOK" ("People Whose Bodies Just Happen to Produce More Melanin, and That's O.K.") as replacement for "people of color" (A31). Rather, what characterizes the remarks of those who specifically see themselves as successors to the Black Power politics of the 1960s and 1970s is their application of the contentious adjective to aesthetics when discussing what Greg Tate in 1986 termed a "postnationalist black arts movement" (206). Taking his cue from writers such as Clarence Major and Ishmael Reed, Trey Ellis proposed a "New Black Aesthetic" (1989) being fashioned by "cultural mulattoes" (235), a "post-bourgeois movement" of the college educated and middle class who recognize racism as "a hard and little-changing constant that neither surprises nor enrages" but are neither shocked by its persistence, like those of the Harlem Renaissance, nor preoccupied with overcoming it, like those of the Black Arts Movement (237, 239–40). Free to make use of any part of their "complicated and sometimes contradictory cultural baggage" (235), these younger practitioners are "shamelessly borrow[ing] and reassembl[ing] across both race and class lines" (234). To that end, Ellis's novel *Platitudes* (1988) opens with an epigraph from Flann O'Brien's *At Swim-Two-Birds* (1939) that conceives of the modern novel as "largely a work of reference" and the "entire corpus of existing literature" a "limbo from which discerning authors could draw" (n. pag.). As Bertram D. Ashe adds, however, when commenting upon a post–Civil Rights aesthetic more descriptive than prescriptive, the cultural hybridity that allows for the targeting of Larry Neal and Amiri Baraka's black nationalist aesthetic for parody is nevertheless done in service of "*blaxploration*, or the propensity to trouble blackness" (614). The eponymous *Angry Black White Boy* (2005) of Adam Mansbach's novel may find himself happily "divorced from his own color" after the whites he robs in his cab report – against all the evidence of their senses – that the perp holding them at gunpoint is black (109). But the riots resulting from the Race Traitor Project of mass apology he later declares force the Jewish hip-hopper (and media darling) to realize that viewing himself as black is "as ridiculous as Toni Morrison calling Bill Clinton the first black president in *The New Yorker*" (264); unlike Malcolm X, on whose corner he launches his campaign, he is unwilling to be black enough to die.

Discussing the subject of race with respect to American novels concerned with black-white relations is not intended to reduce the complexities of race to a simple binary. It springs instead from the long-standing role that those relations have played in the American *literary* imagination, whose artifacts are distinguished as a "coherent entity," as Morrison argues, by an American Africanist "fabricated brew of darkness, otherness, alarm, and desire that is uniquely American" for having arisen out of the nation's collective needs and fears (*Playing* 6, 38). The novels chosen for discussion in the sections that follow thus explore the subject of race by way of familiar genres and established traditions. The first group, by Toni Morrison, John Edgar Wideman, and Edward P. Jones, typify what Bernard W. Bell has termed the neo-slave narrative (285–90), a genre initiated by Margaret Walker's *Jubilee* (1966) and anticipated by Arna Bontemps's *Black Thunder* (1936) (Smith 168–74). These are followed by novels by Ishmael Reed, Percival Everett, and Paul Beatty that update African American satire, a form that emerges in the Harlem Renaissance with works such as Rudolf Fisher's *The Walls of Jericho* (1928), Wallace Thurman's *The Blacker the Berry* (1929) and *Infants of the Spring* (1932), and George Schuyler's *Black No More* (1931). The chapter then turns to portrayals of mixed race, a prominent subject in nineteenth- and early twentieth-century fiction – James Weldon Johnson's *The Autobiography of an Ex-Colored Man* (1912), Nella Larsen's *Passing* (1929) – that reappears in the contemporary period after a steady decline following the Harlem Renaissance (S. Jones 89), joining novels by Colson Whitehead and Emily Raboteau that explore mixed race with novels by Mat Johnson, Danzy Senna, and Richard Powers concerned with mixed race and ethnicity. It concludes with some thoughts on the portrayal of the 2005 event – Hurricane Katrina – that exposed the fissures in all postrace thinking and for which the floods of Hurston and Morrison provide no adequate literary precedent.

Houses Divided, Houses Burned

Inspired by the story of Margaret Garner (1834–1858), an escaped slave who killed her own child when faced with apprehension, and published a year after Sherley Ann Williams's portrait of a captured slave who contemplates strangling the child with which she is pregnant in *Dessa Rose* (1986), Toni Morrison's *Beloved* (1987) establishes its contemporary credentials by opening in 1873, abjuring the linear passage from bondage to freedom that typifies the nineteenth-century slave narrative. Indeed, for all Sethe's attempts to sever herself from the past, the specter of the past continues to haunt her: most obviously in the form of the ghost that has made 124 Bluestone Road a "spiteful" house (3), but no less painfully in those "rememor[ies]" that form the flashbacks that lead up to the act born of desperate "motherlove" that forces Sethe to take a handsaw to her daughter's throat (36, 132). Pivotal to those "rememories" in that it is what prompts Sethe and her husband, Halle, to plan their escape is her happening upon their new master instructing his nephews in the listing of her human and animal "characteristics" (193) – a noun she later learns means "[a] thing that's natural to a thing" (195) – a racial cataloguing that puts into sharp context the measuring of her features that Sethe has previously dismissed as foolery.

More than simply revealing the hypocrisy of a system that profits from sexual relations with women deemed subhuman – Sethe's mother-in-law bears eight children to six different fathers, seven sold while young; her African mother is repeatedly raped by white men both on ship and on shore – such extension of appearance to essence exposes the "special kind of slavery" that supports a Kentucky farm run without beatings or breedings as the "wonderful lie" that it is (140, 221). What the schoolteacher who replaces Mr. Garner upon his death teaches the slaves formerly dubbed "Sweet Home Men," as the sole survivor Paul D finally learns, is that they have been "only Sweet Home men at Sweet Home. One step off that ground and they were trespassers among the human race" (125). This collapsed distinction between benevolent and malevolent ownership, in turn, exposes the fraudulent nature of all those other distinctions – between North and South, pre- and post–Civil War – that have proven so comforting when addressing the history of the peculiar institution. The northern pig port of Cincinnati gains "its status of slaughter and riverboat capital" from serving the entire country (155). The twelve black corpses encountered by a freed slave walking from Selma to Mobile attest that "whitefolks were still on the loose" even after war's end (180) – and remain so. In *Jazz* (1992), the "wave of black people running from want and violence" that "crest[s] in the 1870s" is depicted as continuing well into the next century, as evidenced in 1917 by the two hundred killed in East St. Louis and invitations to see one burned alive in New York City (33).

Yet Morrison, whose portrayal of race relations is complicated by gender relations, refuses to condone the withdrawal from a barbarism of no boundaries that serves as Sethe's response to what her mother-in-law, Baby Suggs, has characterized as a white rout. When the biracial son yearning to be a "free man" instead of a "free nigger" in *Jazz* is bluntly told by the African American father he has tracked to remote Georgia that he can be "white or black" but must surrender any "whiteboy sass" of being neither (173), he opts to remain in the Vienna woods rather than return to Baltimore and becomes a rural legend. When the Mississippi migrants who found the Oklahoma town of Haven in 1890 and, later, Ruby in *Paradise* (1997) compound a separation from whites they hate abstractly with a separation from blacks they actively loathe for refusing the bedraggled group entry into their communities, the African Americans end up enacting their own form of racial discrimination – 8-rock purity – its unspoken blood rule an imitation of the one-drop rule, its worship of coal-black skin one more example of hierarchy based on tonal differences. They also perpetuate a misogyny that bypasses questions of race entirely. In adhering to the Old Fathers' "law of continuance and multiplication" wherein any "visible glitch" is attributable to female promiscuity (279, 196), they project onto the bodies of women all the messiness of life they cannot control, which eventuates in the 1976 lynch mob shooting of women – black *and* white – who occupy the nearby Convent deemed a coven for the unpardonable sin of having chosen their own company over that of men. When Sethe, then, retreats with her surviving daughter, Denver, and the ghost of the slain child embodied in the predatory Beloved into the seclusion of 124, believing that behind its locked door "the women inside were free at last to be what they liked" (*Beloved* 199), she separates herself not just from whites and not just from men. She also separates herself from the community of women that has provided ballast in Morrison's writing from the beginning of her career, from the matriarchs of *The Bluest Eye* (1970) who surround Cholly Breedlove's Aunt Jimmy in her final illness to the "women with seen-it-all eyes" in *Home* (2012) who nurse back to health a young woman on whose womb an Atlanta doctor who takes Madison Grant's *The Passing of the Great Race* (1916) as his bible has experimented (128).

It is these women that Sethe had earlier offended by choosing solitude and self-sufficiency after she emerged from jail for her crime, her "trying to do it all alone with her nose in the air" both "prideful" and "misdirected" (254, 256) – the same women who earlier had reacted with "meanness" to Baby Suggs's perceived "special[ness]" and failed to warn the inhabitants of 124 of the men arriving to reclaim their property (157). Yet it is these same women who, in response to Denver's realization years later that the survival of her shattered family requires that she leave that house, "step off the edge of the world," and "go ask somebody for help" (243), march as a company thirty strong to 124: "Maybe they were sorry for the years of their own disdain. Maybe they were simply nice people who could hold meanness toward each other for just so long and when trouble rode bareback among them, quickly, easily they did what they could to trip him up" (249). Knowing that when trouble takes the form of "past errors taking possession of the present ... you might have to stomp it out" (256), they interject themselves into that historical narrative and change it. When Sethe, forced into endless penance by an embodiment of the past that consumes her to the point of emaciation, rushes with raised ice pick a white man who enters her yard to do in the present what she has been unable to do in the past, she is prevented by the hill of people she joins while leaving behind Beloved. In so doing, those people provide Sethe with the chance to fashion "some kind of tomorrow," to author her life with a man who – in Morrison's deliberate phrasing – longs "to put his story next to hers" (273).

John Edgar Wideman's *The Cattle Killing* (1996), by contrast, eschews linearity only to assert the continuity of past and present for an author best known for his renderings of twentieth-century Pennsylvania yet possessed of a family tree first planted in Pittsburgh by an escaped slave who settled there with her white master's son and their two children (*Damballah* 191–205). Inspired by the account of Philadelphia's 1793 yellow fever epidemic written by Richard Allen and Absalom Jones, two ex-slaves who formed an association of free blacks to tend to the sick and the dead, the novel juxtaposes two *fin-de-siècle* periods to collapse time. Thus the outbreak of one plague ascribed to slaves fleeing Haiti's revolution recalls the etiology of another, AIDS, linked in the popular imagination with Africa. In much the same way, the 1853 slaughter of cattle by South African Xhosa, so desperate to rid themselves of European invaders as to be seduced by false prophecy, gestures backward to an Old World where personal empires are built on the corpses in Liverpool charnel houses and a New World where decapitated animals hang from Philadelphia butcher shops. At the same time, it gestures forward to today's Pittsburgh where black boys shoot each other like "*[p]anicked cattle funneled down the killing chute*"(7), making the history of Africans and people of African descent an "unbroken chain of sausages fed in one end and pulled out the other" (149).

Contributing greatly to that history is the natural science mania for classification that had been extended in the eighteenth century to the classification of human beings based on physiological and mental attributes. Embodied in the figure of Benjamin Thrush, a fictionalized version of the white physician who supervised the black nurses during the 1793 epidemic but remained silent when they later were accused of pilfering and neglect (Lynch 782–83, 787), the practices that make for an "enlightened" man "perfectly suited" for a new age, century, and nation also make for a man who mourns Negroes as a "misunderstood race" while affirming their "natural inclination" to "serve and please" (167, 160). Such regulative categorization was informed by a "spectator theory of knowledge as an epistemological foundation," based on "a passive subject observing a static object" (Cryderman 1049), instances of which abound in Wideman's text. "*Is it* Eye *or* I *or* Ay *or* Aye *or* Aie," asks the contemporary narrator, Isaiah, in the book's opening frame (4). "Did he need someone else's eyes to make him real," queries the former slave turned itinerant preacher (23), a habitual watcher of others himself, whose stories to a dying woman form the book's central narrative.

The most important of those stories concern the interracial couple masquerading as widowed mistress and devoted slave who keep that itinerant preacher from freezing to death by taking him into their home outside Radnor. Asked during his stay to apply liniment to the older woman's skin, the nameless narrator realizes that "[s]he wasn't a white woman" but one whose skin is "variously tinted and grained," with "blushes of red, gold, blue," and is excited to think that his "peeling layers" (as per her request to rub more vigorously) will reveal a "core" with "[b]lack and white gone" (141–42). This, of course, is exactly what her husband has already discovered, as he relates when telling his own story of accompanying his British master, George Stubbs (based on the actual anatomist of that name), to those cadaver dissections that afford the opportunity to "observe and copy nature directly" to a man whose urge to cut and flay is a "backhanded homage" to his currier father's trade (113–14). "No difference beneath the skin," the son asserts to surgeons looking to replace superstition with science but taking the features of the pregnant African woman on the slab before them as proof of a subhuman sensibility (136). In fact, for Wideman, who portrays bodies as mere vessels for African spirits that pass from person to person, what lies beneath the skin is as meaningless a mark of essence as the skin itself. But coming to regard "[b]lack or white" as "unreal" comes only with a willingness to relinquish the "[e]vil dreams of power" supported by conceiving of "[w]hite and black" as hierarchical binaries (141). When the preacher who journeys from Radnor to Philadelphia to assist during the plague later arrives at Thrush's doorstep to ask his help in quelling the backlash against African Americans, he describes Americans of his background as being "of various hues" in response to Mrs. Thrush's repeated queries of whether he is "black" (168), the persistence of which derives from the fact that the woman who turns a blind eye to the husband who creeps into their slave's bed at night is not only literally blind. As one of the orphans this benefactress visits, who scours shelter floors upstairs and sleeps in a locked room downstairs, puts it, "We are . . . children of many colors, but the cellar turns us all black" (187).

The fire that claims the lives of all the children trapped inside that domicile exposes the lie that being spared from fever means being spared a plague that infects a whole nation. For the fire that burns the orphans is the same fire that consumes the black residents of Radnor after a night of rape and murder – a "final reckoning of the peculiar arithmetic," in Wideman's conflation of tabulation and summation, settlement and judgment (149), by which the labor of blacks – free and enslaved – is steadily bled of value until neither it nor the laborer remains with any value at all (112–13). "One day I will tell you about Ramona Africa in her cell," says the preacher who views what happens in Radnor as a prophecy of what transpires in Philadelphia (206), and what transpires in that city in 1793 as a prophecy of what occurs there in 1985, when eleven members of the MOVE liberation group who refuse to vacate their premises at 6221 Osage Avenue are, as Wideman writes in *Philadelphia Fire* (1990), "[s]hot, blowed up, burnt, drowned" in a standoff with city police who "kill them two times, three times, four times" (18). As he goes on to say, "if nothing else works, if evil's still inside, not *out there*, not *them*, if stocks and blocks and locks and pox and rocks and flocks and docks don't work, you can always light a match" (189). Indeed, the match that ignites two blocks of a street named for an Indian tribe recalls the ghosts of all those tribes – Schuylkill, Manayunk, Susquehanna – whose names gild that "ruined city" (159). For the city in which rappers preach the nihilism of "*Dreads coming back / Somebody's gotta pay*" (162) testifies to more than Wideman's dread of a nation moving inexorably toward a "shattering reckoning" (*Fanon* 4). "Spin the globe and touch it wherever it stops," he dares. "You'll get blood on your finger" from the gigantic glass jigsaw that is the world, smashed to smithereens and impossible to reassemble (*Philadelphia* 160).

The kind of reckoning that informs the antebellum Virginia world of Edward P. Jones's *The Known World* (2003) is measured in dollars and cents, and repeatedly so, for in this "world of human property" (34), black bodies are negotiable commodities whose value fluctuates according to "whatever the market would bear" (17). Such property relations derive from a 1662 law modeled on the Roman doctrine of *partus sequitir ventrem*, wherein the condition of the child (slave or free) followed that of the mother, replacing paternity with ownership and trumping all kinship ties (Bassard 409). In Jones's novel, however, the owners in question are black as well as white, a position to which they are entitled because of a 1670 statute that prohibited free blacks and Indians from purchasing Christians while allowing them to buy people of their own kind (Bassard 410). The result, as Jones depicts, are black slaveholders who run the gamut from assuming ownership of family members bought from bondage as a way of circumventing an 1806 act requiring former slaves to leave the Commonwealth to slaveholders who inherit slaves as part of their legacy, justifying their holdings by way of denials ("I did not own my family" [*Known* 109]), dubious distinctions ("they had neighbors who happened to be slaves" [134]), delusions (a housemaid who "adore[s]" her mistress [317]), and declarations regarding the customs of the country ("It was what was done, and so that is what we did" [109]).

Nowhere are those moral ambiguities more clearly displayed than in Henry Townsend, a thirty-one-year-old owner of fifty acres and thirty-three slaves, around whom the book's large cast of characters clusters. Born to a man who buys his freedom and, over time, that of his wife and son, Henry grows up "not yet his [father's] property and so beyond his reach" (18), yet very much within the reach of his original owner, William Robbins, the county's wealthiest man. It is Robbins who instructs Henry in "the value of money, the value of his labors" (113), and, most of all, the importance of maintaining "the line that separates you from your property" after seeing the adult Henry roughhousing on the ground with the man he has just purchased (for $325) as his first investment (123). A quick study, Henry slaps his "[n]igger" for insolently suggesting they work a little longer on the house they are building (124), which eventuates in the man who once imagined himself a "kind of shepherd master" who would provide good food, no whippings, and "short and happy days in the fields" later rationing food (only when God does not provide enough) and administering beatings (only when absolutely necessary) (180). His subordinates follow suit. Moses, the slapped slave who becomes overseer, works field hands on the Sundays they are given to rest. Elias, who has had part of his ear cut off after a failed escape, quickly "fe[els] himself in charge" after being named successor, despite his wife beseeching him not to "go and do what they bought you for" because it "just ain't right" (336).

To which Jones might reply, as he does in interviews, "that's too much like right" ("Interview" 431), for the kind of destabilization that might be expected in a book about black slaveholders and an institution built on the backs of black labor, women slaveholders and an institution that prospers from the violation of their bodies, occurs only up to a point. On the one hand, it does not matter than Henry is two shades darker than Moses; Henry's holdings in 1855 "s[e]t him high above many others, white and black, in Manchester County, Virginia" (*Known* 5). On the other hand, Henry's pre-1850 purchases must still be made through his white former master. Hence "[t]he free men in Manchester knew the tenuousness of their lives . . . they knew they were slaves with just another title" (251–52). Henry's father learns the value of the free papers he carries with him at all times, to the extent of memorizing them because he is illiterate, when he is stopped by a patroller who eats them, remarking, "A nigger's for sale if I say he's for sale," prior to selling Augustus for $50 (down from $200) to a white speculator and his black assistant (214). Robbins's mistress learns the same lesson after threatening to run off to Richmond, claiming her free papers as authorization, when her former master bluntly informs her that "paper meant nothing, that it had only the power that he, Robbins, would give it" (144).

Backed by the power of the federal government, in fact, paper can mean quite a lot, regardless of its accuracy. The 1840 census taker who doubles as a US marshal assesses the children of a Cherokee woman and a white patroller as too dark to be white, as their father claims, and counts them as slaves. The 1860 census taker argues with his wife the day he sends his report to Washington, fails to carry a "1" when doing his calculations, and forever records in error the number of slaves in Manchester County. Paper also can mean a great deal to those northern insurance companies that issue policies on "perishment" of property from Hartford, Connecticut (356). Indeed, paper, as the invented historians cited throughout the book attests, can serve as a medium by which whites – not just southerners and not just Americans – continue to profit from slavery well into the twentieth century, from the Canadian whose 1883 pamphlet on black slave owners goes through ten printings to the University of Virginia academician whose 1979 book nabs her a full professorship at Washington and Lee University.

Yet paper can also burn. The 1912 fire that destroys all the judicial records of Manchester County confirms how little laws inscribed on paper actually mean when power is ultimately a function of whoever holds the gun, as the sheriff who believes "[t]he law always cares" discovers when plugged by the wastrel cousin whose own plantation has, in Jones's linkage of conflagration and plague, gone up in smoke after an outbreak of smallpox (307). More to the point, that 1912 fire confirms the disappearance of a county seat that already had been divided and swallowed up by a Commonwealth that already had surrendered large sections of its land to form eight other states – another wiping off the face of the earth biblical in its resonance. What survives that known world whose exceedingly narrow frame of reference leaves individuals directionless and "world-stupid" when faced with what exists beyond its borders are the worlds unknown for never being recorded and those artifacts that gesture to the possibilities they contain (350). In Texas, people of various hues "not really from any race that was recorded in any of the books" – Mexicans, Asians, mixed-race combinations – talk about states falling off into unknown space (239). In New York City, a dog in a family photo tilts its head to look at "a whole world off to the right that the photograph had not captured" (189). Most of all, in a Washington, D.C., gallery two maps of folk art fashioned by a woman with half a mind who frees herself from bondage offer an alternative in the book's 1861 ending to the 1507 map of America's "Known World" fashioned by Martin Waldseemüller (inaccurate in its dimensions, mistakenly credited to Hans, and leaving North America "nameless") that hangs in the Manchester County jail (174). One, a three-dimensional *"map of life made with every kind of art man has ever thought to represent himself"* and rendering *"what God sees when He looks down on Manchester"* (384), restores in three dimensions what the 1912 conflagration has taken away, a representation completely divorced from its referent. The other, a *"massive miracle on the Western wall,"* in Jones's linkage of Jewish and African American oppression (385), depicts every person of the Townsend plantation, living and dead, resurrected and known by name.

The HooDoo That You Do So Well

The property relations that concern Ishmael Reed involve the pen as much as the plantation, as evidenced by his own neo-slave narrative's outing Harriet Beecher Stowe's "'borrow[ing]'" from Josiah Henson's life story as tantamount to "taking his gris-gris" (*Flight* 8). Against such artistic theft he proposes a Vodun/Voodoo aesthetic derived from West Africa by way of Haiti, what he terms "Neo-HooDoo," that is as syncretic as it is pantheistic, freeing the novel to be "anything it wants to be, a vaudeville show, the six-o'clock news, the mumblings of wild men saddled by demons" (*Yellow* 36), and the African American novel, no longer bound by social realism or calls for black nationalism, free to incorporate European and Native American traditions as easily as African American ones. Such seemingly contradictory views of cultural appropriation reflect not just Reed's awareness of the role played by cultural forms (writing) and state cultural apparatuses (libraries, publishers, museums) in the construction of racial formations and the perpetuation of existing inequities (Rushdy 117, 121). They equally reflect his view of "pure race" as simply absurd in a hemisphere whose residents are "Creole from the Arctic down to Argentina" and a United States that has been multicultural for centuries ("Interview" 130).

In contrast to the "referential frenzy" of his earlier novels (Dickson-Carr 169) – which wildly jump from western (*Yellow Back Radio Broke-Down* [1969]) to detective story (*Mumbo Jumbo* [1972]) to Greek tragedy (*The Last Days of Louisiana Red* [1974]), heedless of time and hell-bent on taking no prisoners when skewing targets that range from Ivy League to Irene Castle – Reed's later fiction focuses more on topical concerns: neoconservatism, rampant consumerism, careerist multiculturalism. To that end, *The Terrible Twos* (1982) and *The Terrible Threes* (1989) chart American history from the murder of John F. Kennedy (the Terrible One), to the 1980s of instant gratification and planned elimination of "surplus people" (*Twos* 55), to the late 1990s revelation of Reagan as a leftist traitor and White House installation of a televangelist chief of staff eager to push the button to hasten the long-awaited Rapture. And because this is a history with no relief in sight, all that the Turkish trickster Saint Nicholas and his Moorish pal Black Peter – different only in that the former favors miracles of the "geostrategic variety" and the latter tends toward "the persecuted and the down-and-out" – can do in a land still ruled by the Colorado cabal behind "too many visionaries" left dead on motel balconies and hotel kitchen floors is accept the failure of their efforts (*Threes* 37–38, 74). One goes "back to the drawing board" after the American president he guides through the American hell where the butchers of Attica (Nelson Rockefeller), Lumumba (Dwight D. Eisenhower), and Hiroshima (Harry S. Truman) dwell is declared incompetent following his moral awakening (*Threes* 2). The other gets turned into a merchandizing phenomenon, a "post-yuppie Black Peter" doll that outsells Cabbage Patch dolls, in an America looking to boost its economy with Christmas all year round run by a North Pole conglomerate that has obtained exclusive rights to Santa Claus (*Threes* 93).

The academicians and aspiring literati of *Reckless Eyeballing* (1986) and *Japanese by Spring* (1993) play for much smaller stakes, of course. But achieving those ends during a time when confrontation is "out" and negotiation is "in" (*Japanese* 20), and racism is dismissed as "something that blacks had made up in order to make whites feel guilty" has been replaced by "Wigger[ism]" wherein "[e]verybody was a nigger" competing for top spot among the oppressed (94, 9), requires a ruthless commitment to nothing beyond self-interest. This is especially the case for those Reed finds subject to the "decade-long drubbing of black men" by a powerful feminist elite (24). When the play that blackballed Ian Ball writes to get his name off a women's "sex list" gets bumped from its venue by a piece that celebrates Eva Braun as "epitomiz[ing] women's universal suffering" (written, it turns out, by the actual Eva Braun), he changes the script of *Reckless Eyeballing* as per his lesbian producer's demands so that the black protagonist lynched for "eye-rap[ing]" a white woman is portrayed as being as guilty as the men who murder him (5, 104). Having been born with a hex to be a "two-head, of two minds" (146), though, he also acts out this double-consciousness by attacking those females responsible for the "blood libel" of black men and, in the manner of the French Resistance, shaving their heads (4). Likewise, when black pathology specialist Benjamin "Chappie" Puttbutt III is denied tenure at Jack London College despite years of playing "intellectual houseboy" (*Japanese* 69), he exacts vengeance on both male and female politically correct colleagues after Japanese who are looking to restore shogun rule take over the school and make him second-in-command. Yet, unlike Ball, Puttbutt discovers that, for all his plans to be well-placed for the new century he assumes will be a "yellow century" (131), he is "too yellow to even do revenge right" (140). For in a world in which racism is a result of "white leaders ... placing little value on nonwhite life" (209), it is not "yellow" that will define an era dominated by Asians with a history of persecuting other Asians deemed inferiors, but, as usual, "white." As Reed, who casts himself as a character in the book, understands when commenting upon the Japanese who may be "acting white" in the 1990s, it is "only a matter of time before the US would humiliate Japan the way the uppity colored men were traditionally humiliated" (206).

All of which reaches new heights in *Juice!* (2011) when O. J. Simpson is tried by the "Jim Crow media jury" more for having "[t]hought that color didn't matter" and forgetting his place than for murder (19, 212). In this presumption Simpson is one of many men cited – Clarence Thomas, Mike Tyson, Tiger Woods, Michael Jackson, Latrell Sprewell, "[e]ven Coz" (191) – whose public spectacles have become the "new form of bread and circuses" for a press that has been making money off black bodies while ignoring the heinous crimes of corporate greed since the 1830s and turning a profit from tales of white women captured by men of color since Mary Rowlandson's 1682 narrative (11). The only difference is that Simpson as central figure has become so "decontextualized" a representative as to extend beyond black men to all men (from Bill Clinton to bin Laden) until finally becoming "a metaphor for [all] things wrong with culture and politics" (266–67, 99). No need to consider whether postrace America trumps "post–O. J.

America" or vice versa (105). With 1995 criminal trial followed by 1997 civil trial followed by 2008 armed robbery trial, "It's O. J. Forever" (243).

"But who am I to point a finger?" asks the cartoonist who signs his work "Bear" (13), the authorial surrogate whose illustration of Simpson's face pasted to a horse's ass nets him a quarter-million-dollar prize. Indeed, his earlier drawing of a trickster O. J. calling plays that energize an America figured as female (mistaken by his boss for O. J. sodomizing America) has put "some kick back into [the] art" of the recently diagnosed diabetic unable to regulate the build-up of sugar (43) – a white substance – in his bloodstream and depleted of fuel (and, arguably, kick-started the imagination of Reed to publish his first work of fiction in eighteen years). A man who had gone "postrace" rather than broke after the alternative television station for which he works goes commercial (60), Bear has been able to avoid the fates of "troublemaker[s]" like Gil Noble and Max Robinson (84), and even the "well-mannered" Bernard Shaw and Bryant Gumbel (217), by reinventing his militant Attitude the Badger as the harmless curmudgeon Koots Badger. Nothing, however, can save the man already an anachronism to a younger generation from viewing his whole profession as equally doomed to obsolescence, a "frill" instead of a shrill (47), once newspapers go fully digital and the cartoon's art of exaggeration that "screams, while an ordinary drawing or painting whispers," is silenced (81). It is not until this self-styled "last man to believe in O. J.'s innocence" comes upon bloggers, unbeholden to advertisers, who depart from the "electronic lynch mob" herd that he realizes that the venue he has viewed as enemy can serve as ally (26, 112). He thus accepts the award named after America's brilliant cartoonist, George Herriman, by quoting the caricaturist who described satire as saving the nation from going to hell, caricature being, in the words of David Levine, a "hopeful statement" that says "I'm drawing this critical look at what you're doing" in the hope "that you will learn something from what I'm doing" (257). Having begun his tale by citing the pressures to go postrace, Bear ends by affirming a mission of "our people" that bypasses race entirely (257).

Thelonious "Monk" Ellison adopts the opposite tactic in Percival Everett's *Erasure* (2001) when faced with the opposite pressures. Informed that his latest novel has yet again been rejected for being "not black enough" (43), and enraged by the runaway success of an Oberlin grad's gritty rendering of "typical Black life" in *We's Lives In Da Ghetto* (based on a few days visiting Harlem), the college professor who does not believe in race, cannot dance, and cannot play basketball produces – almost by way of divine inspiration – *My Pafology*, an uproarious reworking of *Native Son* (1940) that outwrites Wright in saddling its nineteen-year-old protagonist with a vernacular of inverted consonant clusters and four baby mamas with children named after pharmaceuticals, to which he affixes the name "Stagg R. Leigh" (39). Such reworking of form recalls the prolific Everett's own experiments with genre: Greek myth (*For Her Dark Skin* [1990], *Frenzy* [1997]), western (*God's Country* [1994], *Watershed* [1996]), science fiction (*Zulus* [1990]), crime thriller (*Assumption* [2011]), epistolary novel (*A History of the African-American People (proposed) by Strom Thurmond, as told to Percival Everett & James Kincaid* (2004). But unlike the autobiographically averse Everett, who views every novel as experimental by definition while still dependent on the work that has come before it ("Percival" 48), and the fictional Bigger Thomas, who hails his accidental smothering of a young white woman as an act of construction born of unexpressed rage ("He had murdered and had created a new life for himself" [R. Wright 105]), Monk mourns the sellout that comprises his "self-murder" as an act of aesthetic despair (*Erasure* 139). For once the book intended as a parody becomes a bestseller itself and this Ellison is forced to wear the mask of his nom de plume, a pathologically shy ex-con straight out of the joint, he must perform his alter ego in much the same way that his literary namesake Ralph has the Invisible Man (allusions to which punctuate the text) play the role of the ever-fluid Rinehart. When he finds himself hiding behind a screen while an Oprah-clone swoons over how it "doesn't get any more real" than the portrayals in the book (retitled *Fuck*), Monk realizes that "assert[ing] the individuality of Stagg Leigh" in order to play with and disrupt racial expectations has ended in "annihilating" his own presence (251, 248). In fact, the kind of layering that adds texture to parodic literature (*Finnegans Wake* is the example cited) by calling attention to the conventions it seeks to challenge, what Linda Hutcheon has termed its "double process of installing and ironizing" (93), has turned the man who adopts that practice for his life into a palimpsest in reverse.

In this erasure, however, Monk is luckier that the protagonists of other Everett novels; he, a least, is ascribed woodworking skills to make functional objects that occupy actual space and the discovery of a financially strapped half-sister to whom the giving of a large check from his advances is "real" in a way that his hall-of-mirrors shenanigans are not (*Erasure* 243). Named Not Sidney by a mother who leaves him orphaned at the age of seven, the hero of *I Am Not Sidney Poitier* (2009) can only affirm himself – in the book's running joke – by way of denying himself ("not only was I Not Sidney Poitier, but also ... I was not Sidney Poitier" [92]) – and *not*, moreover, by way of his resemblance to Poitier the person but to the Poitier persona. To that end, the book traces his sentimental education, overseen by Ted Turner (master of the non sequitur) and Percival Everett (Philosophy of Nonsense professor), by way of situations that deliciously upend the actor's most famous films: *The Defiant Ones* (1958), relocated to Peckerwood County; *Lilies of the Field* (1963), in Smuteye, Alabama; *A Patch of Blue* (1965), and fellating blind ingénue; *Guess Who's Coming to Dinner* (1967), for Thanksgiving in D.C. with the moneyed Talented Tenth. It is only when he sees, in Everett's recycling of *In the Heat of the Night* (1967), the body of a young man mistakenly killed for being Not Sidney Poitier that the living double can envision himself as more than representation divorced from referent, for "if that body in the chest was Not Sidney Poitier, then I was not Not Sidney Poitier and that by all I know of logic and double negatives, I was therefore Sidney Poitier" (212). With his identity thus confirmed, he can travel to Los Angeles at the book's end to accept a special award for "Most Dignified Figure in American Culture," presented by Elizabeth Taylor – in Everett's sly punning – in tribute to an "icon of American character" (234).

The Los Angeles of Paul Beatty's work is the Los Angeles of the 1992 riots, the latest in a history of violent outbreaks (1943 zoot-suit riots, 1965 Watts riots), less postrace than post–Rodney King. This is not, significantly, the City of Angels in which the narrator of *The White Boy Shuffle* (1996) grows up: Gunnar Kaufman only moves from the Santa Monica of all-white schools devoted to multicultural "Eracism" to the gated (to divide 'hood from suburban hamlet) community of Hillside after his mother hears her three children refer to blacks as "different from us" (29, 37). In this renunciation, Gunnar is but the latest in a long line of Kaufman race traitors, from the "sell-out" Euripides, who helps "jump-start" the American Revolution by dodging a redcoat's shot that comes to rest in Crispus Attucks, to the freeman Swen, who hops a fence into slavery thinking field hands at work will provide inspiration for his dance opera, to the LAPD cop Rölf, who views the King beating as self-defense on the part of the officer who confused the Jheri curl activator that got in his eyes with Mace (10). But when a jury exonerates the attackers who have jammed 50,000 volts of Taser democracy into King's body, the sixteen-year-old wordsmith who has considered himself a "cultural alloy, tin-hearted whiteness wrapped in blackened copper plating," finds himself with a "glistening anger" that "couldn't be dealt with in a poem" (63, 131). Asking "[w]hat happens to a dream deferred?" receives a blunt reply: "Fuck Langston Hughes" (134). Unfortunately, he also finds himself with no venue to express that anger meaningfully. As the local barbershop elders know, without feces to rub on themselves in the manner of defiant slaves looking to throw off dogs following their scent, blacks in LA are out of luck: "Lots o' chickenshit niggers, no real chicken shit. Couldn't run away from Los Angeles if you wanted to" (91).

Even worse, when Gunnar himself runs from LA to Boston for college, and encounters cornrowed blondes named Negritude carrying coffee-table copies of his collected verse and a black student union staging fashion shows to promote literacy ("Afro-chic to uplift the Afro-weak" [184]), he realizes that the commodification of blackness has deprived not just his own voice but all black protest of any impact. Hardly "passé," as the protagonist of Beatty's *Slumberland* (2008) initially thinks, "black is the new black" (4, 234). With political activism reduced to the civil disobedience of days past, which is to say teach-ins led by Dead Heads to refrains of "We Shall Overcome," Gunnar invokes another seminal dreamer when he takes to the stage in protest of South Africa's National Party, only to invert Martin Luther King, Jr.'s admonition: "If a man hasn't discovered something he will die for, he isn't fit to live" (*White Boy* 199–200). Taking his cue from Yukio Mishima's notion of *hara-kiri* as an act of winning, he challenges those unwilling to die for anything to just not live. Having thus proclaimed an "Emancipation Disintegration" by which "mass suicide will be the ultimate sit-in" (2), the new messiah returns to LA, where he can lead his flock to glory while standing – in Beatty's conflation of Hollywood and helicopter, Searchlight Pictures and police searchlight – in "the world's biggest spotlight" (217).

More constructive is the solution at which the titular hero of *The Sellout* (2015) arrives after the loss of both father and hometown – one shot while running from cops after a traffic stop, the other struck from maps to keep property values in areas that surround the alleged "Murder Capital" from declining (67). At first, the man devoted to no unit larger than himself, a character surnamed "Me" who writes "Californian" for race on official forms, has "no idea who I was, and no clue how to become myself" (40). But when an elderly neighbor he saves from hanging himself with a bungee cord, a Little Rascal whose career as a Hollywood "stunt coon" has left him a "Living National Embarrassment" (71, 76), becomes his slave for life in gratitude, he realizes that the only way of extricating himself from the role of massa – even a massa who works harder than the slave who limits his labor to posing as a lawn jockey – is to bring back the city of Dickens, the disappearance of which has prompted Hominy Jenkins's act of despair in the first place. Only restoring the integrity of a city founded to stay free of all but blacks and zoned for farming (Beatty's version of forty acres and a mule) means more than simply spray-painting white lines to delineate borders. It also means, as the judge who rules on the violation of the many acts, amendments, and biblical commandments that finally gets the narrator hauled into court (and, eventually, before the Supreme Court) understands, "reintroducing precepts, namely segregation and slavery, that, given [its] cultural history, have come to define his community despite the supposed unconstitutionality and non-existence of these concepts" (265–66). Simply put, it means admitting "'[r]acism' in a post-racial world" (262).

Such efforts are anathema to those Dum Dum Donut intellectuals who form the closest thing the former town has to a representative government – "wereniggers" who drop gerundial "*g*"s when professionally advantageous (96), but expunge American literature of all offensive words so as to produce a *"Pejorative-Free Adventures and Intellectual and Spiritual Journeys of African-American Jim and His Young Protégé"* with "warriors" instead of "niggers" and "dark-skinned volunteers" instead of "slaves" (95). And yet they work. PRIORITY SEATING FOR WHITES signs promote civility and courtesy on public buses. COLORED ONLY signs in storefronts make customers feel special. Perhaps most important, signs for an all-white (fake) Academy Charter Magnet School result in higher grades earned by African American and Latino students in Chaff Middle School. Affirming, uncomfortably, Booker T. Washington's call for buckets cast where they are as farsighted and racism's power to inspire the best efforts of people taken "back" only to "realize how far we have to go" (163), these successes also confirm the narrator's view of the Civil Rights movement as a "collective 16 mm" gag reel of Keystone Negroes in Selma slipping on affirmative-action banana peels and Washington, D.C., zombies marching one hundred thousand strong that has gotten people only so far (18–19). As he notes when describing "After the Fact," a game in which players shown famous historical photos are asked "So what happened next?" (255), the 1957 integration of Little Rock Central High School was followed by the governor shutting down every high school in the city a year later.

Ultimately, they query whether the entire principle of integration, a concept "[n]o one's ever defined," is "a natural or an unnatural state," "social entropy or social order" (168). To farmers, like the narrator who separates fruit trees by color, the question is moot: "we segregate in an effort to give every tree, every plant, every poor Mexican, every poor nigger, a chance for equal access to sunlight and water; we make sure every living organism has room to breathe" (214). To the Supreme Court Justice who asks "the first question that makes any sense" during his hearing (274), the cultivation of America's garden is far more complicated. Reminding her audience that *Plessy v. Ferguson* (1896) was overturned when *Brown v. Board of Education* (1954) deemed separate as never being equal, Elena Kagan enumerates the challenges that *Me v. the United of America* poses to all Americans: to query "separate and not quite equal, but infinitely better off than ever before"; to examine the very terms "separate" and "equal"; finally, to grapple with the "nitty-gritty" question of what we mean by "black" (274). And while the defense attorney responds by listing the four stages of Quintessential Blackness ("Neophyte Negro," "Capital *B* Black," "Race Transcendentalism," "Unmitigated Blackness") devised by his client's Liberation Psycholog[ist] father, complete with pictures unrestricted by phenotype, the narrator ends with two memories that convey his own ongoing uncertainty. He recalls his failure to ask a comedian who ejected a white couple from a club the exact nature of the sacrosanct "*our thing*" they had presumed upon (288), and, in a chapter titled "Closure," he recalls the inauguration of "the black dude" as failing to instill in him any sense that the book on the subject of race has in any way been closed (289).

The Color Beige

Part detective novel, sci-fi fiction, allegory, and fable, Colson Whitehead's *The Intuitionist* (1999) mixes genres as deftly as underlying motives when it comes to the philosophy that takes the idea of racial uplift quite literally and applies it to elevators. To Lila Mae Watson, who in man's suit negotiates the book's temporally indeterminate New York City where skyscrapers pierce the clouds and African Americans are still called "colored," Intuitionism offers the hope of transcending the barriers of race and gender that have left her the only black woman inspector among civil servants who pledge allegiance to a Guild that holds elections every four years. For in contrast to the Empiricism based on physical examination of an elevator's exterior ("the skin of things"), born of "[w]hite people's reality [that] is built on what things appear to be" (239), the Intuitionism derided as "voodoo" entails "communicating with the elevator on a nonmaterial basis" (57, 62). More posthuman than postracial in anthropomorphically attributing to elevators memory lapses and moods, Intuitionism aspires to convey believers beyond the "tumultuous modernity" of Elisha Graves Otis's 1853 "first elevation," and technology's promise to obliterate the distances that separate nations (158), to the "shining city" of its founder's "second elevation," a completely disembodied "heliopolis" floating free of spine and steel (198, 199).

Such transcendence of spatial/racial binaries, of course, is predicated on a whole other set of binaries – North and South, elevator and subway – that the history of New York refutes. Far from functioning in opposition, elevators (first dubbed "perpendicular railways") and subways functioned symbiotically: the erection of taller buildings that required more trains to transport workers increased land values and led to the construction of taller towers

(Brooks 116). And as Lila Mae's father reminds her before she leaves for Vertical Transport school, "They have the same white people up there they got down here" (234). Yet it is not until an elevator she has recently inspected goes into total free fall, and clearing her name means locating the blueprint for the "perfect elevator" drawn by the founder of Intuitionism prior to his death (61), that Lila Mae's faith in Intuitionism – as well as her confidence that she is "never wrong" (9) – comes crashing to the ground. What Lila Mae discovers is that James Fulton has been neither white nor black but a mixed-race product of rape, and the doctrine derived from a lifetime of passing has originated as one "big joke" (232). The joke, however, is not only on those whites who mistake his writings on "*horizontal thinking in a vertical world [to be] the race's curse*" as generalized exhortations rather than code because they "do not see colored people" (151, 134), but on Lila Mae herself. Having assumed the man in a library window at whom she once waved from her dorm room to be just a codger with a cane, she never considers that the conundrum regarding the "perfect elevator" applies as much to its designer as it does to the black box that is its core: "We don't know because we can't see inside it, it's something we cannot imagine" (61).

And when it comes to the future relieved of race that Fulton's contributions are meant to deliver, neither can Whitehead. This is less because of the conspiratorial politics of inspectors, manufacturers, and enforcers in various alignment that surrounds Lila Mae, men at a "level of commerce" for whom Fulton's ancestry will not "change the fact that there's money to be made from his invention," as an industrial spy who has pretended to be his nephew informs her (250). Rather, it is because Whitehead never loses sight of the fact that his book's vehicle of uplift only exists by virtue of its human cargo, that without that freight elevators remain mere boxes, coffins as it were, no different from those narrow rooms that Lila Mae habitually occupies. Emboldened by the "new literacy" she gains from rereading Fulton's writings "like a slave does, one forbidden word at a time," in light of his real identity (230), Lila Mae ends by assuming Fulton's voice in order to turn the fragments of the notebooks she is given by his housekeeper into a completed manuscript. But in reclaiming the trope of one African American genre (the slave narrative), she comes up against of the demands of another, the ignoring of which has led Fulton to be seduced by his own satire: "A joke has no purpose if you cannot share it with anyone" (241). Having "learned to read [where] there was no one she could tell" (151), Lila Mae succumbs to the allure of the perfect elevator that "reached out to her" and the prospects of being "a citizen of the city to come" (255). Her conviction that she is "never wrong" renewed (255), she forgets the fate to which all acts of passing – vehicular (the elevator "pretend[ing] to be what it was not," i.e., healthy), racial (the inventor pretending to be what he is not, i.e., white), authorial (the writer pretending to be what she is not, i.e., male) – are subject and the eventuality that Intuitionism can never anticipate (229): "the catastrophic accident the elevator encounters at that unexpected moment on that quite ordinary ascent, the one who will reveal the device for what it truly is" (231).

Less concerned with identity revealed than determined are works that take *Loving v. Virginia*, the Supreme Court decision that decriminalized interracial marriage, as given but query its presumptive freeing of children – no longer "mixtries," in Langston Hughes's conflation of mysterious and mixed parentage (46) – to believe they can be anything they wish. In Mat Johnson's *Loving Day* (2015), where "mixies" celebrate the 1967 decision each year as "Mulatto Christmas" (159), the end result – for all its satiric swipes at Mulattopians and mismatched socks, Oreos and sunflowers, and a Mélange Center that quizzes parents of prospective students on O. J. Simpson's guilt and Jesus's race – is affirmation. The half-Irish and half–African American illustrator who claims tribes real but race nonexistent in his lifelong fight to be a member of *Team Blackie* learns through the discovery of a daughter raised as white and Jewish (18) – a "black girl who looks like a white girl with a tan and a bad hair day" (52) – that the seemingly slight difference between saying "I'm mixed" instead of "I'm white" is the difference between "the comfort of wearing shoes that fit as opposed to bearing the blisters of shoes just one size too small" (240). In Rosellen Brown's *Half a Heart* (2000), the teen taken as a babe from her white mother to be raised by a recent-convert-to-Black-Power father in the only community he thinks will accept her discovers that the whiteness she has always deemed "a nothing, an absence" (84), in fact has presence after a classmate from Zimbabwe finds her "ineligible" as a mate because her blood is "impure" (83, 82), and that the mother who embraces "the simpler fact of her" has always been "the only one, in the end, who didn't see her color first," the only one who, for all her liberal stumbling and bumbling, sees essence and existence as "indivisible" (394). In Emily Raboteau's *The Professor's Daughter* (2005), by contrast, where parental desires to transcend race spring from race trauma, the presumption ends in fatalist confirmation or expatriation. The mixed-race son, hailed "The *New* New Negro" in Princetonian print (22), becomes part of the "vegetable race" after a freak electrical accident "burn[s] him from the inside out" (20, 23), as well as heir to the father that schoolboys have tried to burn alive and the grandfather actually burned alive. The sister who develops rashes after her skin starts "rebelling against itself" comes to recognize her illness as symptomatic of more than what an herbalist diagnoses as her inner disharmony (97).

Last seen in Brazil, a place where everyone "looked like some permutation of her[self]," after concluding "there wasn't anything wrong with her head, but rather something wrong with her country" (270, 271), she is left "discovering herself in a new language" but still described as "missing" (275, 270).

Replacing transcendence with performance, Danzy Senna's *Caucasia* (1998) introduces its narrator born the year of the *Loving* decision as the child (much like Senna herself) of a Massachusetts blue-blood mother and African American father of uncertain lineage, only to complicate the familiar racial scenario of "mad scientists, embarking on this marvelous, ambitious experiment" by interrogating the degree to which all bases for community are enacted (299). In fact, when the father convinced the US is suicide for a black man departs Boston for Brazil with the daughter whose darker skin offers proof that his own "blackness hadn't been completely blanched" (47), and the mother fearing arrest for her radical politics goes underground with the child whose lighter skin provides "the key to [their] going incognito" (109), Birdie Lee discovers that ethnicity, sexuality, and family are as easily constructed as race. When she agrees to be Jewish as per her mother's suggested alias, however, she does so not to pass as white: the nine-year-old mistaken for Sicilian, French, Puerto Rican, Native American, and Pakistani already suspects from playing with her sister at being Elemenos, a "shifting people" who change "form, color, pattern, in a quest for invisibility," that a species survival based on disappearance makes no sense (7). She does so with the understanding that Jews, a people historically "joined at the hip" with African Americans as far as representation in America is concerned (Elam 112), "weren't really white, more like an off-white," in which case being Jewish is the closest she is "going to get to black and still stay white" (119), with the added benefit that performing as Jesse Goldman, child of the conveniently dead David, provides her with a "lighter-skinned version" of her own absent father (111). Perhaps more important, she does so assuming that her "real self" is "safely hidden beneath [her] beige flesh," that "when the right moment came, I would reveal her, preserved, frozen solid in the moment in which I had left her" (199).

Senna exposes such surface/depth thinking for the error it is when the unnamed narrator of *Symptomatic* (2004), another mixed-race child with illnesses of unknown etiology, looks at the hospital X-rays that comprise an art project and finds no evidence of underlying authenticity in fractures that could belong to anyone. Yet she remains acutely aware, in fiction filled with mirrors and doubles, of the dangers of viewing identity solely as a function of what she terms "[c]ontexts": "Once you put them in the picture, they took over" (*Symptomatic* 5). Indeed, for all the emphasis on the "real me" that constitutes herself in *Caucasia*, Birdie always defines herself in conjunction with others, beginning with the older sister in whom the child with no name on her birth certificate (her parents cannot agree on one) finds the "reflection that proved my own existence" (5), and remains subject to a desire to belong to a community larger than herself. When girls in the New Hampshire town where she and her mother settle look askance at the Star of David she wears, Birdie removes it, remarking that she is not "*really* Jewish" because "to be really a Jew" one must have a Jewish mother (210). But when she applies that reasoning to race, wondering if being "really black" requires a black mother in her attempts to divorce herself further from the mixed-race classmate ostracized for having darker skin (242), she ends up severing the link between family and genealogy that forms the basis of her own "real" identity: the only mother the student abandoned at birth knows is the white Quaker woman who has adopted her. By the time she flees New Hampshire for Boston, in effect orphaning herself, and discovers that living as Jesse for six years has left her estranged from those who knew her as Birdie during her earliest years, she realizes that the Roxbury Black Power school where she first learns the "art of changing" that would become "second nature" has taught its coercive lesson all too well (53). Wondering if "whiteness were contagious," she concludes that "surely I had caught it" (280).

She refuses, however, the patient's passivity when finally reunited in 1982 with the lost half of her family in California, a place where people like herself are a "dime a dozen" (351), in the book's last pages. Negotiating a path between the American reinvention of the self (held by a mother who never strays far from her New England ancestral home) and the fatalist conviction that mulattoes remain canaries in the American coal mine (held by a father who cannot stay outside the US for even two years), Birdie realizes that the freedom to "be anything" comes with the imperative to choose to be something (110), "[b]ecause there are consequences if you don't" (349). When she opts, in the book's last lines, not to wave at the "mixed girl" she sees through a Berkeley bus window, the narrator who has measured herself by way of likeness to others asserts that simply being "black like me" is insufficient grounds for selfhood (353).

Richard Powers's *The Time of Our Singing* (2003) is predicated on that assumption. To the extent that the African American soprano and German Jewish physicist at its center liken their "[c]hildren of the coming age" to anything, it is to the first "[c]harter citizens of the postrace place, ... blending unblended" – in the language of the book's governing discipline – "like notes stacked up in a chord" (345). Such musical analogizing is hardly unusual for an author whose works, beginning with his first, *Three Farmers on Their Way to a Dance* (1985), have taken disciplinary interconnectivity as a given; *The Gold Bug Variations* (1991) blends four notes of a Bach aria, four nucleotides of DNA, and four-letter Hebrew name of God. In this later sprawling saga framed chronologically by Marian Anderson's 1939 Washington, D.C., concert and the 1995 Washington Million Man March, however, performance of identity and musical performance are synchronized to test the foundational faith that *"we will transform the jangling discords of our nation into a symphony"* (277). In other words – namely, those of the science to which Powers weds music – if time can be conceived as an "enormous polytonal cluster that has the whole horizontal tune stacked up inside it" (93), does the arrow of time that indicates "which way the melody is running" point to a "[b]reaking," or "[m]ixing," that always signals "[g]rowing disorder" (88)? Or do curves in time that violate causality allow for the possibility of events that "move continuously into their own local future while turning back onto their own past" (476)?

It is faith in a universe that prefers counterclockwise to clockwise rotation that sustains Delia Daley and David Strom, who meet at the 1939 concert, marry, and school their children in the art of "Crazed Quotations," a call-and-response game that produces the "wildest mixed marriages, love matches that even the heaven of half-breeds looked sidelong at": Brahms and Dixieland, Cherubini and Cole Porter (13). They continue in that faith despite all the evidence of race thinking to the contrary – Delia rejected by a music conservatory because of her color, David's family annihilated during the Holocaust because of their ancestry – and in defiance of those who surround them. When the atom-bombing of Japan based on what he feels is its inhabitants' race prompts Delia's father – a physician who proclaims himself "not black" ("black" being the color of shoe soles) in the same way that David proclaims himself "not white" (because a secular Jew) (79, 304) – to condemn the idea of raising grandchildren *"[b]eyond color"* (even though "Colored" is exactly what it says on their birth certificates) as raising them to pass as white (425), the severing of relations between the Stroms and their only living family forces them to retreat into "the circle of that smallest race" that is their nuclear family (464).

Their three musical prodigies are another story. Unwilling to remain a "mulatto bel canto castrato" in a US where people see a black artist first and tenor second (128), the eldest, Jonah, takes off for opera's European capitals (where he ironically makes his signature piece a Michael Tippett oratorio inspired historically by the Jewish boy whose killing of a Nazi diplomat precipitated the *Kristallnacht* and musically by African American spirituals), eventually to the medieval city of Ghent. There his efforts to "sing

his way back *before*" – instead of "beyond" – race through pre-1610 poly-
phony yield a voice of such "disembodied grace," such "pure, voluptuous
power of indifference," as to catapult him "beyond being anything at all" (530,
596). Traumatized by their mother's death in a suspicious fire, the youngest,
Ruth, rejects music entirely for Black Panther militancy. It thus is left for the
uncommitted sibling who trades Julliard accompanist for Atlantic City lounge
pianist to grapple with the book's most interesting aesthetic questions. For in
desiring to compose rather than just channel music, Joseph must deal with not
just the paradoxical nature of written music – "fixed instructions on how to
re-create the simultaneous" (537) – but the ownership and purpose of music
itself.

At issue, as Powers makes clear, is more than genealogy, the fact that "[n]o
two songs are further apart than half cousins by incest" (433), a cross-
fertilization that Joseph's adult niece later dubs "mutual theft," resulting in
"[m]ore for everybody" and "more kinds of everybody" and making being
"anti-Europe" as much an amputation as not being "pro-Africa" (573). When
the Julliard dropout Miles Davis transcribes for trumpet a guitar *concierto* of
Joaquín Rodrigo and ballet of Manuel de Falla, he produces, with *Sketches of
Spain* (1960), a record of "all cultures picking one another's pockets, not to
mention the pockets of those who only stand and listen" (262). But as Powers
goes on to argue, an audience attentive to the real joy of music – Joseph
listening to a John Coltrane pickup quartet that plays "[m]usic for the sheer
making" (200), his girlfriend singing the music she cannot read "[b]y heart"
and arranging her record collection "by happiness" (461, 441) – is not enough.
As the niece that cuts right to the heart of the frustrated composer's core by
asking Joseph, "Are you happy?," understands (573), the same music that
admittedly "never cured anyone" needs to be more than an exercise in self-
expression (574). "Nothing without that," she replies to Joseph's suggestion
that we sing for ourselves. "But nothing if only that. We need a music that
sings to anyone. That makes them sing. No audience!" (574). Hearing her,
Joseph chooses to become a music teacher in an Oakland elementary school,
an institution with "no separate audience" and "no separate musics," where
music is taught not as a "separate cry called music" and children are
surrounded by "[j]ust song everywhere" (587).

Powers the historical novelist has no illusions regarding the limited role of
such endeavors in a world he early characterizes as a "howl" (50). In a book
that references the too many names burned into consciousness – Emmett Till,
Medgar Evers, Martin Luther King, Malcolm X, Rodney King – within
a nonlinear narrative of "recursive revision" and temporally juxtaposed scenes
(LA in 1965, LA in 1992), the actuality of tragedy gives way to the inevitability

of tragedy (LeClair 19). Indeed, it is that same sense of the past still informing, if not determining, the future that marks the fiction that goes beyond Power's time frame to frame Hurricane Katrina as the latest disaster to confirm the persistence of race in America. Mat Johnson and Simon Gane's graphic novel *Dark Rain* (2010) opens by comparing the levees that flood the Lower Ninth Ward in 2005 to the levees allegedly blown up in 1965 by whites trying to save their own neighborhoods; it ends with the Confederate bills judged worthless by looters fetching enough from "racist types [who] pay top dollar" to fund the hero's new charter boat business (n. pag.). Dave Eggers's *Zeitoun* (2009) details the experiences of a man dragged at gunpoint and caged in a Guantánamo-like facility built by prisoners from Angola, a penitentiary resting on land once used as a plantation to breed slaves. Jesmyn Ward's *Salvage the Bones* (2011) juxtaposes the assertion that "[e]verything deserve[s] to live," regardless of race or even species (213), with the reality that African Americans in the town of Bois Sauvage "don't run" in response to imminent catastrophe but "prepare" their homes much like squirrels and rabbits (215). When the catastrophe of 2005 that recalls those of 1969 and 1985 finally recedes, it leaves the motherless girl who narrates the book casting Katrina as a latter-day Medea, "the mother we will remember until the next mother with large, merciless hands, committed to blood, comes" (255). Of this eventuality Ward has no doubts. Her account of the five young African American men she knows who die violent deaths between 2000 and 2004 in *Men We Reaped* (2013) ends with the conclusion: "Life is a hurricane" (250).

All of which makes Powers's decision to end his own work by returning once more to the 1939 event at the nation's capital at which Delia and David meet all the more poignant. This time the return to a union being born in love follows pages set in 1995 in which calls for "a more perfect union" – the same words Barack Obama would invoke thirteen years later when abjuring racial division as endemic – are being directed at a fractured African American community by a man convinced that white supremacy is systemic. Yet Joseph, who recognizes the term "union" as undoing all Louis Farrakhan's cries for separatist allegiance, can divorce the words of a man he remembers is also a trained concert violinist from their meaning and affirm: "I have seen the future, and it is mongrel" (*Time* 624). As does Powers, who juxtaposes the grandchild lost, then found, at the Million Man March, the true child of the future who celebrates wavelengths of infinite colors, and the child lost, then found, by Delia and David in the past, an African American child whose singing of birds and fish falling in love puts to music lines that David has always assumed belonged to a Jewish folk saying, and with this first Crazed Quotation silences all the "impossibles" of Delia's demurrals (629). And so the novel does not close on a requiem – to recall the title of its penultimate chapter – to the older son beaten during the 1992 riots but dying when the man torn between being beyond and of race simply erases himself in bed and stops breathing. It ends instead with a song of acclamation – Anderson's soaring rendition of "America" – in which, for one moment at least, "I" and "thee" merge in one nation. As Duke Ellington, who deemed "good music" and "the other kind" the only melodic binary he recognized ("Where"), predicted, "Soon it'll all be just music" ("Jazz").

Conclusion: Postscripts and Post-Postmodernism

Rebecca was an academic star. Her new book was on the phenomenon of word casings, a term she'd invented for words that no longer had meaning outside quotation marks. English was full of these empty words – "friend" and "real" and "story" and "change" – words that had been shucked of their meanings and reduced to husks. Some, like "identity," "search," and "cloud," had clearly been drained of life by their Web usage. With others, the reasons were more complex; how had "American" become an ironic term? How had "democracy" come to be used in an arch, mocking way?

– Jennifer Egan, *A Visit from the Goon Squad* (2010)

How, indeed. For the novel that opens with epigraphs from Marcel Proust's *In Search of Lost Time* (1913–1927) and takes its title from the depiction of time as a "goon" is not just Jennifer Egan's contemplation of the impact of time on characters who wonder if they became gray and pot-bellied suddenly or incrementally (127, 332). Spanning the years 1973 to the early 2020s, the book that joins them by way of a music industry that offers an extreme case of the changes time's passing forces on any kind of aesthetic productivity locates the earliest of its thirteen disjointed chapters in the year cited by Brian McHale as the beginning of postmodernism's "peak" phase (7). The questions about "word casings" that Egan asks in this final chapter set at an outdoor concert being held at what was once Ground Zero, then, can be seen as querying the legacy of an entire cultural movement whose moment has clearly passed (323–24). Less immediately clear is Egan's stance, however. In surrounding those same words eviscerated of meaning with quotation marks in her own book, is Egan adhering to postmodern irony or ironizing that which is already ironic, which is to say making a positive out of two negatives? Likewise, in opening the conclusion of my new book with reference to a passage that concerns an academic star and her new book, am I being metacritical or simply delusional?

Critical commentary offers no consensus when addressing whether the reported end of postmodernism has produced an actual corpse or, in Stephen J. Burn's words, been bent "toward the end of *more* postmodernism" (221). Such indecision, of course, is hardly surprising given that the phenomenon in question follows one whose very name, as McHale notes, testifies to a dialectic of continuity with and break from the modernism of an earlier era (6). Hence the scholarly emphasis on the former in reassessing postmodernism as "long modernism" (Amy Hungerford) or "technomodernism" (Mark McGurl) is matched by descriptions of its successor as "late postmodernism" (Jeremy Green), "post-postmodernism" (Jeffrey T. Nealon), and "second- and third-generation postmodernism" (David Cowart). At the same time, the replacement of "post" with "new" when targeting the elements that distinguish that successor – "New Sincerity" (Adam Kelly), "new humanism" (Mary K. Holland), "renewalism" (Josh Toth) – signals the latter. The publicist in Egan's novel whose career, literally and figuratively, has gone down in flames after lit trays suspended above the New Year's party meant to outdo Truman Capote's Black and White party start to rain scalding oil on the 500 beautiful bodies assembled thus recognizes her real error as having had less to do with design and more with sell-by dates: "she'd overlooked a seismic shift – had conceived of an event crystallizing an era that had already passed" (143). Stumped when trying to identify what kind of "event or convergence" will define the "new world" in which she now finds herself, the chastened woman leaves it to the generation of her nine-year-old daughter, Lulu, "to decide" (143).

That Lulu certainly does by the end of the novel. Typifying the new deskless and paperless "'handset employee'" who scoffs at the words "viral" and "connect" as having nothing to do with an information-age paradigm of "reach" and finds the idea of anything being "inherently wrong" an example of "calcified morality" (317, 320), Lulu is the poster child for what her music producer boss – who once served cow pies to corporate bigwigs in protest of the shit they sold – earlier deemed the "*aesthetic holocaust*" produced by digitization that "sucked the life out of everything that got smeared through its microscopic mesh" (23). This, after all, is a young woman who prefers to "T" a man standing in front of her than talk to him. And yet Egan, who fashioned a gothic novel, *The Keep* (2006), to explore the concept of reality in the light of new communications technology and released "Black Box" (2012) in ten installments on *The New Yorker*'s Twitter feed ("Interview" 443), does not portray the Internet as Antichrist to unmediated authenticity. The novel opens with a character whose shrink employs a couch to relieve both doctor and patient of the burden of eye contact – the same character who later reconnects via Facebook with the man who eventually becomes her husband. In fact, Egan's pitching the book's penultimate chapter as a PowerPoint presentation makes her one of the many novelists who, as Jessica Pressman argues (256–57), engage with the digital and its presumed threat by acts of remediation that, on the one hand, reaffirm the representational powers of print fiction while, on the other hand, recalling the larger systems in which print operates. Far from being "postscripts" in the manner of those e-books created and meant to be read on computers – such as the early examples of Michael Joyce's *afternoon, a story* (1987) and Shelley Jackson's *Patchwork Girl* (1995) – these "technotexts," as N. Katherine Hayles calls them, display a "heightened sense of their materiality" so as to "foreground the inscription technologies that produce them" (794), and to various degrees. The "Young Lady's Illustrated Primer" in Neal Stephenson's *The Diamond Age* (1995) that is designed to promote independent thinking in a neo-Victorian future combines elements of print, audio, and video games but is distinguished from the surrounding text only by changed font. The word "house" in Mark Z. Danielewski's *House of Leaves* (2000) that appears in blue so as to approximate a hyperlink is housed in a typographically riotous work (composed entirely in pencil) whose footnotes and appendices offer the reader-turned-player alternative ways of moving through it in the manner of hypertext.

The fact that Egan formally eschews linearity in a book devoted to the inexorable passage of time thus testifies no more to any paradox at the heart of the novel than her refusal to include the word "novel" on its cover when it was first published implies any wholesale repudiation of the genre itself. It testifies instead to a willingness to withhold judgment when it comes to what that passage has wrought, to view progression and progress as not inextricably linked. For every flash forward in the book that jettisons a present moment of triumph with a future fall from grace – into drugs, suicide, death – there is a seemingly inescapable fall averted – and against all odds – by amazing resurrection. The rock 'n' roll relic looking to "*flame* away" rather than "fade away" ends up owning a dairy farm (129). The journalist jailed for assaulting a starlet writes a best-selling bio. The washed-up starlet emerges a rom-com sweetheart. Even the genocidal Latin American dictator gets a "fresh start" (164). It is a similar predilection that makes Andrew Hoberek's emphasis on the "uneven transformations" displayed by an American fiction of "as-yet-uncategorized diversity" such a considered, not cautious, assessment of what has come "after postmodernism" (240, 233), for recognizing, in effect, the need to pause in order to reflect. Egan, in fact, offsets her PowerPoint exposure of pauses in songs that deceive with fake endings with a slide that offers "Proof of the Necessity of Pauses" (306). To the character who feels that "everything is ending," she juxtaposes a character who responds with "everything is ending, . . . but not yet" (131, 132). In that same spirit, I want to (fake) end my book by turning, with a discussion of Junot Díaz and Michael Chabon, to the wholesale deployment of popular genres in contemporary American fiction that scholars view as different from an earlier knowing allusiveness in order to (really) end with discussion of a writer, David Foster Wallace, who transcends categorization by genre entirely.

Perhaps the biggest – in every sense of the word – genre enthusiast in that fiction is the character whose *Brief Wondrous Life of Oscar Wao* is chronicled in Junot Díaz's 2007 novel. A "fat sci-fi-reading nerd" from Paterson whose interest in what he terms "the more speculative genres" spans all media (19, 43), Oscar de León dreams of becoming the "Dominican Stephen King" or the "Dominican Tolkien" (27, 192), his social ineptness making a heroic future as "some kind of plátano Doc Savage" highly unlikely (27). As the macho foil, Yunior, who recounts the history of the de León–Cabral family shows, however, the appeal of such marginalized artifacts is not "synonymous with being a loser with a capital L" (17). For all his dismissal of the unreal, from a world that "ain't no fucking Middle-earth" to a narrative that "ain't no Marvel Comics" (194, 270), this "postmodern plátano" who writes fiction devoted to robberies and drug deals still assumes the guise of a *Fantastic Four* figure when introducing himself as "your humble Watcher" (144, 4), admits to throwing "a lot of fantasy and sci-fi into the mix" (285), and wonders whether his own book "ain't a zafa of sorts" or his "very own counterspell" (7). The difference, as T. S. Miller points out (94–95), is that Oscar's "absolute" commitment to "the Genres" (upper-case) accords them master narrative status whereas Yunior's employment of them along with works by Homer, Aeschylus, Flaubert, Wilde, and Hemingway treats them as one of many weapons in his arsenal (*Brief* 20).

For Díaz, a self-described "ghetto nerd supreme" growing up in a military family that emigrated from the Dominican Republic to New Jersey, those marginalized genres speak directly to his own diasporic experience: time-travel making sense of going from "latrines and no lights" to "MTV and a car in every parking space," X-Men mutants serving as a potent metaphor for both race and any perceived "erased condition" ("Junot" 90, 92). The boy from outside Ocoa in *Drown* (1996) who wears a mask to cover a face mutilated by a pig, and suffers accordingly at the hands of Yunior and his brother in that story collection, thus imagines himself "fighting evil" with powers of "INVISIBILITY" and "STRENGTH" (160, 155, 156), much like the orphaned superhero Kaliman in his comic books. And the apocalyptic variants that the fictional surrogates in *Oscar Wao* favor are particularly well-suited to depicting a Fall of the House of Cabral that coincides – in Yunior's conflation of Greek myth, Genesis, and nuclear holocaust – with atomic bombs that fall on Japan. In fact, the "End" awaited by Oscar's surgeon grandfather for running afoul of the Dominican regime only begins the fallout experienced by the "daughter of the Fall, recipient of its heaviest radiations," who grows up to be Oscar's mother (223, 126), from the "world-scar like those of a hibakusha" left on her scalded back by strangers in Outer Azua's "irradiated terrains" that buy the child nobody wants (257, 256), to the beating that later nearly kills her for daring to love "atomically" a man married to a politically well-connected woman (126). Even more appropriate are they to a Santo Domingo introduced as the "Ground Zero of the New World" and a nation ruled for thirty-one years (1930–1961) by a dictator "so outlandish, so perverse, so dreadful that not even a sci-fi writer could have made his ass up" (1, 2). For unlike Sauron, the Tolkien villain he most approximates, whose evil is dispersed by a great wind, Trujillo is "too toxic a radiation to be dispelled" (156), as evidenced by footnotes that chronicle the evil perpetrated by henchmen long after his death and a book that ends with the youngest member of the Cabral family – born and bred in the US – still wearing three azabaches around her neck as shields against his Eye.

Ramón Saldívar proposes "speculative realism" and "historical fantasy" to denote this seemingly oxymoronic blending of genres displayed by much twenty-first-century US ethnic writing ("Second" 3–6; "Historical" 584–87): Yxta Maya Murray's *The Conquest* (2002), Salvador Plascencia's *The People of Paper* (2005), Gary Shteyngart's *Super Sad True Love Story* (2010), Chang-rae Lee's *On Such a Full Sea* (2014). In this sense, Díaz's portrayal of the Dominican Republic under Trujillo as an unending *Twilight Zone* episode anticipates Colson Whitehead's depiction of Manhattan after 9/11 as a postapocalyptic *Zone One* (2011). In that book, which weds the familiar elements of the 9/11 novel – decimated skyline, falling ash, Marine patrols, patriotic admonitions – to the genre of zombie fiction, the point is not just that the barriers hastily erected in response to a plague simply make "more literal" those personal barriers meant to "keep other people out" on which the nation was founded (102). It is that the flesh-eating skels looking to feed are the realization of an economy built on consumers deemed "meat" in a city prone to "devour" newcomers (150, 206), in other words, that the undead on the loose in Manhattan are the repressed returned to a metropolis that has "long carried its own plague" with regard to anyone deemed "mis-fitting" (121). When the barriers inevitably fall in the book's last chapter, the zombies incapable of speech who parade down Broadway declare in no uncertain terms "what the city had always told its citizens" from the first settlers onward: "I am going to eat you up" (244).

What distinguishes Díaz's novel among such works in which the fantastic is less exaggeration than actualization is the heroic role it accords the intellectual who transcribes – in whatever form – that history. "What is it with Dictators and Writers, anyway?" Yunior asks when recounting the murder of the "Basque supernerd" Jesús de Galíndez (*Brief* 97, 96), kidnapped from his New York apartment and returned to Santo Domingo for writing a dissertation deemed offensive to El Jefe. As Yunior goes on to suggest, in fact, it is arguably not the failure of Oscar's grandfather to produce his eldest daughter for the predatory dictator's delight (a tale as "common as krill" and rejected for being one of those "easy stories" that purportedly *"explains it all"* [244]) or the imprudent joke he makes about dead bodies in a Packard's trunk (its punch line hotly disputed) that leads to the prominent man's downfall. Rather, it is the book the doctor allegedly is writing about the president's supernatural powers, one of the many lost books cited as unavailable for review or even authentication after every scrap of paper in Abelard's house is confiscated by a regime that, in contrast to its Nazi twin, "didn't leave a paper trail," preferring instead "páginas en blanco" (243, 119).

In the end, however, even Yunior must concede to the presence of blank pages in the reconstructed history he offers in place of Trujillo's univocal history, given that the government's suppression of alternative stories is exacerbated by his own protagonists' resistance to certain kinds of stories: the doctor uninterested in the "fates of Unfortunate People" whose "stories in his house" would upset his "Tao of Dictator Avoidance" (227, 215); the daughter intent on re-creating herself anew in a new country whose embrace of Islands amnesia consists of "five parts denial, five parts negative hallucination" (259). "[Y]ou'll have to decide for yourself," Yunior tells his reader, as to whether the brief wondrous life of Oscar testifies to accident, conspiracy, or fukú curse (243). To that end, he portrays Oscar's return to the Dominican Republic that concludes the book in such a way as to support completely opposed interpretations. On the one hand, the assassination that follows the beating Oscar suffers in the cane fields for being so unwise as to fall crazy in love with a "semiretired puta" whose military police boyfriend is "one of those very bad men that not even postmodernism can explain away" both recapitulates and exceeds in brutality anything his mother experiences (279, 294). On the other hand, the "miracles" that begin when Oscar is approached by a woman who asks him what he is reading, and continue during the twenty-seven days he works on the four-part space opera ("J. R. R. Tolkien meets E. E. 'Doc' Smith") planned as his "crowning achievement" (280, 269), grant

Oscar, at gunpoint, the courage to assert the rarity of "great love" and the removal of it from the world as punishable by a haunting that he as avenging angel will administer (321). On the one hand, the package in which Oscar promises "the cure to what ails us" is never received (333), and the copy of *Watchmen* that Yunior is able to retrieve from his belongings includes – in a panel that tries to justify the destruction of New York City by the saving of the world – the one instance of Oscar defacing a book: the triply circled phrase "Nothing ever ends" (331). On the other hand, the final letter from Oscar that arrives safely, which details his finally being able to express his love sexually, ends with words that exchange the horror of Conrad's heart of darkness for a celebration of "The beauty! The beauty!" of two hearts joined in intimacy (335).

The diaspora portrayed in Michael Chabon's fiction has a much longer history, extending as far back as the eighth century BCE, sixth century BCE, or first century CE, depending on which conqueror of Judaea – Assyrian, Babylonian, or Roman – is used. In contrast to the "virtually escape-proof" Dominican Alcatraz that imprisons Díaz's characters, a "Plátano Curtain" with no "Houdini holes" (*Brief* 80), the characters in Chabon's work are offered – however infrequently and temporarily – peepholes through which they can slip. It is his training in the escapistry of the "Mysteriarch" (533), as Houdini is called in *The Amazing Adventures of Kavalier & Clay* (2000), that enables Josef Kavalier in 1939 to escape German-occupied Czechoslovakia in a coffin holding the Golem of Prague and to pair up in New York with his cousin, Sammy, to create the Escapist, a comic book hero modeled on Superman – the ultimate Wandering Jew, in Jerry Siegel and Joe Shuster's rendering, for having "[c]om[e] over from the old country" and, with the exchange of Kal-El for Clark Kent, chosen a name "only a Jew would pick" for himself (585). More than just chronicling the evolution of the comic book from newspaper strip reprint to graphic novel, from trashy "devolution of American culture" to curated artifact auctioned at Sotheby's (156), Chabon presents the history of that "bastard, wide-open art form" as typifying all those genres dismissed as "mongrel art forms" whose value he asserts in essays that reclaim pleasure and entertainment as worthwhile goals for literature (176, 75). As he reminds readers whose "idea of genre" is "of a thing fundamentally, perhaps inherently debased" because its presumed adherence to a set of conventions limits any such work from "ris[ing] to the masterful heights of true literature, free (it is to be supposed) of all formulas and templates" (*Maps* 20), the genre known as "'literary fiction'" has its own rules, conventions, and formulas (22). The key for writers is to "*play*" with those rules (22), to "pl[y] their trade in the spaces between genres," so as to create a "Trickster literature" of "unending crossroads" (25), or, to return to *Kavalier & Clay*, to escape the chains of strict compliance in the manner of the "escape artist" (37), whose acts of "autoliberation" eventuate in acts of "*transformation*" (32, 3), as presaged by the man born Erich Weiss who transformed himself into Harry Houdini and whose first magic act was called "Metamorphosis" (3).

Such blending of high and low is embodied in the partnership between the illustrator trained at a European fine arts academy and the scripter working at an American novelties company that gives birth to the Escapist – Joe, ironically, alert from the start to the celebration of the human form in motion that comic books offer; Sammy, a frustrated "epic novelist," ever plagued by a need to move from comic books into "something really *legit*" (480, 356) – to which Chabon adds those inkers, colorists, engravers, even printers who also contribute to the superhero's realization. That initial cross-fertilization – anticipated, as Hillary Chute notes ("*Ragtime*" 288–90), by the Surrealist tenet that "[n]o medium is inherently better than any other" and those mixed-media works of Joseph Cornell made from "the commonplace, the neglected, the despised" (*Kavalier* 363, 319) – is only enhanced over time by a cross-fertilization between different media. As the character of the Escapist is adapted by radio and Hollywood serial, his comic book, in turn, steadily incorporates the techniques of film and, especially, the particular film, *Citizen Kane* (1941), whose "total blending of narration and image" results in *Radio Comics* #19's "daring use of perspective and shading," "radical placement of word balloons and captions," and "artfully disarranged, dislocated panels" that "unreeled themselves like the frames of a film" (362, 369). With the publication of an actual comic book series titled *Michael Chabon Presents: The Amazing Adventures of the Escapist*, that remediation goes on to extend beyond the novel's covers.

That the "genuine magic of art" that infuses such artifacts should have been "so universally despised" – vilified as perverting morality in books like Fredric Wertham's *Seduction of the Innocent* (1954), prosecuted as leading to juvenile delinquency by 1954 Senate subcommittee – is proof to Chabon of how blind American society is, a sign of how "fucked-up and broken" the world itself is (576). At the same time, Chabon remains acutely aware of the economics of comic books (their written texts born of the requirements for second-class postal rates, their superheroes grounded by circulation figures more than senatorial floggings) and the politics of comic books (Joe waging a personal war against Hitler in the Escapist's pages for destroying his family). He knows how easily the art employed in the service of democracy can inadvertently glorify vengeful brutality: Will Eisner's heroic Blackhawk Squadron pilots did don uniforms modeled on those of the Waffen SS; the Escapist's exploits do inspire a Nazi sympathizer to try to bomb a bar mitzvah while in the guise of his Saboteur alter ego. He therefore locates the primary importance of that art form conceived by immigrant artists, and their children, with no chance of working at the *Saturday Evening Post* in stories that, "for all their anti-fascist fisticuffs and screaming Stukas," were really "stories of orphans threatened, peasants abused, poor factory workers turned into slavering zombies" (360). For in expressing the abstract longings of "an entire generation of weaklings, stumblebums, and playground goats" (177), those tales of heroes and their wards addressed the specific yearnings for "absent, indifferent, vanishing fathers" depicted as endemic among "the comic-book-reading boys of America" (631). Defying sales counts because of their habit of passing comic books among themselves – so different from the legal wrangling over copyrights and contracts that left Superman's creators with a mere $130 and the Escapist's with nary a cent from any corporate tie-ins – these readers bespeak an ownership that transcends tabulation.

Such filial relationships lie at the heart of the novel that follows Chabon's argument for genre fiction with the wholesale appropriation of genre. In fact, in the counterfactual novel–detective novel that is *The Yiddish Policemen's Union* (2007), fathers who merely abandon their sons are joined by fathers willing to sacrifice their sons, from the biblical "sandal-wearing idiot . . . ready to cut his own son's throat for the sake of a hare-brained idea" to the twenty-first-century Verbover rebbe forcing his son to continue as Tzaddik Ha-Dor in order to have the messianic idea of a restored Temple in Jerusalem realized (368). In the alternative history of this novel set in late 2007, within which the slaughtered of World War II combine with the outnumbered of a three-month-old Jewish state "routed, massacred, and driven into the sea" (29), and the 1940 King-Havenner bill to resettle refugees in Alaska that was killed in Senate committee is actually passed by Congress, this idea of a return to a promised land has special urgency. With sovereignty of the District of Sitka due to revert, in accordance with a sixty-year agreement, back to the US in eight weeks, residents are scurrying to obtain green cards and scouting out the few places willing to take them (Canada, Argentina, Madagascar, the moon), even those places "tired of hearing about pogroms secondhand" and "hoping to throw one for themselves" (19), making it "strange times to be a Jew" as the book's refrain asserts (4).

But no stranger, as Chabon's hard-boiled detective, Meyer Landsman, understands, than all those other times when Jews living "on sufferance" are about to be dumped "like goldfish in a bag" back "into the big black lake of Diaspora" (375, 202). The son and grandson of suicidal fathers, and prospective father who "sacrificed to the god of his own dark hunches" the son that prenatal tests revealed as possibly having chromosomal defects (376), the world-weary Landsman has no religious faith and less than zero faith in the Middle East providing any kind of homeland much less a home when "Jews have been tossed out of the joint three times now – in 586 BCE, in 70 CE and with savage finality in 1948" (17). What prompts this forty-two-year-old noz with a sholem in his holster and the "balls of a fireman" in his pants (2) – in Chabon's stylized Yiddish patois – into action when presented with the "yid" found dead in Room 208 as the book opens is no illusion that solving the crime will make any difference – especially once every Sitka police case gets shoved into a file cabinet upon the January 1 Reversion – or that justice will ever be served. Even in that remote Alaskan outpost, institutional corruption thrives (Chasids running a criminal empire collude with right-wing American Christians), political intrigue flourishes (FBI provocateurs foment riots on disputed land), and all manner of aberrant behaviors and physical deformities, as per the genre's dictates, are on display (a grotesquely obese religious leader, a heroin addict that ties off with tefillin). It is instead the fact that the crime occurs in the Hotel Zamenhof, the "dump [that] is my house" where Landsman has made his home since his divorce, and to one of the hard-luck transients sleeping on pull-down beds that he takes as "my people" (166). Hence "finding out the truth" and "getting the story right" are superseded by the noir detective's more personal imperative – "to pay those fuckers back" (287–88) – that and a promise made to the victim's mother to uncover her son's killer.

But in also casting his neo-noir antagonists as adhering to different stances with respect to literary conventions, Chabon embellishes the genre conventions set down by writers like Raymond Chandler, Dashiell Hammett, and James M. Cain (and later adapted to the screen by European refugees like Fritz Lang, Robert Siodmak, and Billy Wilder). The conspirators that, even without a living messiah, go on to bomb the mosque in Palestine that inconveniently rests where the Jewish Temple had in order to hasten the coming of the Messiah, remain literalists bound to "the paper that God left the Jews holding" (331). They rejoice in an end-time violently unfolding "just the way it was written" in the (upper-case) "Book" (388, 366), making up for any shortfall between prophecy and actuality by imagining the murdered Mendel Shpilman awaiting them in Jerusalem. In so settling to be just "part of the story," though, they forfeit the chance to participate in "telling" a story (365). The "[p]eople of the book" (lower-case) police who uphold human rather than divine law, by contrast, assume a much more self-determining role (390). Indeed, what makes Landsman's ex-wife, Bina, such a good detective is her ability to fashion her own narratives: "She does not solve cases so much as tell the stories of them" (158). When Landsman, then, declares near the book's end, "Fuck what is written," prior to phoning a reporter with the story he has been blackmailed into keeping hidden (368), it is with the understanding that breaking his silence will leave him with "no home, no future" (411). Yet it also is with the diasporic subject's knowledge that his homeland is in his hat and his only home is with the woman introduced as carrying her own in a bulging tote bag.

A "Great White Male" derived from "plain old American WASPS," as he writes of one of his surrogates (*Girl* 303), David Foster Wallace abjured any classification of fiction by genre. As even the fledgling writer Mark Nechtr in "Westward the Course of Empire Takes Its Way" (1989) recognizes, "dividing this fiction business into realistic and naturalistic and surrealistic and modern and postmodern and new-realistic and meta- is like dividing history into cosmic and tragic and prophetic and apocalyptic," a "dumb" endeavor that leads to "blind supplication" (*Girl* 346). Worse still, it completely misses the point that fiction's importance lies not in what it is called – "Maybe it's called metalife. Or metafiction. Or realism. Or gfhrytytu. ... Maybe it's not called anything" (333) – but from where it springs, what Wallace elsewhere termed "the art's heart's purpose" ("Interview" 148), a moral imperative aligned in his writing with words like "integrity," "honor," and "love." It was a descent into solipsistic recursion that he viewed as compromising metafiction's once valuable exposure of fiction as mediated, just as it was postmodernism's television-assisted deterioration into an irony of "hip cynicism" that ruined irony's earlier service in piercing the legacy of 1950–1960s hypocrisies ("Interview" 147). With the funhouse of John Barth's 1968 collection turned into a franchise by 1989, and metafiction purveyed like "*[m]eatfiction*" in the novella's nod to Ray Kroc's golden arches (*Girl* 310), it is no wonder that Nechtr views himself as part of a "generation whose eyes have moved fish-like to the sides of its head, forward vision usurped by a numb need to survive the now, side-placed eyes scanning for any *garde* of which to be *avant*" (304), or that Wallace would describe his own generation of writers as ambivalently patricidal. Having come to realize that, with their parents' demise, "*we're going to have to be the parents*," these "literary orphans" shoulder a burden compounded by the fact that, as the first generation for whom pop images are less elements of mood than mimesis, they are fully implicated in the very phenomenon against which they battle ("Interview" 150).

The dead father who hovers over *Infinite Jest* (1996), much as Hamlet's does in the play from which the novel takes its name, is a "genre-dysphoric" filmmaker whose propensity to parody established genres is part of the "very self-consciously American" quality of all his work (682, 1011). It is, in fact, the search by Québecois Separatists for the ironized "so-called perfect Entertainment" made by James O. Incandenza prior to his untimely suicide by microwave (his mind literally blown by the kitchen appliance) that loosely forms the closest thing to a plot in this encyclopedic novel that is also part dystopian novel, family saga, coming-of-age novel, ecofiction, and sports novel (318). For in this end-of-history near future that outdoes Fukuyama's in being both "post-Soviet and -Jihad" (382), and in which the US, Mexico, and Canada have formed an interdependent Organization of North American Nations (really a "three-country continental Anschluss" [1020]), it is in Canada's postmillennial American protectorate that President (and former Famous Crooner) Johnny Gentle has found a way to solve America's waste problem while satisfying the need for "some cohesion-renewing Other" against which fractious Americans can unite (384). By replacing imperialism with Experialism, and ceding upper New England's "Great Concavity" (or "Convexity," depending on one's side of the border), the US can "dump pretty much everything we don't want" onto its northern neighbor (1032). By instituting Subsidized Time in addition to Standard Time, the US can recoup any revenue lost from its gifting from corporate sponsors bidding for the right to name each new year. If such bidding leaves the Statue of Liberty holding a Depend Adult Undergarment, as per each winner's contractual agreement, during the year in which most of the novel takes place, so be it.

Unlike Chabon, however, who works to redress the American suspicion of pleasure, Wallace addresses the American pursuit of pleasure as an inalienable right that has eventuated in a nation of addicts – slaves to drugs, booze, sugar, suicide, sex, even *M*A*S*H* – as exemplified by the two on whom the book most focuses: the seventeen-year-old Incandenza son, Hal, a tennis prodigy with a growing dependence on marijuana; and the recovering addict Don Gately, a live-in staffer at the halfway house down the hill from the Enfield, Massachusetts, tennis academy at which Hal resides. As Wallace recognizes, an addict's "second most meaningful relationship is always with his domestic entertainment unit" (834). It is to bombard those pleasure-seeking Americans into a state of catatonia that the Québecois Separatists search for the Master copy of Incandenza *père*'s "U.S.A. production" (also named *Infinite Jest*) that so satisfies the "U.S.A. drive for spectation" as to leave anyone who sees it "want[ing] nothing else ever in life but to see it again, and then again, and so on" (318, 548), thus forcing Ottawa to accede to their secessionist demands rather than face "the wrath of a neighbor struck down by its own inability to say '*Non*' to fatal pleasures" (722). Hardly aberrations, though, the lost souls already locked in wards are merely extreme cases of a TV docility only exacerbated by the shift to digital TP (teleputer), advances in technology that have joined private spectation to passive spectation and resulted in 94 percent of all entertainment being absorbed at home and 50 percent of all education and work conducted at home by individuals devoted only to the self and "citizen[s] of nothing" (620, 108). In other words, a nation of infants, of which Wallace's US abounds: from grown men who still cherish "Mummykins" and Men's Group members who clutch teddy bears to the Incandenza child traumatized by a narcissist "Moms" unwilling to change a diaper and the Gately toddler left in a crib beneath a leaky ceiling by an alcoholic mother.

But not, for all the hints of substance abuse as "genetically hard-wired" (395), doomed to remain infants, as the non-American characters are quick to assert. The German tennis coach Gerhardt Schtitt, who views athletics as "training for citizenship," trains his student-athletes to "sacrifice the hot narrow imperatives of the Self ... to the larger imperatives of a team" (82). The Québecois Rémy Marathe, who sacrifices his politics for his severely disabled wife's medical care, distinguishes between the lack of choice that comes from a first viewing of the Entertainment and the "deci[sion] to be this pleasurably entertained in the first place" (430). His repeated admonition that U.S.A.s "[c]hoose with care" (107, 318) their attachments is, in fact, exactly what Wallace reiterated in his 2005 Kenyon College commencement address in which he urged graduates to replace the "default setting" of self-centeredness with the "choice" of adopting another's perspective (*This* 38, 89). As illustrated by the "maximally unironic" model of Boston AA (*Infinite* 369), this means replacing irony with empathy, and the pursuit of pleasure or, more to the point, the anesthetic dulling of sensation that is the real under-lying desire of the addict, as Hal's anhedonia confirms, with the opening up to pain that is the route to recovery. As the group's long-term Crocodiles, who have no patience for the blame game of "causal attribution" but "sincere compassion about fucking up that empathy makes possible" (370, 356), do not mention among the truisms they spout, "the way it gets better and you get better is through pain" (446). Or as the doctor treating Gately for a Grade-II trauma suffered while "simply doing the best he could" while "trying to stand up for himself and for a resident of the House" states when trying to convince the former Demerol addict to consent to an analgesic, "The laws of trauma dictate the pain will intensify as healing begins to commence" (817, 887).

This extension of empathy that was, to Wallace, part of being human is portrayed as not limited to humans. The flies maimed by his mother's boyfriend that an intubated Gately desperately hopes he put out of their misery when a child are no different in their pain and fear from the lobsters frantically clinging to the edges of pots to avoid being plunged into boiling water that Wallace asked the readers of *Gourmet* magazine to consider. As the "confus[ion]" with which he ended that contemplation of the crustacean's plight also indicates (*Consider* 253), Wallace was well aware of the complications, if not contradictions, of the practices he preached: the "proto-fascist" element behind the surrender of individual will required by both team tennis and Boston AA (82, 374); the substance abuse program that becomes a substitute for the addictive drug itself. Perhaps most paradoxical is the way that the fiction meant, as he famously stated, to inculcate "what it is to be a fucking *human being*," to create collaborative rather than passive readers, ultimately to move beyond postmodernism's diagnosis of all that is wrong toward "redeeming what's wrong" ("Interview" 131, 147), employed those same practices of fragmentation, self-consciousness, and authorial pyrotechnics to, as A. O. Scott remarks, "Janus-faced" excess (40). Not in the spirit of the four-day debauch by which one of the halfway house residents had imagined "cur[ing]" himself by excess" (*Infinite* 22), but in the manner of those parodies of "commercial-type genre modes" whose "formulaic shticks" Hal's father "so grotesquely exaggerated" as to become "ironic metacinematic parodies on the genres" themselves (703). It is in those films that the director whose work typically suggested a "very smart person conversing with himself" revealed the early flashes of "something more than cold hip technical abstraction" that interjected an "almost *moral* thesis" to his "campy abstract[ions]" (740, 742), leading to the particular film most favored by his sons: the one in which a habitually late bureaucrat ensures his own firing because he takes the time to minister to a child, a film distinguished by its "unhip earnestness" (689).

Artistic "*askesis*" is the term used by the lecturer describing the "battle-to-the-death with the loved dead" that forms the climax of the last film of his father's that Hal screens for himself, its intimation of a "contest proper" making it a more appropriate paradigm than *clinamen*'s revival and *kenosis*'s repression of the dead ancestor (911). Not that Wallace portrays that battle to replace irony with empathy as definitely won: Hal is left lying on the floor staring at a bathroom tumbler at book's end, Gately in a hospital bed recalling a Dilaudid binge chosen in lieu of helping the supplier he knows will pay heavily for his scamming. Indeed, when addressing "Fictional Futures" the year that my study of contemporary American fiction takes as its rough starting point, Wallace conceded that "1987's America is not a nice place to be" and that his generation of "Conspicuously Young" writers, "Watergate's children, television's audience, Reagan's draft-pool, and everyone's market," inhabited "[a]n age between" (52, 51). Yet as someone with an "abiding faith" that the artist of any age "retains the power to effect change," he also recognized that a grey time need not give way to a nihilistic grey art, that, in fact, "fiction in a grey time *may not be grey*" (52). And so the "Year of Glad" prologue from which the rest of *Infinite Jest* emerges as extended flashback does not end with Hal, having suffered a complete breakdown during a college interview, merely entreating others, in his own mind, to see him as someone who can "feel and believe" (12). It ends with Hal imagining one of the invisible blue-collar others at the hospital to which he is being taken looking down at him and asking: "So yo then man what's *your* story? (17).

Works Cited

Abdullah, Shaila. *Saffron Dreams*. Ann Arbor: Modern History P, 2009.

Abish, Walter. *Eclipse Fever*. 1993. Boston: Nonpareil-Godine, 1995.

Abrams, David. *Fobbit*. New York: Black Cat–Grove/Atlantic, 2012.

Adams, Henry. *The Education of Henry Adams*. 1906. Boston: Houghton, 1961.

Agamben, Giorgio. *State of Exception*. Trans. Kevin Attell. Chicago: U of Chicago P, 2005. Trans. of *Stato di eccezione*. 2003.

Akhtiorskaya, Yelena. *Panic in a Suitcase*. New York: Riverhead-Penguin, 2014.

Alcoff, Linda. "The Problem of Speaking for Others." *Cultural Critique* 20 (1991–1992): 5–32.

Allen, Irving Lewis. *The City in Slang: New York and Popular Speech*. New York: Oxford UP, 1993.

Alvarez, Julia. *How the García Girls Lost Their Accents*. 1991. Chapel Hill, NC: Algonquin-Workman, 2010.

In the Time of the Butterflies. 1994. Chapel Hill, NC: Algonquin-Workman, 2010.

Something to Declare. Chapel Hill, NC: Algonquin-Workman, 1998.

Anaya, Rudolfo. *Alburquerque*. 1992. New York: Warner, 1994.

Anderson, Benedict. *Imagined Communities: Reflections on the Origin and Spread of Nationalism*. London: Verso, 1983.

Annesley, James. *Fictions of Globalization*. London: Continuum, 2006.

Anzaldúa, Gloria. *Borderlands/La Frontera: The New Mestiza*. San Francisco: Spinsters–Aunt Lute, 1987.

Appadurai, Arjun. "Disjuncture and Difference in the Global Cultural Economy." *Theory, Culture & Society* 7 (1990): 295–310.

Apter, Emily. "On Oneworldedness: Or Paranoia as a World System." *American Literary History* 18 (2006): 365–89.

Ashe, Bertram D. "Theorizing the Post-Soul Aesthetic: An Introduction." *African American Review* 41 (2007): 609–23.

Auster, Paul. *Leviathan*. 1992. New York: Penguin, 1993.

Man in the Dark. New York: Picador-Holt, 2008.

Banks, Russell. *Affliction*. 1989. New York: HarperPerennial–HarperCollins, 1990.

Cloudsplitter. 1998. New York: HarperPerennial–HarperCollins, 1999.

Continental Drift. 1985. New York: HarperPerennial–HarperCollins, 1994.

The Sweet Hereafter. 1991. New York: HarperPerennial–HarperCollins, 1992.

Barth, John. "The Literature of Exhaustion." *Atlantic Monthly* Aug. 1967: 29–34.

"The Literature of Replenishment." *Atlantic Monthly* Jan. 1980: 65–71.

Lost in the Funhouse: Fiction for Print, Tape, Live Voice. 1968. New York: Bantam, 1969.

Barthelme, Donald. *The Dead Father.* 1975. New York: Penguin, 1986.

Barthes, Roland. *Empire of Signs.* Trans. Richard Howard. New York: Hill and Wang–Farrar, 1982. Trans. of *L'empire des signes.* 1970.

Bassard, Katherine Clay. "Imagining Other Worlds: Race, Gender, and the 'Power Line' in Edward P. Jones's *The Known World.*" *African American Review* 42 (2008): 407–19.

Baudrillard, Jean. *The Spirit of Terrorism and Requiem for the Twin Towers.* Trans. Chris Turner. London: Verso, 2002. Trans. of *L'esprit du terrorisme* and *Requiem pour les Twin Towers.* 2002.

Beattie, Ann. *The Burning House.* 1982. New York: Ballantine, 1983.

Chilly Scenes of Winter. 1976. New York: Vintage–Random, 1991.

Mrs. Nixon: A Novelist Imagines a Life. New York: Scribner–Simon, 2011.

Beattie, Tina. "The End of Postmodernism: The 'New Atheists' and Democracy." *Open Democracy,* 20 Dec. 2007, www.opendemocracy.net/article/faith_ideas/the_new_atheists. Accessed 22 Jan. 2016.

Beatty, Paul. *The Sellout.* New York: Farrar, 2015.

Slumberland. New York: Bloomsbury, 2008.

The White Boy Shuffle. Boston: Houghton, 1996.

Bell, Bernard W. *The Afro-American Novel and Its Tradition.* Amherst: U of Massachusetts P, 1987.

Bellow, Saul. *Dangling Man.* 1944. New York: Bard-Avon, 1975.

Bender, Thomas, and William R. Taylor. "Culture and Architecture: Some Aesthetic Tensions in the Shaping of Modern New York City." *Visions of the Modern City: Essays in History, Art, and Literature.* Ed. William Sharpe and Leonard Wallock. Baltimore: Johns Hopkins UP, 1987. 189–219.

Bennett, Bridget. "The Crisis of Restoration: Mary Rowlandson's Lost Home." *Early American Literature* 49 (2014): 327–56.

Bevis, William. "Native American Novels: Homing In." *Recovering the Word: Essays on Native American Literature.* Ed. Brian Swann and Arnold Krupat. Berkeley: U of California P, 1987. 580–620.

Bhabha, Homi. "The World and the Home." *Social Text* 31–32 (1992): 141–53.

Boxall, Peter. *Twenty-First-Century Fiction: A Critical Introduction.* New York: Cambridge UP, 2013.

Boyers, Robert. *Atrocity and Amnesia: The Political Novel since 1945.* New York: Oxford UP, 1985.

Boyle, T. Coraghessan. *The Inner Circle.* 2004. New York: Penguin, 2005.

The Road to Wellville. 1993. New York: Penguin, 1994.

The Tortilla Curtain. 1995. New York: Penguin, 1996.

The Women. New York: Viking-Penguin, 2009.

Bradbury, Malcolm, and Sigmund Roy, eds. *Contemporary American Fiction.* London: Edward Arnold, 1987.

Bradford, William. *Of Plymouth Plantation 1620–1647.* Ed. Samuel Eliot Morison. New York: Borzoi-Knopf, 1952.

Brooks, Michael W. *Subway City: Riding the Trains, Reading New York.* New Brunswick, NJ: Rutgers UP, 1997.

Brown, Rosellen. *Half a Heart.* New York: Farrar, 2000.

Buell, Lawrence. "Ecoglobalist Affects: The Emergence of U.S. Environmental Imagination on a Planetary Scale." *Shades of the Planet: American Literature as World Literature.* Ed. Wai Chee Dimock and Lawrence Buell. Princeton: Princeton UP, 2007. 227–48.

Buford, Bill. Editorial. *Granta* 8: "Dirty Realism: New Writing from America" (1983): 4–5.

Burn, Stephen J. "The End of Postmodernism: American Fiction at the Millennium." *American Fiction of the 1990s: Reflections of History and Culture.* Ed. Jay Prosser. London: Routledge, 2008. 220–34.

Busch, Frederick. *Girls.* 1997. New York: Fawcett Columbine–Ballantine, 1998.

The Mutual Friend. 1978. New York: New Directions, 1994.

The Night Inspector. 1999. New York: Ballantine-Random, 2000.

North. New York: Norton, 2005.

When People Publish: Essays on Writers and Writing. Iowa City: U of Iowa P, 1986.

Butler, Judith. *Precarious Life: The Powers of Mourning and Violence.* 2004. London: Verso, 2006.

Butler, Octavia E. *Adulthood Rites.* New York: Warner, 1988.

Dawn. New York: Warner, 1987.

Imago. 1989. New York: Aspect-Warner, 1990.

Kindred. 1979. Boston: Beacon, 1988.

Cantor, Jay. *The Space Between: Literature and Politics.* Baltimore: Johns Hopkins UP, 1981.

Cantor, Jay, and James Romberger. *Aaron and Ahmed: A Love Story.* New York: Vertigo–DC Comics, 2011.

Caruth, Cathy. "Recapturing the Past: Introduction." *Explorations in Memory.* Ed. Cathy Caruth. Baltimore: Johns Hopkins UP, 1995. 151–57.

Castiglia, Christopher. *Bound and Determined: Captivity, Culture-Crossing, and White Womanhood from Mary Rowlandson to Patty Hearst.* Chicago: U of Chicago P, 1996.

Castillo, Ana. *The Mixquiahuala Letters.* Binghamton, NY: Bilingual Press/ Editorial Bilingüe, 1986.

So Far from God. 1993. New York: Plume-Penguin, 1994.

Chabon, Michael. *The Amazing Adventures of Kavalier & Clay.* 2000. New York: Picador–St. Martin's, 2001.

Maps and Legends: Reading and Writing along the Borderlands. San Francisco: McSweeney's, 2008.

Michael Chabon Presents: The Amazing Adventures of the Escapist. Milwaukie, OR: Dark Horse Comics, 2004–2005.

The Yiddish Policemen's Union. New York: HarperCollins, 2007.

Chan, Sucheng. "The Exclusion of Chinese Women, 1870–1943." *Entry Denied: Exclusion and the Chinese Community in America, 1882–1943.* Ed. Sucheng Chan. Philadelphia: Temple UP, 1991. 94–146.

Chen, Tina. *Double Agency: Acts of Impersonation in Asian American Literature and Culture.* Stanford: Stanford UP, 2005.

Chénetier, Marc. *Beyond Suspicion: New American Fiction since 1960.* Trans. Elizabeth A. Houlding. Philadelphia: U of Pennsylvania P, 1996. Trans of *Au-delà du soupçon: La nouvelle fiction américaine de 1960 à nos jours.* 1989.

Chin, Frank. *The Chinaman Pacific & Frisco R.R. Co.* Minneapolis: Coffee House, 1988.

"Come All Ye Asian American Writers of the Real and the Fake." 1990. *The Big Aiiieeeee!: An Anthology of Chinese American and Japanese American Literature.* Ed. Jeffery Paul Chan, Frank Chin, Lawson Fusao Inada, and Shawn Wong. New York: Meridian-Penguin, 1991. 1–92.

The Confessions of a Number One Son. Ed. Calvin McMillin. Honolulu: U of Hawai'i P, 2015.

Donald Duk. 1991. Minneapolis: Coffee House, 1997.

Gunga Din Highway. Minneapolis: Coffee House, 1994.

Choi, Susan. *American Woman.* 2003. New York: Perennial–HarperCollins, 2004.

A Person of Interest. 2008. New York: Penguin, 2009.

Chute, Hillary. "Comics as Literature? Reading Graphic Narrative." *PMLA* 123 (2008): 452–65.

"*Ragtime, Kavalier & Clay*, and the Framing of Comics." *Modern Fiction Studies* 54 (2008): 268–301.

Cisneros, Sandra. *Caramelo.* New York: Knopf, 2002.

The House on Mango Street. 1984. Rev. 1989. New York: Vintage-Random, 1991.

Coates, Ta-Nehisi. *Between the World and Me.* New York: Spiegel & Grau–Random, 2015.

Cole, Teju. *Every Day Is for the Thief.* 2007. New York: Random, 2014.

Open City. 2011. New York: Random, 2012.

Coover, Robert. "And Hypertext Is Only the Beginning. Watch Out!" *New York Times Book Review* 29 Aug. 1993: 8–9.

Cotter, Holland. "Beyond Multiculturalism, Freedom?" *New York Times* 29 July 2001, late ed., sec. 2: 1+.

Cowart, David. *Trailing Clouds: Immigrant Fiction in Contemporary America.* Ithaca: Cornell UP, 2006.

The Tribe of Pyn: Literary Generations in the Postmodern Period. Ann Arbor: U of Michigan P, 2015.

Coyne, Andrew. *National Post* 12 Sept. 2001.

Crèvecoeur, J. Hector St. John de. *Letters from an American Farmer*. 1782. New York: Everyman-Dutton, 1957.

Crouch, Stanley. "Race Is Over: Black, White, Red, Yellow – Same Difference." *New York Times* 29 Sept. 1996: 170–71.

Cryderman, Kevin. "Fire for a Ghost: Blind Spots and the Dissection of Race in John Edgar Wideman's *The Cattle Killing*." *Callaloo* 34 (2011): 1047–67.

Cunningham, Michael. *The Hours*. New York: Farrar, 1998.

 Specimen Days. New York: Farrar, 2005.

Dandicat, Edwidge. *The Farming of Bones*. New York: Soho, 1998.

Danielewski, Mark Z. *House of Leaves*. New York: Pantheon, 2000.

Däwes, Birgit. *Ground Zero Fiction: History, Memory, and Representation in the American 9/11 Novel*. Heidelberg: Universitätsverlag Winter, 2011.

Delgadillo, Theresa. "The Criticality of Latino/a Fiction in the Twenty-First Century." *American Literary History* 23 (2011): 600–24.

DeLillo, Don. "American Blood: A Journey through the Labyrinth of Dallas and JFK." *Rolling Stone* 8 Dec. 1983: 21–22, 24, 27–28, 74.

 Americana. Boston: Houghton, 1971.

 Cosmopolis. New York: Scribner, 2003.

 Falling Man. New York: Scribner, 2007.

 Great Jones Street. Boston: Houghton, 1973.

 "In the Ruins of the Future: Reflections on Terror and Loss in the Shadow of September." *Harper's* Dec. 2001: 33–40.

 Libra. 1988. New York: Penguin, 1989.

 Mao II. New York: Viking, 1991.

 The Names. New York: Knopf, 1982.

 Underworld. New York: Scribner, 1997.

Derrida, Jacques. "Autoimmunity: Real and Symbolic Suicides: A Dialogue with Jacques Derrida." Trans. Pascale-Anne Brault and Michael Naas. *Philosophy in a Time of Terror: Dialogues with Jürgen Habermas and Jacques Derrida*. By Giovanna Borradori. Chicago: U of Chicago P, 2003. 85–136.

Dewey, Joseph. *Novels from Reagan's America: A New Realism*. Gainesville: UP of Florida, 1999.

Díaz, Junot. *The Brief Wondrous Life of Oscar Wao*. 2007. New York: Riverhead-Penguin, 2008.

 Drown. New York: Riverhead-Putnam's, 1996.

 "Junot Díaz." Interview with Edwidge Dandicat. *BOMB* 101 (2007): 88–95.

Dickson-Carr, Darryl. *African American Satire: The Sacredly Profane Novel*. Columbia: U of Missouri P, 2001.

Didion, Joan. *After Henry*. 1992. New York: Vintage-Random, 1993.

 The White Album. 1979. New York: Pocket-Simon, 1980.

Dimock, Wai Chee. "Planet and America, Set and Subset." Introduction. *Shades of the Planet: American Literature as World Literature*. Ed. Wai Chee Dimock and Lawrence Buell. Princeton: Princeton UP, 2007. 1–16.

Doctorow, E. L. *The Book of Daniel*. 1971. New York: Signet–New American Library, 1972.

    Homer & Langley. New York: Random, 2009.

Dorfman, Ariel. "America's No Longer Unique." *Counterpunch*, 3 Oct. 2001, www.counterpunch.org/2001/10/03/america-s-no-longer-unique/. Accessed 22 Jan. 2016.

Douglass, Frederick. "The Heroic Slave." *Autographs for Freedom*. Boston: John P. Jewett, 1853. 174–239.

Dubus, Andre, III. *The Garden of Last Days*. 2008. New York: Norton, 2009.

    House of Sand and Fog. 1999. New York: Norton, 2011.

Duvall, John N., ed. *The Cambridge Companion to American Fiction after 1945*. Cambridge: Cambridge UP, 2012.

    "Witnessing Trauma: *Falling Man* and Performance Art." *Don DeLillo: Mao II, Underworld, Falling Man*. Ed. Stacey Olster. London: Continuum, 2011. 152–68.

Egan, Jennifer. "Black Box." @NYerFiction. 24 May–2 June 2012.

    "An Interview with Jennifer Egan." With Charlie Reilly. *Contemporary Literature* 50 (2009): 439–60.

    The Keep. New York: Knopf, 2006.

    A Visit from the Goon Squad. 2010. New York: Anchor-Random, 2011.

Eggers, Dave. *A Heartbreaking Work of Staggering Genius*. 2000. New York: Vintage-Random, 2001.

    A Hologram for the King. San Francisco: McSweeney's, 2012.

    What Is the What. 2006. New York: Vintage-Random, 2007.

    You Shall Know Our Velocity! 2002. New York: Vintage-Random, 2003.

    Zeitoun. San Francisco: McSweeney's, 2009.

Elam, Michele. *The Souls of Mixed Folk: Race, Politics, and Aesthetics in the New Millennium*. Stanford: Stanford UP, 2011.

Ellington, Duke. "Where Is Jazz Going?" *Music Journal* (Mar. 1962). Rpt. in *The Duke Ellington Reader*. Ed. Mark Tucker. New York: Oxford UP, 1993. 324–26.

Ellis, Trey. "The New Black Aesthetic." *Callaloo* 38 (1989): 233–43.

    Platitudes. New York: Vintage-Random, 1988.

Ellison, Ralph. *Invisible Man*. New York: Random, 1952.

Emerson, Ralph Waldo. *The Complete Essays and Other Writings of Ralph Waldo Emerson*. Ed. Brooks Atkinson. New York: Modern Library–Random, 1950.

"The Encyclopedia of 9/11." *New York* 5–12 Sept. 2011: 33–138.

Erdrich, Louise. *Love Medicine*. 1984. New York: Bantam, 1989.

    The Master Butchers Singing Club. 2003. New York: Harper Perennial–HarperCollins, 2004.

    The Plague of Doves. New York: HarperCollins, 2008.

The Round House. New York: HarperCollins, 2012.

"Where I Ought to Be: A Writer's Sense of Place." *New York Times Book Review* 28 July 1985: 23–24.

Everett, Percival. *Assumption*. Minneapolis: Graywolf, 2011.

Erasure. Hanover, NH: UP of New England, 2001.

For Her Dark Skin. 1990. Ann Arbor: Dzanc, 2014.

Frenzy. Saint Paul: Graywolf, 1997.

God's Country. 1994. Boston: Beacon, 2003.

A History of the African-American People (proposed) by Strom Thurmond, as told to Percival Everett & James Kincaid. New York: Akashic, 2004.

I Am Not Sidney Poitier. Minneapolis: Graywolf, 2009.

"Percival Everett." Interview with Rone Shavers. *BOMB* 88 (2004): 46–51.

Watershed. 1996. Boston: Beacon, 2003.

Zulus. Sag Harbor, NY: Permanent, 1990.

Fadda-Conrey, Carol. "Arab American Citizenship in Crisis: Destabilizing Representations of Arabs and Muslims in the US after 9/11." *Modern Fiction Studies* 57 (2011): 532–55.

Firmat, Gustavo Pérez. "Rum, Rump, and Rumba: Cuban Contexts for *The Mambo Kings Play Songs of Love*." *Dispositio* 16.41 (1991): 61–69.

Fishkin, Shelley Fisher. "Crossroads of Cultures: The Transnational Turn in American Studies – Presidential Address to the American Studies Association, November 12, 2004." *American Quarterly* 57 (2005): 17–57.

Fiske, John. *Television Culture*. London: Routledge, 1987.

Fitzgerald, F. Scott. *The Great Gatsby*. New York: Scribner's, 1925.

Fluck, Winfried. "Surface Knowledge and 'Deep' Knowledge: The New Realism in American Fiction." *Neo-Realism in Contemporary American Fiction*. Ed. Kristiaan Versluys. Amsterdam: Rodopi, 1992. 65–85.

Foer, Jonathan Safran. *Everything Is Illuminated*. Boston: Houghton, 2002.

Extremely Loud & Incredibly Close. 2005. Boston: Mariner-Houghton, 2006.

Ford, Richard. *Independence Day*. 1995. New York: Vintage-Random, 1996.

The Lay of the Land. London: Bloomsbury, 2006.

Let Me Be Frank with You. New York: Ecco–HarperCollins, 2014.

The Sportswriter. 1986: New York: Vintage-Random, 1995.

Fountain, Ben. *Billy Lynn's Long Halftime Walk*. New York: Ecco–HarperCollins, 2012.

Franzen, Jonathan. *The Corrections*. New York: Farrar, 2001.

Freedom. New York: Farrar, 2010.

How to Be Alone: Essays. New York: Farrar, 2002.

Fukuyama, Francis. "The End of History?" *The National Interest* 16 (Summer 1989): 3–18.

The End of History and the Last Man. New York: Free-Macmillan, 1992.

García, Cristina. *Dreaming in Cuban*. 1992. New York: Ballantine-Random, 1993.

George, Nelson. *Buppies, B-Boys, Baps & Bohos: Notes on Post-Soul Black Culture*. New York: HarperCollins, 1992.

Gibson, William. *Neuromancer*. New York: Ace-Berkley, 1984.

Pattern Recognition. New York: Putnam's, 2003.

Giddens, Anthony. *Runaway World: How Globalization Is Reshaping Our Lives.* 1999. New York: Routledge, 2000.

Giles, Paul. *The Global Remapping of American Literature.* Princeton: Princeton UP, 2011.

Gilroy, Paul. *Against Race: Imagining Political Culture beyond the Color Line.* Cambridge: Belknap–Harvard UP, 2000.

Golden, Thelma. Introduction. *Freestyle.* Ed. Christine Y. Kim and Franklin Simans. New York: Studio Museum in Harlem, 2001. 14–15.

Goldenberger, Paul. *Up from Zero: Politics, Architecture, and the Rebuilding of New York.* New York: Random, 2004.

Gómez, Alma, Cherríe Moraga, and Mariana Romo-Carmona, eds. *Cuentos: Stories by Latinas.* New York: Kitchen Table: Women of Color, 1983.

Gómez-Vega, Ibis. "Hating the Self in the 'Other' or How Yolanda Learns to See Her Own Kind in Julia Alvarez's *How the García Girls Lost Their Accents.*" *Intertexts* 3.1 (1999): 85–96.

González, Bill Johnson. "The Politics of Translation in Sandra Cisneros's *Caramelo.*" *Differences* 17.3 (2006): 3–19.

Gray, Richard. *After the Fall: American Literature since 9/11.* Chinchester: Wiley-Blackwell, 2011.

Green, Jeremy. *Late Postmodernism: American Fiction at the Millennium.* New York: Palgrave Macmillan, 2005.

Groff, Lauren. *Arcadia.* New York: Voice-Hyperion, 2012.

Hagedorn, Jessica. *Dogeaters.* 1990. New York: Penguin, 1991.

Dream Jungle. New York: Viking-Penguin, 2003.

"An Interview with Jessica Hagedorn." With Kay Bonetti. *Missouri Review* 18.1 (1995): 89–114.

Halaby, Laila. *Once in a Promised Land.* Boston: Beacon, 2007.

Hall, Stuart. "Encoding/Decoding." *Culture, Media, Language: Working Papers in Cultural Studies, 1972–79.* Centre for Contemporary Cultural Studies, University of Birmingham. London: Hutchinson, 1980. 128–38.

Hamid, Mohsin. *The Reluctant Fundamentalist.* Orlando: Harcourt, 2007.

Hardt, Michael, and Antonio Negri. *Empire.* 2000. Cambridge: Harvard UP, 2001.

Hayles, N. Katherine. "Saving the Subject: Remediation in *House of Leaves.*" *American Literature* 74 (2002): 779–806.

Heise, Ursula K. *Sense of Place and Sense of Planet: The Environmental Imagination of the Global.* New York: Oxford UP, 2008.

Hemingway, Ernest. *A Farewell to Arms.* New York: Scribner's, 1929.

Hemon, Aleksandar. *Nowhere Man.* New York: Talese-Doubleday, 2002.

Herman, Judith. *Trauma and Recovery.* New York: BasicBooks–HarperCollins, 1992.

Hersey, John. *Hiroshima.* 1946. New York: Bantam, 1975.

Hijuelos, Oscar. *The Mambo Kings Play Songs of Love.* 1989. New York: Harper-Perennial, 1990.

Hoberek, Andrew. "Introduction: After Postmodernism." *Twentieth-Century Literature* 53 (2007): 233–47.

Hoffman, Joan M. "'She Wants to Be Called Yolanda Now': Identity, Language, and the Third Sister in *How the García Girls Lost Their Accents*." *Bilingual Review/La Revista Bilingüe* 23.1 (1998): 21–27.

Hogan, Linda. *Mean Spirit*. New York: Atheneum-Macmillan, 1990.

   People of the Whale. New York: Norton, 2008.

   Power. New York: Norton, 1998.

   Solar Storms. New York: Scribner, 1995.

Holland, Mary K. *Succeeding Postmodernism: Language & Humanism in Contemporary American Literature*. New York: Bloomsbury, 2013.

Hollinger, David A. *Postethnic America: Beyond Multiculturalism*. New York: BasicBooks–HarperCollins, 1995.

Hornung, Alfred. "'Flying Planes Can Be Dangerous': Ground Zero Literature." *Science, Technology, and the Humanities in Recent American Fiction*. Ed. Peter Freese and Charles B. Harris. Essen: Die Blaue Eule–Verlag, 2004. 383–403.

Howe, Irving. "Anarchy and Authority in American Literature." 1967. Rpt. in *Selected Writings 1950–1990*. San Diego: Harcourt, 1990. 103–18.

   Politics and the Novel. Cleveland: Meridian-World, 1957.

Hughes, Langston. *Mulatto*. 1930. Rpt. In *The Collected Works of Langston Hughes: The Plays to 1942*. Vol. 5. Ed. Leslie Catherine Sanders with Nancy Johnston. Columbia: U of Missouri P, 2002. 17–50.

Hume, Kathryn. *American Dream, American Nightmare: Fiction since 1960*. Urbana: U of Illinois P, 2000.

Hungerford, Amy. "On the Period Formerly Known as Contemporary." *American Literary History* 20 (2008): 410–19.

Hutcheon, Linda. *The Politics of Postmodernism*. London: Routledge, 1989.

Hutchison, Anthony. *Writing the Republic: Liberalism and Morality in American Political Fiction*. New York: Columbia UP, 2007.

Irr, Caren. *Toward the Geopolitical Novel: U.S. Fiction in the Twenty-First Century*. New York: Columbia UP, 2014.

Jackson, Shelley. *Patchwork Girl; or, A Modern Monster*. Watertown, MA: Eastgate Systems, 1995. CD-ROM.

Jacobson, Sid, and Ernie Colón. *The 9/11 Report: A Graphic Adaptation*. New York: Hill-Farrar, 2006.

Jameson, Fredric. *Postmodernism, or, The Cultural Logic of Late Capitalism*. Durham: Duke UP, 1991.

"Jazz Goes to College." *Time* 7 June 1971: 67.

Jen, Gish. *Mona in the Promised Land*. 1996. New York: Vintage-Random, 1997.

   Tiger Writing: Art, Culture, and the Interdependent Self. Cambridge: Harvard UP, 2013.

   Typical American. 1991. New York: Plume-Penguin, 1992.

Johnson, Charles. *Being and Race: Black Writing since 1970*. Bloomington: Indiana UP, 1988.

Middle Passage. 1990. New York: Plume-Penguin, 1991.

Oxherding Tale. 1982. New York: Plume-Penguin, 1995.

Johnson, Mat. *Loving Day.* New York: Spiegel & Grau–Random, 2015.

Johnson, Mat, and Simon Gane. *Dark Rain: A New Orleans Story.* New York: Vertigo–DC Comics, 2010.

Jones, Edward P. "An Interview with Edward P. Jones." With Maryemma Graham. *African American Review* 42 (2008): 421–38.

The Known World. New York: Amistad–HarperCollins, 2003.

Jones, Suzanne W. "Tragic No More? The Reappearance of the Racially Mixed Character." *American Fiction of the 1990s.* Ed. Jay Prosser. London: Routledge, 2008. 89–103.

Joyce, Michael. *afternoon, a story.* Watertown, MA: Eastgate Systems, 1987. CD-ROM.

Kalfus, Ken. *A Disorder Peculiar to the Country.* New York: Ecco–HarperCollins, 2006.

Kaplan, Amy. "Homeland Insecurities: Reflections on Language and Space." *Radical History Review* 85 (2003): 82–93.

Karl, Frederick R. *American Fictions, 1940–1980: A Comprehensive History and Critical Evaluation.* New York: Harper, 1983.

Keller, Julia. "After the Attack, Postmodernism Loses Its Glib Grip." *Chicago Tribune*, 27 Sept. 2001, www.articles.chicagotribune.com/2001–09–27/features/0109270018_1_postmodernism-military-personnel-field-in-southwestern-pennsylvania. Accessed 22 Jan. 2016.

Kellner, Douglas. "TV, Ideology, and Emancipatory Popular Culture." *Socialist Review* 45 (May–June 1979): 13–53.

Kelly, Adam. "David Foster Wallace and the New Sincerity in American Fiction." *Consider David Foster Wallace: Critical Essays.* Ed. David Hering. Los Angeles: Sideshow Media Group P, 2010. 131–46.

Keniston, Ann, and Jeanne Follansbee Quinn, eds. *Literature after 9/11.* New York: Routledge, 2008.

King, Stephen. *11/22/63.* New York: Scribner-Simon, 2011.

Kingsolver, Barbara. *Animal Dreams.* 1990. New York: HarperPerennial–HarperCollins, 1991.

The Bean Trees. New York: Harper, 1988.

Hide Tide in Tucson. New York: HarperCollins, 1995.

The Lacuna. New York: Harper–HarperCollins, 2009.

The Poisonwood Bible. 1998. New York: HarperPerennial–HarperCollins, 1999.

Prodigal Summer. New York: HarperCollins, 2000.

Klay, Phil. *Redeployment.* New York: Penguin, 2014.

Knapp, Kathy. "Richard Ford's Frank Bascombe Trilogy and the Post–9/11 Suburban Novel." *American Literary History* 23 (2011): 500–28.

Kushner, Rachel. *The Flamethrowers.* 2013. New York: Scribner-Simon, 2014.

Telex from Cuba. 2008. New York: Scribner-Simon, 2009.

LaCapra, Dominick. *Writing History, Writing Trauma.* Baltimore: Johns Hopkins UP, 2001.

Lahiri, Jhumpa. *The Namesake.* 2003. Boston: Mariner-Houghton, 2004.

Laub, Dori. "Bearing Witness, or the Vicissitudes of Listening." *Testimony: Crises of Witnessing in Literature, Psychoanalysis, and History.* Ed. Shoshana Felman and Dori Laub. New York: Routledge, 1992. 57–74.

LeClair, Tom. "The Prodigious Fiction of Richard Powers, William Vollmann, and David Foster Wallace." *Critique* 38 (1996): 12–37.

Lee, Chang-rae. *Native Speaker.* New York: Riverhead-Putnam's, 1995.

Leise, Christopher. "'That Little Incandescence': Reading the Fragmentary and John Calvin in Marilynne Robinson's *Gilead.*" *Studies in the Novel* 41 (2009): 348–67.

Lethem, Jonathan. *Dissident Gardens.* New York: Doubleday-Random, 2013.

———. "The Ecstasy of Influence: A Plagiarism." *Harper's Magazine* Feb. 2007: 59–71.

———. *The Fortress of Solitude.* New York: Doubleday-Random, 2003.

———. *Motherless Brooklyn.* 1999. New York: Vintage-Random, 2000.

Levinas, Emmanuel. "Peace and Proximity." 1984. *Basic Philosophical Writings.* Ed. Adriaan T. Peperzak, Simon Critchley, and Robert Bernasconi. Bloomington: Indiana UP, 1996. 161–69.

Lewis, Sinclair. *It Can't Happen Here.* Garden City, NY: Doubleday, 1935.

Limón, José E. *American Encounters: Greater Mexico, the United States, and the Erotics of Culture.* Boston: Beacon, 1998.

Link, Alex. "Global War, Global Capital, and the Work of Art in William Gibson's *Pattern Recognition.*" *Contemporary Literature* 49 (2008): 209–31.

London, Jack. *The Iron Heel.* New York: Macmillan, 1908.

Lowe, Lisa. *Immigrant Acts: On Asian American Cultural Politics.* Durham: Duke UP, 1996.

Lukács, Georg. *The Historical Novel.* Trans. Hannah and Stanley Mitchell. 1962. Boston: Beacon, 1963. Trans. of *A történelmi regény.* 1937.

Lynch, Lisa. "The Fever Next Time: The Race of Disease and the Disease of Racism in John Edgar Wideman." *American Literary History* 14 (2002): 776–804.

Lyotard, Jean-François. *The Postmodern Condition: A Report on Knowledge.* Trans. Geoff Bennington and Brian Massumi. Minneapolis: U of Minnesota P, 1984. Trans. of *La Condition postmoderne: rapport sur le savoir.* 1979.

Mailer, Norman. *The Armies of the Night: History as a Novel/The Novel as History.* New York: New American Library, 1968.

———. *Barbary Shore.* New York: Holt 1951.

———. *Cannibals and Christians.* 1966. New York: Dell, 1967.

———. *The Executioner's Song.* 1979. New York: Warner, 1980.

———. *The Naked and the Dead.* New York: Holt, 1948.

———. *Oswald's Tale: An American Mystery.* New York: Random, 1995.

———. *The Presidential Papers.* 1963. New York: Berkley, 1970.

"The White Negro: Superficial Reflections on the Hipster." 1957. *Advertisements for Myself.* 1959. New York: Berkley-Putnam, 1976. 299–320.

Mansbach, Adam. *Angry Black White Boy, or, The Miscegenation of Macon Detornay.* New York: Three Rivers, 2005.

Maso, Carole. "Rupture, Verge, and Precipice/Precipice, Verge, and Hurt Not." *Barcelona Review,* 20 (Sept.–Oct. 2000), www.barcelonareview.com/20/e_cm.htm. Accessed 15 Jan. 2016.

Mason, Bobbie Ann. *In Country.* 1985. New York: Perennial-Harper, 1986.

McCann, Colum. "A Conversation with Colum McCann and Elizabeth Strout." 2014. *TransAtlantic.* 2013. New York: Random, 2014. 307–15.

"A Conversation with Colum McCann and Nathan Englander." *Let the Great World Spin.* New York: Random, 2009. 361–71.

Dancer. 2003. New York: Picador–Henry Holt, 2009.

Let the Great World Spin. New York: Random, 2009.

This Side of Brightness. 1998. New York: Picador–Henry Holt, n.d.

TransAtlantic. 2013. New York: Random, 2014.

McCarthy, Cormac. *All the Pretty Horses.* 1992. London: Picador–Pan Macmillan, 2012.

Blood Meridian, or, The Evening Redness in the West. 1985. New York: Vintage-Random, 1992.

Cities of the Plain. 1998. London: Picador–Pan Macmillan, 2011.

The Crossing. 1994. London: Picador–Pan Macmillan, 2011.

No Country for Old Men. 2005. London: Picador–Pan Macmillan, 2011.

The Road. 2006. London: Picador–Pan Macmillan, 2010.

McGurl, Mark. "The Program Era: Pluralisms of Postwar American Fiction." *Critical Inquiry* 32 (2005): 102–29.

McHale, Brian. *The Cambridge Introduction to Postmodernism.* Cambridge: Cambridge UP, 2015.

McInerney, Jay. *The Good Life.* New York: Knopf, 2006.

Melville, Herman. *Moby-Dick: or, The Whale.* 1851. Ed. Alfred Kazin. Cambridge: Riverside-Houghton, 1956.

Messud, Claire. *The Emperor's Children.* New York: Knopf, 2006.

Michaels, Walter Benn. "Political Science Fictions." *New Literary History* 31 (2000): 649–64.

The Shape of the Signifier: 1967 to the End of History. Princeton: Princeton UP, 2004.

Millard, Kenneth. *Contemporary American Fiction: An Introduction to American Fiction since 1970.* Oxford: Oxford UP, 2000.

Miller, Arthur. *Death of a Salesman.* 1949. New York: Viking, 1958.

Miller, T. S. "Preternatural Narration and the Lens of Genre Fiction in Junot Díaz's *The Brief Wondrous Life of Oscar Wao.*" *Science Fiction Studies* 38 (2011): 92–114.

Mishra, Pankaj. "The End of Innocence." *The Guardian*, 18 May 2007, www.the
guardian.com/books/2007/may/19/fiction.martinamis. Accessed 22 Jan.
2016.

Modelski, George. *Principles of World Politics*. New York: Free-Macmillan, 1972.

Moody, Rick. *The Ice Storm*. 1994. New York: Back Bay–Little, 2002.

Purple America. Boston: Little, 1997.

Moore, Lorrie. *Who Will Run the Frog Hospital?* New York: Knopf, 1994.

Morales, Alejandro. *The Rag Doll Plagues*. Houston: Arte Publico, 1992.

Moraru, Christian. *Cosmodernism: American Narrative, Late Globalization, and
the New Cultural Imaginary*. Ann Arbor: U of Michigan P, 2011.

"Speakers and Sleepers: Chang-rae Lee's *Native Speaker*, Whitman, and the
Performance of Americanness." *College Literature* 36.3 (2009): 66–91.

Morrison, Toni. *Beloved*. 1987. New York: Plume-Penguin, 1988.

The Bluest Eye. 1970. New York: Washington Square–Simon, 1972.

Home. New York: Knopf, 2012.

Jazz. New York: Knopf, 1992.

A Mercy. New York: Knopf, 2008.

"On the Backs of Blacks." *Time* 18 Nov. 1993: 57.

Paradise. 1997. New York: Plume-Penguin, 1999.

Playing in the Dark: Whiteness and the Literary Imagination. Cambridge:
Harvard UP, 1992.

"Toni Morrison Finds 'A Mercy' in Servitude." Interview, with
Michele Norris. *All Things Considered*. *NPR.org*. Natl. Public Radio,
27 Oct. 2008, www.npr.org/templates/story/story.php?storyId=95961382.
Accessed 13 Nov. 2013.

Mukherjee, Bharati. "A Four-Hundred-Year-Old Woman." *Critical Fictions: The
Politics of Imaginative Writing*. Ed. Philomena Mariani. Seattle: Bay,
1991. 24–28.

The Holder of the World. New York: Knopf, 1993.

"Holders of the Word: An Interview with Bharati Mukherjee." With Tina
Chen and S. X. Goudie. *Jouvert* 1.1 (1997): 1–22.

"Immigrant Writing: Give Us Your Maximalists!" *New York Times Book
Review* 28 Aug. 1998: 1, 28–29.

Jasmine. 1989. New York: Fawcett-Ballantine, 1991.

Naqvi, H. M. *Home Boy*. New York: Shaye Areheart–Crown, 2009.

Neal, Mark Anthony. *Soul Babies: Black Popular Culture and the Post-Soul
Aesthetic*. New York: Routledge, 2002.

Nealon, Jeffrey T. *Post-Postmodernism: or, The Cultural Logic of Just-in-Time
Capitalism*. Stanford: Stanford UP, 2012.

"The New Face of America." *Time* 18 Nov. 1993: cover.

Norris, Frank. *The Octopus*. 1901. New York: Penguin, 1986.

Oates, Joyce Carol. *Black Water*. 1992. New York: Plume-Penguin, 1993.

Blonde. 2000. New York: Ecco–Harper, 2001.

Carthage. New York: Ecco–HarperCollins, 2014.

Obama, Barack. "A More Perfect Union." National Constitution Center, Philadelphia, 18 Mar. 2008, www.constitutioncenter.org/amoreperfect union/docs/Race_Speech_Transcript.pdf. Accessed 5 Jan. 2016.

O'Brien, Tim. *The Things They Carried.* 1990. New York: Penguin, 1991.

O'Donnell, Patrick. *The American Novel Now: Reading Contemporary American Fiction since 1980.* Chichester: Wiley-Blackwell, 2010.

Omi, Michael, and Howard Winant. *Racial Formation in the United States: From the 1960s to the 1990s.* 2nd ed. New York: Routledge, 1994.

O'Neill, Joseph. *Blood-Dark Track: A Family History.* 2001. New York: Vintage-Random, 2010.

The Dog. New York: Pantheon-Random, 2014.

Netherland. 2008. New York: Vintage-Random, 2009.

Parkes, Adam. "History, Bloodshed, and the Spectacle of American Identity in *Blood Meridian*." *Cormac McCarthy: New Directions.* Ed. James D. Lilley. Albuquerque: U of New Mexico P, 2002. 103–24.

Patterson, Orlando. "Race Over." *New Republic* 10 Jan. 2000: 6.

Perrotta, Tom. *The Abstinence Teacher.* New York: St. Martin's, 2007.

Election. New York: Berkley–Penguin Putnam, 1998.

Little Children. New York: St. Martin's, 2004.

Phillips, Caryl. *Dancing in the Dark.* 2005. New York: Vintage-Random, 2006.

Powers, Kevin. *The Yellow Birds.* New York: Little, 2012.

Powers, Richard. *The Gold Bug Variations.* New York: William Morrow, 1991.

Three Farmers on Their Way to a Dance. New York: Beech Tree–William Morrow, 1985.

The Time of Our Singing. New York: Farrar, 2003.

Pressman, Jessica. "Conclusion: Whither American Fiction?" *The Cambridge Companion to American Fiction after 1945.* Ed. John N. Duvall. Cambridge: Cambridge UP, 2012. 256–64.

Prosser, Jay, ed. *American Fiction of the 1990s: Reflections of History and Culture.* London: Routledge, 2008.

Pynchon, Thomas. *Against the Day.* 2006. New York: Penguin, 2007.

Bleeding Edge. New York: Penguin, 2013.

The Crying of Lot 49. 1966. New York: Bantam, 1967.

Gravity's Rainbow. New York: Viking, 1973.

Inherent Vice. New York: Penguin, 2009.

Mason & Dixon. New York: Holt, 1997.

Vineland. Boston: Little, 1990.

Raboteau, Emily. *The Professor's Daughter.* New York: Henry Holt, 2005.

Radway, Janice. "What's in a Name? Presidential Address to the American Studies Association, 20 November, 1998." *American Quarterly* 51 (1999): 1–32.

Rebein, Robert. "Contemporary Realism." *The Cambridge Companion to American Fiction after 1945.* Ed. John N. Duvall. Cambridge: Cambridge UP, 2012. 30–43.

Redfield, Marc. "Virtual Trauma: The Idiom of 9/11." *Diacritics* 37.1 (2007): 55–80.

Reed, Ishmael. *Flight to Canada*. 1976. New York: Atheneum-Macmillan, 1989.
    "An Interview with Ishmael Reed." With Peter Nazareth. *Iowa Review* 13.2
        (1982): 117–31.
    Japanese by Spring. 1993. New York: Penguin, 1996.
    Juice! Champaign, IL: Dalkey Archive, 2011.
    The Last Days of Louisiana Red. New York: Random, 1974.
    Mumbo Jumbo. 1972. New York: Atheneum-Macmillan, 1988.
    Reckless Eyeballing. New York: St. Martin's, 1986.
    The Terrible Threes. 1989. London: Allison & Busby–Wilson & Day, 1993.
    The Terrible Twos. 1982. Normal, IL: Dalkey Archive, 1999.
    Yellow Back Radio Broke-Down. Garden City, NY: Doubleday, 1969.
Reynolds, David S. *Walt Whitman's America: A Cultural Biography*. New York:
    Knopf, 1995.
Robbins, Bruce. "The Worlding of the American Novel." *The Cambridge History
    of the American Novel*. Ed. Leonard Cassuto, Clare Virginia Eby, and
    Benjamin Reiss. Cambridge: Cambridge UP, 2011. 1096–106.
Robertson, Roland. "Glocalization: Time-Space and Homogeneity-Heterogeneity."
    Global Modernities. Ed. Mike Featherstone, Scott Lash, and Roland
    Robertson. London: Sage, 1995. 25–44.
Robinson, Marilynne. *The Death of Adam: Essays on Modern Thought*. Boston:
    Houghton, 1998.
    Gilead. New York: Farrar, 2004.
    Home. New York: Farrar, 2008.
    Housekeeping. 1980. New York: Bantam, 1982.
    Lila. New York: Farrar, 2014.
Rosaldo, Renato. *Culture & Truth: The Remaking of Social Analysis*. Boston:
    Beacon, 1993.
Rosenbaum, Thane. "Art and Atrocity in a Post-9/11 World." *Jewish American
    and Holocaust Literature: Representation in the Postmodern World*. Ed.
    Alan L. Berger and Gloria L. Cronin. Albany: State U of New York P,
    2004. 125–36.
Rosenblatt, Roger. "The Age of Irony Comes to an End." *Time* 24 Sept.
    2001: 79.
Roth, Philip. *American Pastoral*. Boston: Houghton, 1997.
    The Human Stain. Boston: Houghton, 2000.
    I Married a Communist. Boston: Houghton, 1998.
    The Plot against America. Boston: Houghton, 2004.
    "The Story Behind 'The Plot against America.'" *New York Times Book Review*
        19 Sept. 2004: 10–12.
Rothstein, Edward. "Attacks on U.S. Challenge the Perspectives of Postmodern
    True Believers." *New York Times* 22 Sept. 2001, late ed.: A17.
Rumbaut, Rubén G. "Ages, Life Stages, and Generational Cohorts: Decomposing
    the Immigrant First and Second Generations in the United States."
    International Migration Review 38 (2004): 1160–205.

Rushdy, Ashraf H. A. *Neo-slave Narratives: Studies in the Social Logic of a Literary Form*. New York: Oxford UP, 1999.

Russo, Richard. *Empire Falls*. 2001. New York: Vintage-Random, 2002.

Rzepka, Charles J. "Race, Region, Rule: Genre and the Case of Charlie Chan." *PMLA* 122 (2007): 1463–81.

Sadowski-Smith, Claudia. *Border Fictions: Globalization, Empire, and Writing at the Boundaries of the United States*. Charlottesville: U of Virginia P, 2008.

Saldívar, José David. *Border Matters: Remapping American Cultural Studies*. Berkeley: U of California P, 1997.

Saldívar, Ramón. *Chicano Narrative: The Dialectics of Difference*. Madison: U of Wisconsin P, 1990.

"Historical Fantasy, Speculative Realism, and Postrace Aesthetics in Contemporary American Fiction." *American Literary History* 23 (2011): 574–99.

"The Second Elevation of the Novel: Race, Form, and the Postrace Aesthetic in Contemporary Narrative." *Narrative* 21 (2013): 1–18.

Schulman, Helen. *A Day at the Beach*. Boston: Houghton, 2007.

Schwartz, Lynne Sharon. *The Writing on the Wall*. New York: Counterpoint-Perseus, 2005.

Scott, A. O. "The Panic of Influence." *New York Review of Books* 10 Feb. 2000: 39–40, 42–43.

Senna, Danzy. *Caucasia*. New York: Riverhead–Penguin Putnam, 1998.

"The Mulatto Millennium." *Half and Half: Writers on Growing Up Biracial and Bicultural*. Ed. Claudine Chiawei O'Hearn. New York: Pantheon, 1998. 12–27.

Symptomatic. 2004. New York: Riverhead-Penguin, 2005.

Shirley, Paula W. "Reading Desi Arnaz in *The Mambo Kings Play Songs of Love*." *MELUS* 20.3 (1995): 69–78.

Shreve, Anita. *A Wedding in December*. New York: Little, 2005.

Shteyngart, Gary. *Absurdistan*. New York: Random, 2006.

Little Failure: A Memoir. New York: Random, 2014.

The Russian Debutante's Handbook. 2002. New York: Riverhead-Berkley, 2003.

Silko, Leslie Marmon. *Almanac of the Dead*. New York: Simon, 1991.

Ceremony. 1977. New York: Penguin, 1986.

Yellow Woman and a Beauty of the Spirit: Essays on Native American Life Today. New York: Simon, 1996.

Simpson, David. *9/11: The Culture of Commemoration*. Chicago: U of Chicago P, 2006.

Smiley, Jane. *A Thousand Acres*. 1991. New York: Fawcett Columbine–Ballantine, 1992.

Smith, Valerie. "Neo-slave Narratives." *The Cambridge Companion to the African American Slave Narrative*. Ed. Audrey Fisch. Cambridge: Cambridge UP, 2007. 168–85.

Sollors, Werner. *Beyond Ethnicity: Consent and Descent in American Culture.* New York: Oxford UP, 1986.

Song, Min Hyoung. "Becoming Planetary." *American Literary History* 23 (2011): 555–73.

Sontag, Susan. *The Benefactor.* 1963. New York: Picador-Farrar, 2002.

    Death Kit. 1967. New York: Picador-Farrar, 2002.

    The Volcano Lover: A Romance. New York: Farrar, 1992.

Sorrentino, Christopher. *Trance.* New York: Farrar, 2005.

Spiegelman, Art. *In the Shadow of No Towers.* New York: Pantheon-Random, 2004.

    Maus: A Survivor's Tale. New York: Pantheon-Random, 1986, 1991.

Spiotta, Dana. *Eat the Document.* New York: Scribner, 2006.

Spivak, Gayatri Chakravorty. "Planetarity." *Death of a Discipline.* New York: Columbia UP, 2003. 71–102.

Stephenson, Neal. *The Diamond Age: or, A Young Lady's Illustrated Primer.* New York: Bantam Spectra, 1995.

Sundquist, Eric J. "*Benito Cereno* and New World Slavery." *Reconstructing American Literary History.* Ed. Sacvan Bercovitch. Cambridge: Harvard UP, 1986. 93–122.

    "The Country of the Blue." Introduction. *American Realism: New Essays.* Ed. Eric J. Sundquist. Baltimore: Johns Hopkins UP, 1982. 3–24.

Tanner, Tony. *City of Words: American Fiction, 1950–1970.* New York: Harper, 1971.

Tate, Greg. "Cult-Nats Meet Freaky-Deke." 1986. Rpt. in *Flyboy in the Buttermilk: Essays on Contemporary America.* New York: Fireside-Simon, 1992. 198–210.

Tocqueville, Alexis de. *Democracy in America.* Vol. 2. 1835. Ed. Phillips Bradley. New York: Vintage-Random, 1945.

Toth, Josh. *The Passing of Postmodernism: A Spectroanalysis of the Contemporary.* Albany, NY: SUNY P, 2010.

Touré. *Who's Afraid of Post Blackness?: What It Means to Be Black Now.* New York: Free-Simon, 2011.

Trilling, Lionel. "Reality in America." 1946. Rpt. in *The Liberal Imagination: Essays on Literature and Society.* New York: Doubleday Anchor, 1950. 1–19.

Tuchman, Barbara W. *The First Salute: A View of the American Revolution.* New York: Knopf, 1988.

Ulinich, Anya. *Lena Finkle's Magic Barrel.* New York: Penguin, 2014.

    Petropolis. 2007. New York: Penguin, 2008.

Updike, John. *Assorted Prose.* New York: Knopf, 1965.

    Hugging the Shore: Essays and Criticism. New York: Knopf, 1983.

    Odd Jobs: Essays and Criticism. New York: Knopf, 1991.

    Picked-Up Pieces. New York: Knopf, 1975.

    Rabbit at Rest. New York: Knopf, 1990.

    Rabbit Is Rich. 1981. New York: Fawcett Crest-Ballantine, 1982.

Rabbit Redux. 1971. New York: Fawcett Crest–Ballantine, 1972.

"Rabbit Remembered." *Licks of Love.* New York: Knopf, 2000. 177–359.

Rabbit, Run. Greenwich, CT: Fawcett Crest, 1960.

Terrorist. 2006. New York: Ballantine-Random, 2007.

"Varieties of Religious Experience." *The Atlantic* Nov. 2002: 93–104.

Vapnyar, Lara. *There Are Jews in My House.* New York: Pantheon, 2003.

Versluys, Kristiaan. Introduction. *Neo-Realism in Contemporary American Fiction.* Ed. Kristiaan Versluys. Amsterdam: Rodopi, 1992. 7–12.

Out of the Blue: September 11 and the Novel. New York: Columbia UP, 2009.

Vidal, Gore. *The Golden Age.* New York: Doubleday-Random, 2000.

Washington, D.C. Boston: Little, 1967.

Vollmann, William T. "American Writing Today: A Diagnosis of the Disease." 1990. Rpt. In *Expelled from Eden: A William T. Vollmann Reader.* Ed. Larry McCaffery and Michael Hemmingson. New York: Thunder's Mouth–Avalon, 2004. 329–32.

Europe Central. New York: Viking-Penguin, 2005.

Waldman, Amy. *The Submission.* New York: Farrar, 2011.

Wallace, David Foster. *Consider the Lobster and Other Essays.* New York: Back Bay–Little, 2005.

"E Unibus Pluram: Television and U.S. Fiction." *Review of Contemporary Fiction* 13.2 (1993): 151–94.

"Fictional Futures and the Conspicuously Young." *Review of Contemporary Fiction* 8.3 (1988): 36–53.

Girl with Curious Hair. 1989. New York: Avon, 1991.

Infinite Jest. 1996. New York: Back Bay–Little, 2006.

"An Interview with David Foster Wallace." With Larry McCaffery. *Review of Contemporary Fiction* 13.2 (1993): 127–50.

This Is Water: Some Thoughts, Delivered on a Significant Occasion, about Living a Compassionate Life. New York: Little, 2009.

Walter, Jess. "A Conversation with Jess Walter." Rpt. in *The Zero.* 2006. New York: Harper Perennial–HarperCollins, 2007. 3–7.

The Zero. 2006. New York: Harper Perennial–HarperCollins, 2007.

Ward, Jesmyn. *Men We Reaped.* London: Bloomsbury, 2013.

Salvage the Bones. London: Bloomsbury, 2011.

White, Hayden. *Metahistory: The Historical Imagination in Nineteenth-Century Europe.* Baltimore: Johns Hopkins UP, 1973.

Whitehead, Colson. *The Intuitionist.* New York: Anchor-Doubleday, 1999.

"The Year of Living Postracially." *New York Times* 4 Nov. 2009, late ed.: A31.

Zone One. New York: Doubleday, 2011.

Whitman, Walt. *Leaves of Grass.* 1891–1892. Ed. Sculley Bradley and Harold W. Blodgett. New York: Norton, 1973.

"Slang in America." *November Boughs.* Philadelphia: David McKay, 1888. 68–72.

Specimen Days & Collect. 1882. New York: Dover, 1995.

Wideman, John Edgar. *The Cattle Killing.* Boston: Houghton, 1996.

Damballah. 1981. Boston: Mariner-Houghton, 1998.

Fanon. Boston: Houghton, 2008.

Philadelphia Fire. New York: Henry Holt, 1990.

Wilhite, Keith. "Contested Terrain: The Suburbs as Region." *American Literature* 84 (2012): 617–44.

Williams, Sherley Ann. *Dessa Rose.* 1986. New York: Harper Perennial–HarperCollins, 1999.

Wills, Garry. *Inventing America: Jefferson's Declaration of Independence.* Garden City, NY: Doubleday, 1978.

Winthrop, John. "A Modell of Christian Charity." 1630. *The Puritans.* Ed. Perry Miller and Thomas H. Johnson. Vol. 1. 1938. New York: Harper, 1963. 195–99.

Wolfe, Tom. *The Bonfire of the Vanities.* 1987. New York: Bantam, 1988.

"Stalking the Billion-Footed Beast: A Literary Manifesto for the New Social Novel." *Harper's Magazine* Nov. 1989: 45–56.

Wright, Frank Lloyd. *An Autobiography.* 1943. Petaluma, CA: Pomegranate, 2005.

Wright, Richard. *Native Son.* 1940. New York: Harper Perennial–HarperCollins, 1998.

Yamashita, Karen Tei. *Brazil-Maru.* Minneapolis: Coffee House, 1992.

Through the Arc of the Rain Forest. Minneapolis: Coffee House, 1990.

Tropic of Orange. Minneapolis: Coffee House, 1997.

Yunis, Alia. *The Night Counter.* New York: Shaye Areheart–Crown, 2009.

Žižek, Slavoj. *Welcome to the Desert of the Real!: Five Essays on September 11 and Related Dates.* London: Verso, 2002.

Index

Cambridge Introductions to . . .

Authors

Topics